NEW AVENGERS

THE REUNION

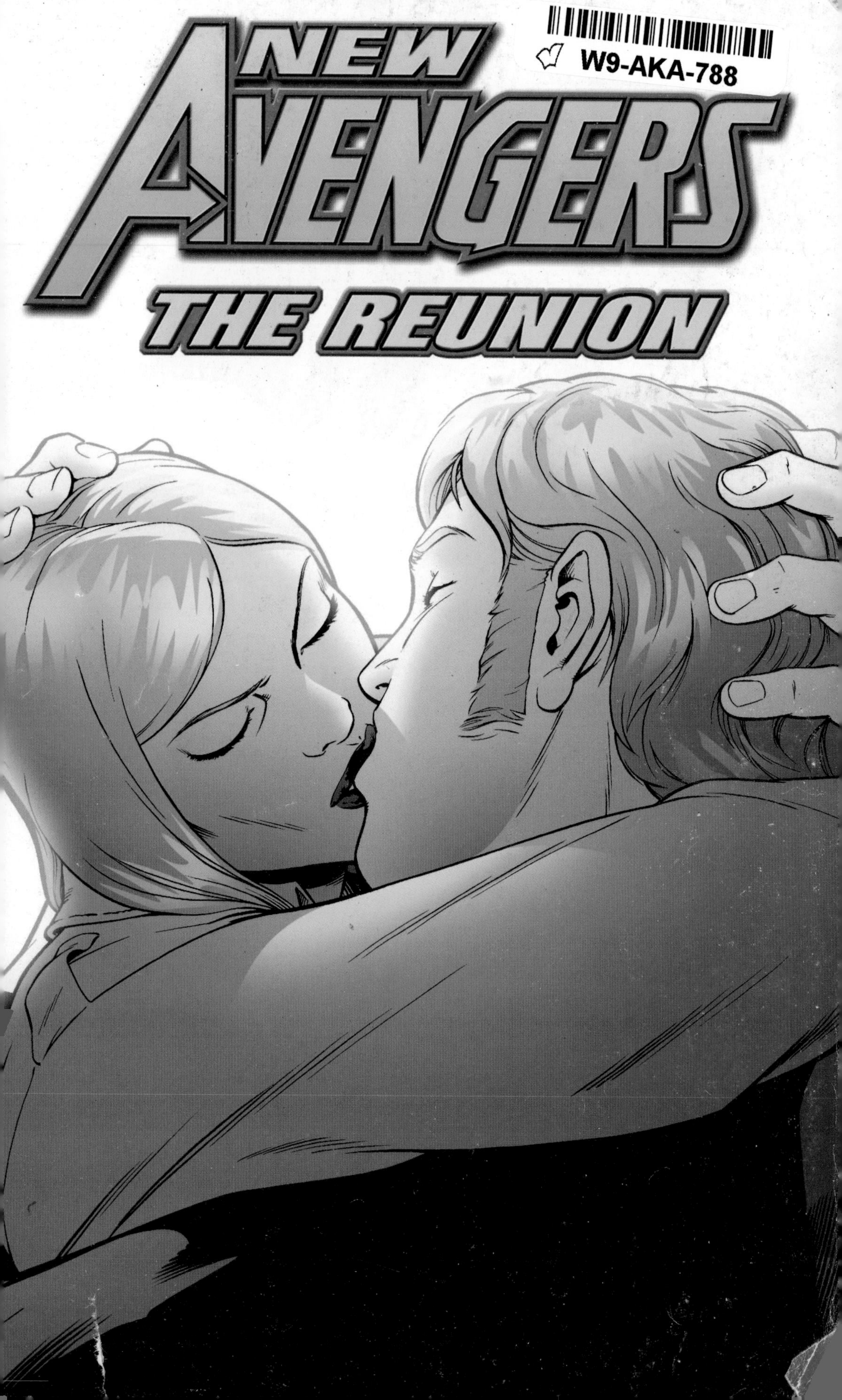

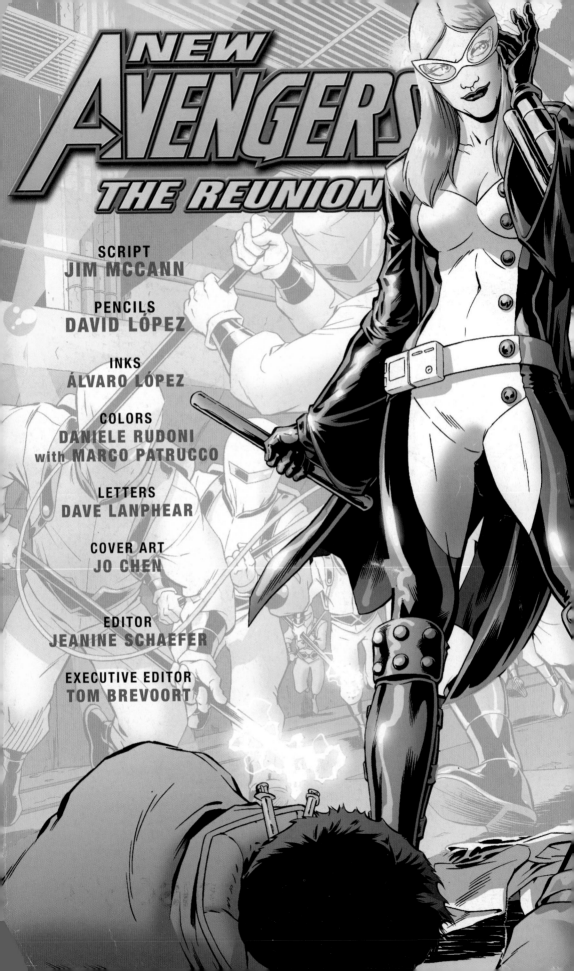

NEW AVENGERS
THE REUNION

SCRIPT
JIM McCANN

PENCILS
DAVID LÓPEZ

INKS
ÁLVARO LÓPEZ

COLORS
DANIELE RUDONI
with **MARCO PATRUCCO**

LETTERS
DAVE LANPHEAR

COVER ART
JO CHEN

EDITOR
JEANINE SCHAEFER

EXECUTIVE EDITOR
TOM BREVOORT

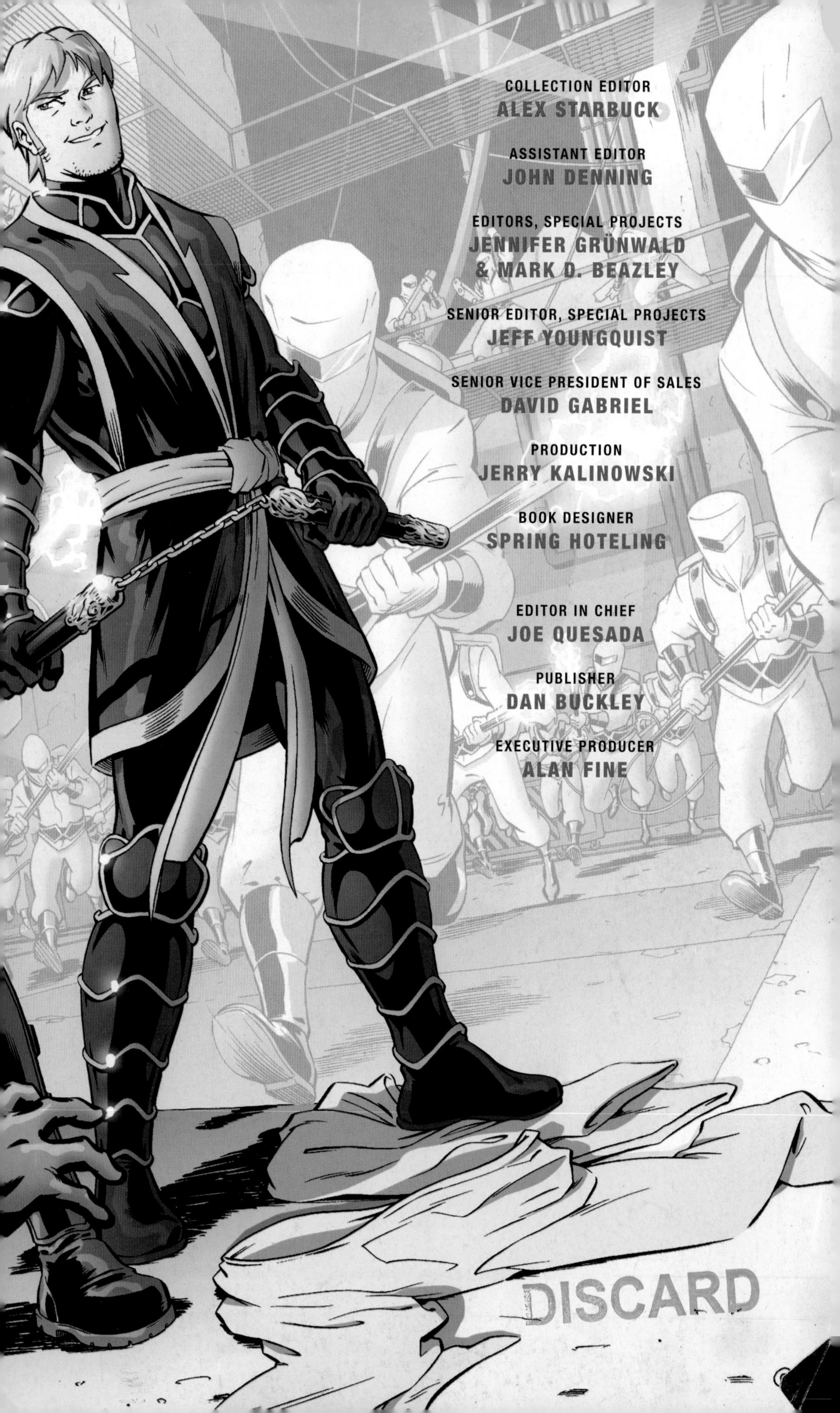

COLLECTION EDITOR
ALEX STARBUCK

ASSISTANT EDITOR
JOHN DENNING

EDITORS, SPECIAL PROJECTS
JENNIFER GRÜNWALD
& MARK D. BEAZLEY

SENIOR EDITOR, SPECIAL PROJECTS
JEFF YOUNGQUIST

SENIOR VICE PRESIDENT OF SALES
DAVID GABRIEL

PRODUCTION
JERRY KALINOWSKI

BOOK DESIGNER
SPRING HOTELING

EDITOR IN CHIEF
JOE QUESADA

PUBLISHER
DAN BUCKLEY

EXECUTIVE PRODUCER
ALAN FINE

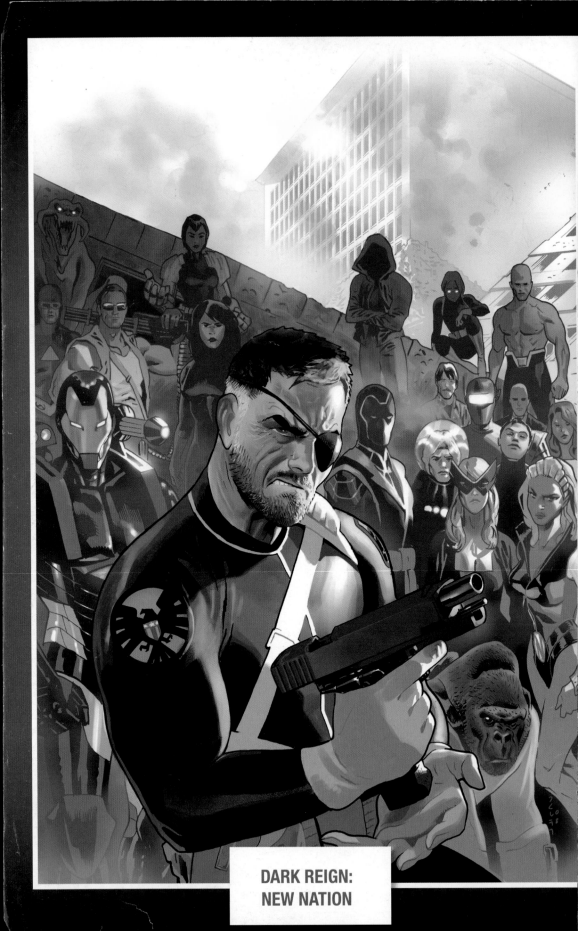

DARK REIGN:
NEW NATION

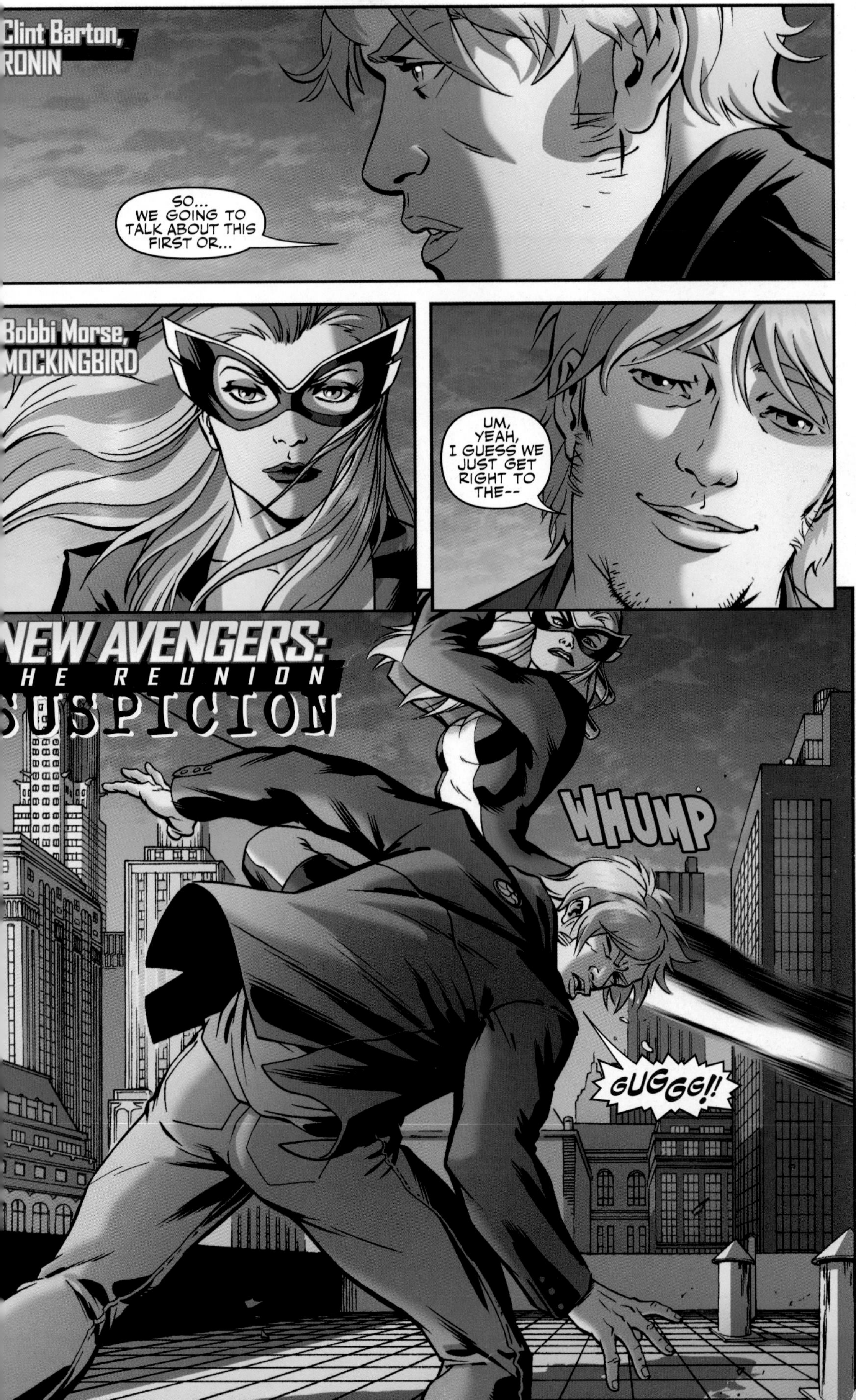
Clint Barton, RONIN
SO... WE GOING TO TALK ABOUT THIS FIRST OR...
Bobbi Morse, MOCKINGBIRD
UM, YEAH, I GUESS WE JUST GET RIGHT TO THE--
NEW AVENGERS: THE REUNION
SUSPICION
WHUMP
GUGGG!!

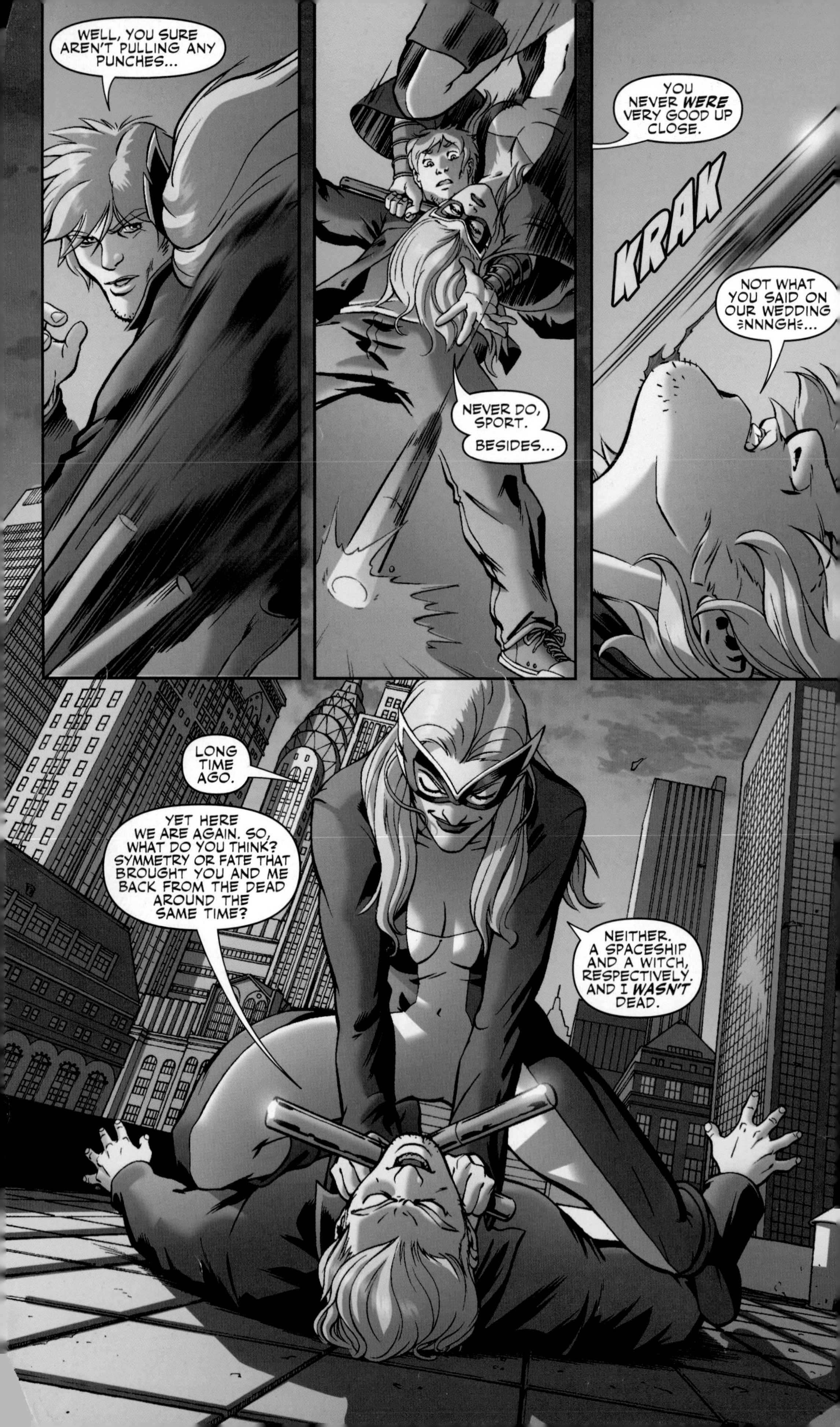
WELL, YOU SURE AREN'T PULLING ANY PUNCHES...
NEVER DO, SPORT.
BESIDES...
YOU NEVER *WERE* VERY GOOD UP CLOSE.
KRAK
NOT WHAT YOU SAID ON OUR WEDDING -NNNGH-...
LONG TIME AGO.
YET HERE WE ARE AGAIN. SO, WHAT DO YOU THINK? SYMMETRY OR FATE THAT BROUGHT YOU AND ME BACK FROM THE DEAD AROUND THE SAME TIME?
NEITHER. A SPACESHIP AND A WITCH, RESPECTIVELY. AND I *WASN'T* DEAD.

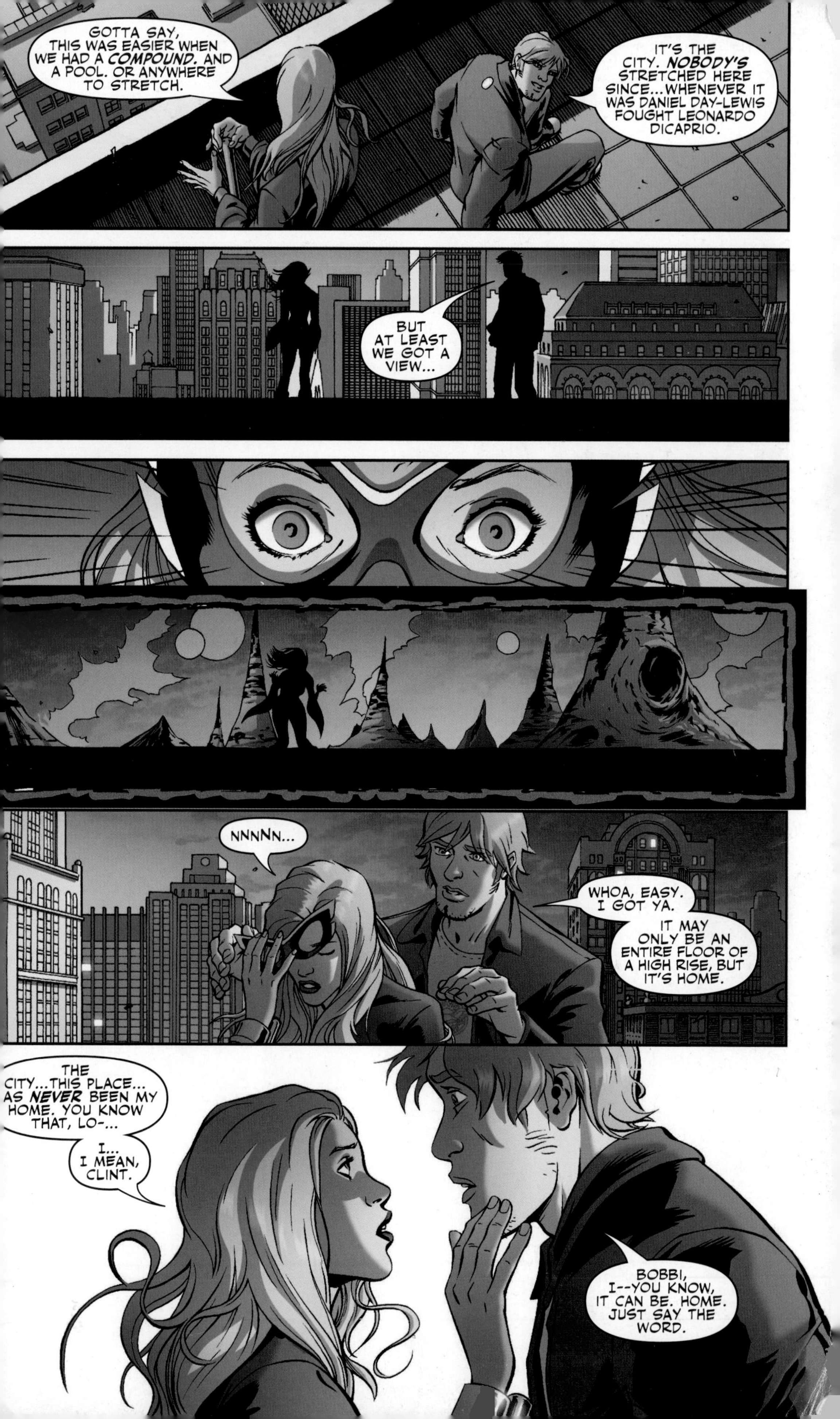
GOTTA SAY, THIS WAS EASIER WHEN WE HAD A *COMPOUND.* AND A POOL. OR ANYWHERE TO STRETCH.
IT'S THE CITY. *NOBODY'S* STRETCHED HERE SINCE... WHENEVER IT WAS DANIEL DAY-LEWIS FOUGHT LEONARDO DICAPRIO.
BUT AT LEAST WE GOT A VIEW...
NNNNN...
WHOA, EASY. I GOT YA.
IT MAY ONLY BE AN ENTIRE FLOOR OF A HIGH RISE, BUT IT'S HOME.
THE CITY... THIS PLACE... AS *NEVER* BEEN MY HOME. YOU KNOW THAT, LO-...
I... I MEAN, CLINT.
BOBBI, I--YOU KNOW, IT CAN BE. HOME. JUST SAY THE WORD.

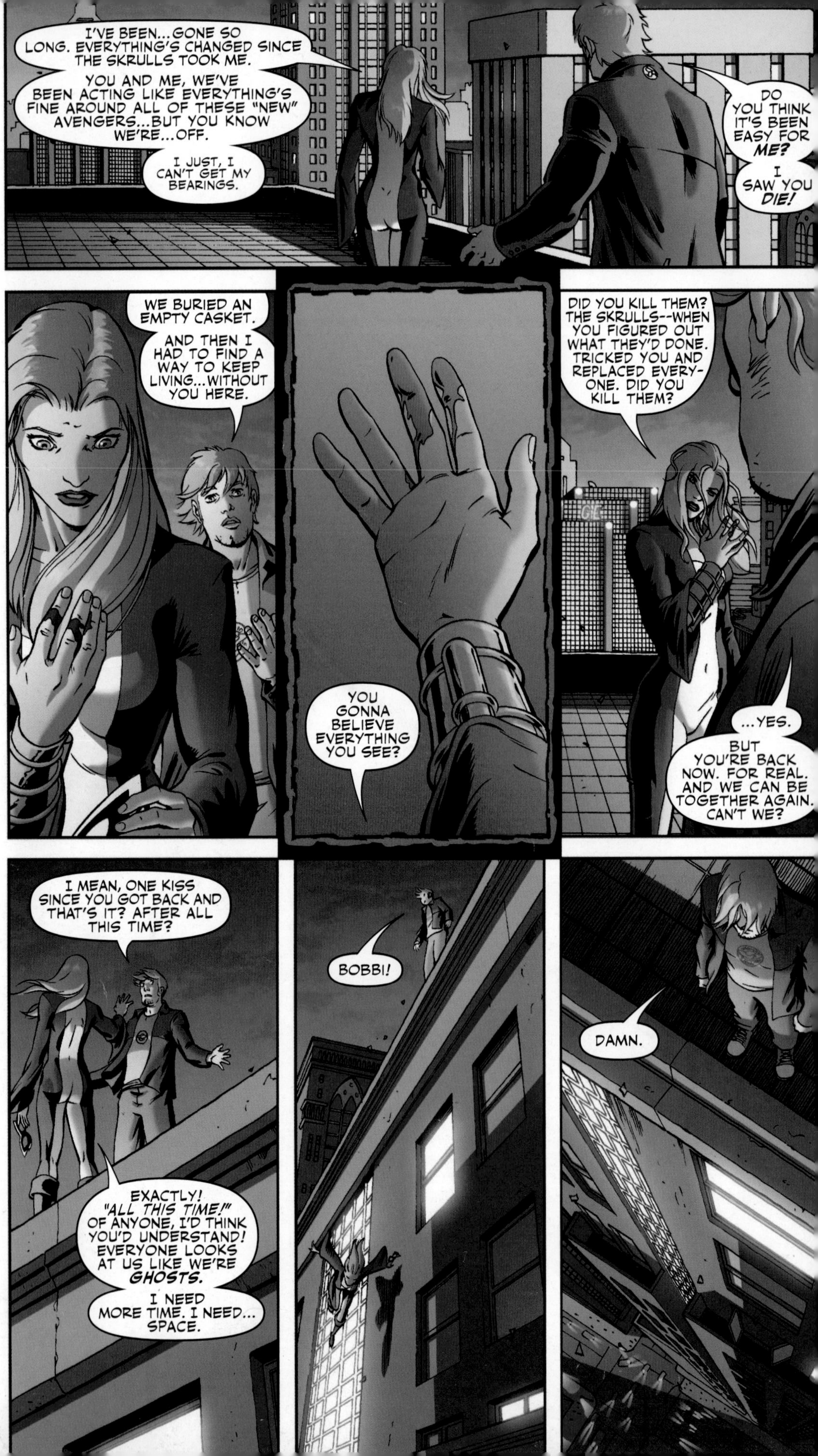
I'VE BEEN...GONE SO LONG. EVERYTHING'S CHANGED SINCE THE SKRULLS TOOK ME.
YOU AND ME, WE'VE BEEN ACTING LIKE EVERYTHING'S FINE AROUND ALL OF THESE "NEW" AVENGERS...BUT YOU KNOW WE'RE...OFF.
I JUST, I CAN'T GET MY BEARINGS.
DO YOU THINK IT'S BEEN EASY FOR ME?
I SAW YOU DIE!
WE BURIED AN EMPTY CASKET.
AND THEN I HAD TO FIND A WAY TO KEEP LIVING...WITHOUT YOU HERE.
YOU GONNA BELIEVE EVERYTHING YOU SEE?
DID YOU KILL THEM? THE SKRULLS--WHEN YOU FIGURED OUT WHAT THEY'D DONE. TRICKED YOU AND REPLACED EVERY-ONE. DID YOU KILL THEM?
...YES.
BUT YOU'RE BACK NOW. FOR REAL. AND WE CAN BE TOGETHER AGAIN. CAN'T WE?
I MEAN, ONE KISS SINCE YOU GOT BACK AND THAT'S IT? AFTER ALL THIS TIME?
EXACTLY! "ALL THIS TIME!" OF ANYONE, I'D THINK YOU'D UNDERSTAND! EVERYONE LOOKS AT US LIKE WE'RE GHOSTS.
I NEED MORE TIME. I NEED... SPACE.
BOBBI!
DAMN.

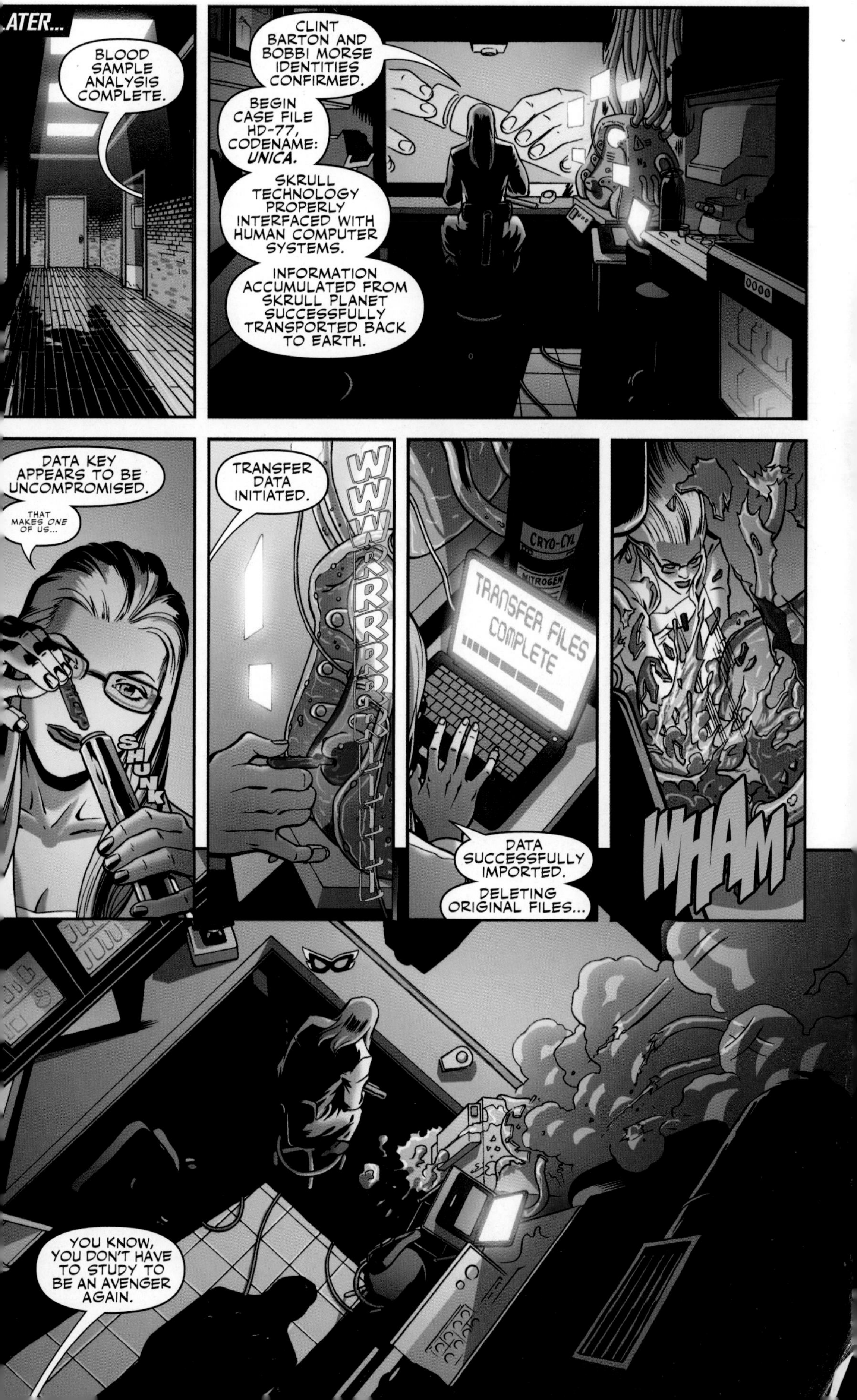
LATER...
BLOOD SAMPLE ANALYSIS COMPLETE.
CLINT BARTON AND BOBBI MORSE IDENTITIES CONFIRMED.
BEGIN CASE FILE HD-77, CODENAME: *UNICA.*
SKRULL TECHNOLOGY PROPERLY INTERFACED WITH HUMAN COMPUTER SYSTEMS.
INFORMATION ACCUMULATED FROM SKRULL PLANET SUCCESSFULLY TRANSPORTED BACK TO EARTH.
DATA KEY APPEARS TO BE UNCOMPROMISED.
THAT MAKES *ONE* OF US...
SHUNK
TRANSFER DATA INITIATED.
WWWRRRRRRLLLLLLL
CRYO-CYL
NITROGEN
TRANSFER FILES COMPLETE
DATA SUCCESSFULLY IMPORTED.
DELETING ORIGINAL FILES...
WHAM
YOU KNOW, YOU DON'T HAVE TO STUDY TO BE AN AVENGER AGAIN.

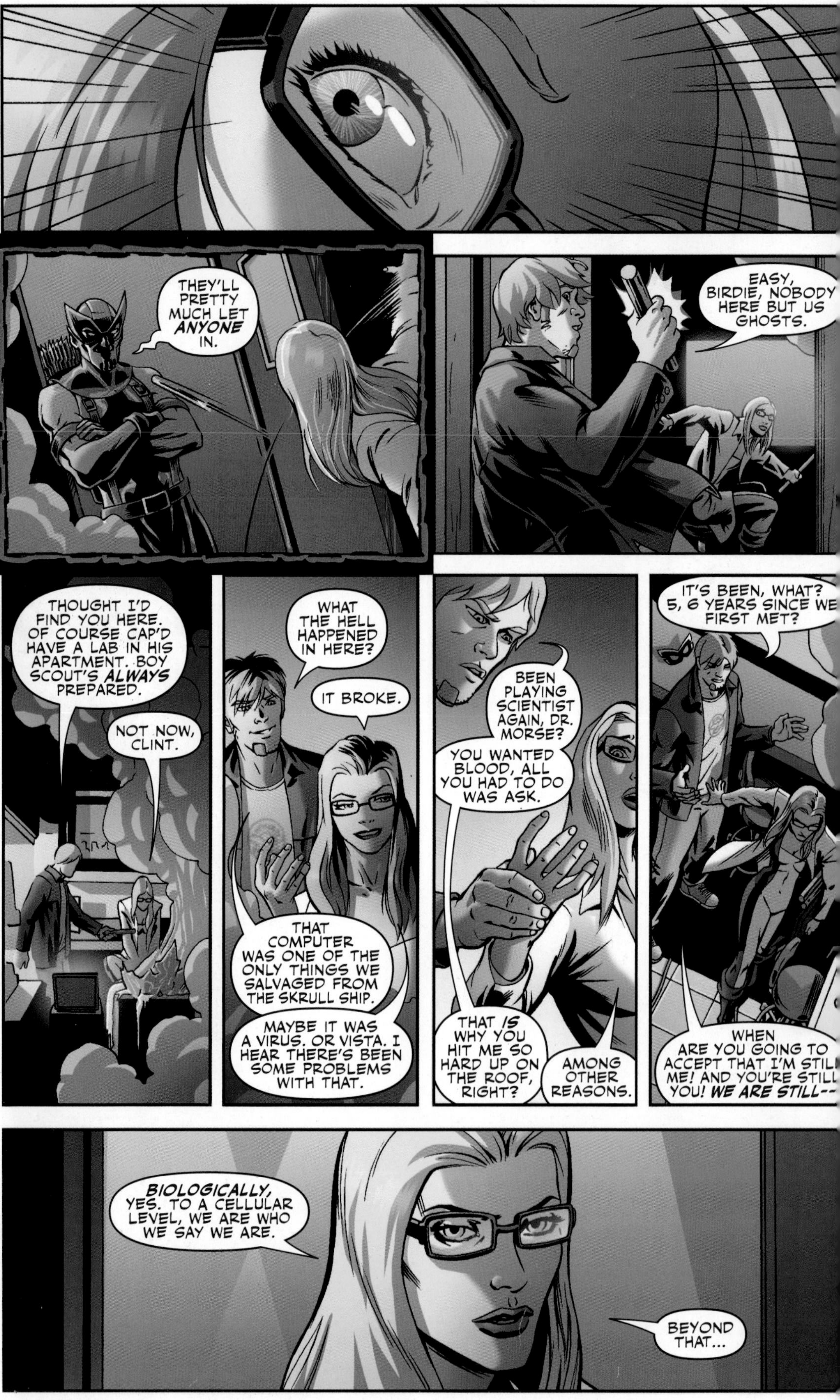

THEY'LL PRETTY MUCH LET ANYONE IN.
EASY, BIRDIE, NOBODY HERE BUT US GHOSTS.
THOUGHT I'D FIND YOU HERE. OF COURSE CAP'D HAVE A LAB IN HIS APARTMENT. BOY SCOUT'S ALWAYS PREPARED.
NOT NOW, CLINT.
WHAT THE HELL HAPPENED IN HERE?
IT BROKE.
THAT COMPUTER WAS ONE OF THE ONLY THINGS WE SALVAGED FROM THE SKRULL SHIP.
MAYBE IT WAS A VIRUS. OR VISTA. I HEAR THERE'S BEEN SOME PROBLEMS WITH THAT.
BEEN PLAYING SCIENTIST AGAIN, DR. MORSE?
YOU WANTED BLOOD, ALL YOU HAD TO DO WAS ASK.
THAT IS WHY YOU HIT ME SO HARD UP ON THE ROOF, RIGHT?
AMONG OTHER REASONS.
IT'S BEEN, WHAT? 5, 6 YEARS SINCE WE FIRST MET?
WHEN ARE YOU GOING TO ACCEPT THAT I'M STILL ME! AND YOU'RE STILL YOU! WE ARE STILL--
BIOLOGICALLY, YES. TO A CELLULAR LEVEL, WE ARE WHO WE SAY WE ARE.
BEYOND THAT...

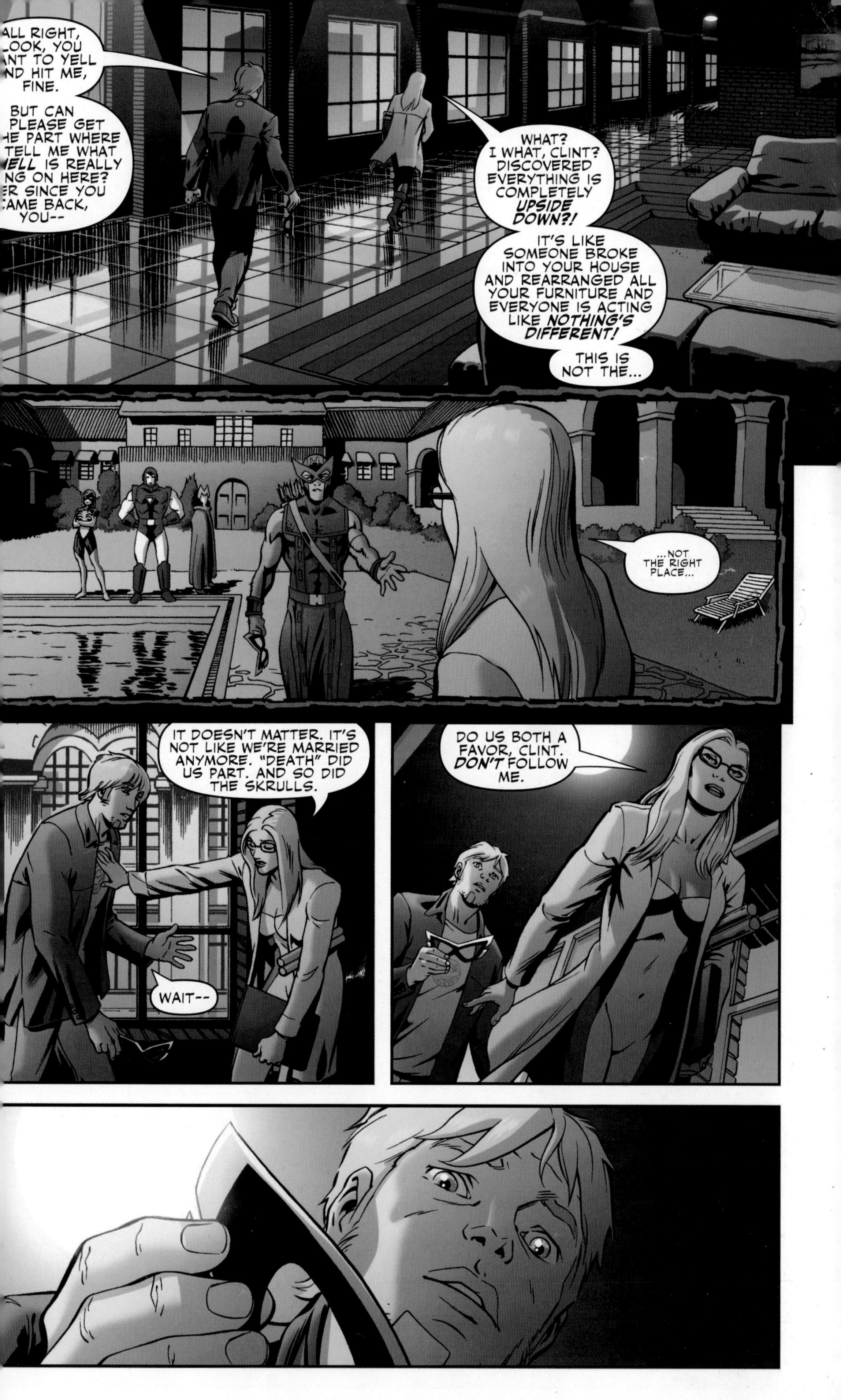

ALL RIGHT, LOOK, YOU ANT TO YELL ND HIT ME, FINE.
BUT CAN PLEASE GET HE PART WHERE TELL ME WHAT ELL IS REALLY NG ON HERE? R SINCE YOU CAME BACK, YOU--
WHAT? I WHAT, CLINT? DISCOVERED EVERYTHING IS COMPLETELY UPSIDE DOWN?!
IT'S LIKE SOMEONE BROKE INTO YOUR HOUSE AND REARRANGED ALL YOUR FURNITURE AND EVERYONE IS ACTING LIKE NOTHING'S DIFFERENT!
THIS IS NOT THE...
...NOT THE RIGHT PLACE...
IT DOESN'T MATTER. IT'S NOT LIKE WE'RE MARRIED ANYMORE. "DEATH" DID US PART. AND SO DID THE SKRULLS.
WAIT--
DO US BOTH A FAVOR, CLINT. DON'T FOLLOW ME.

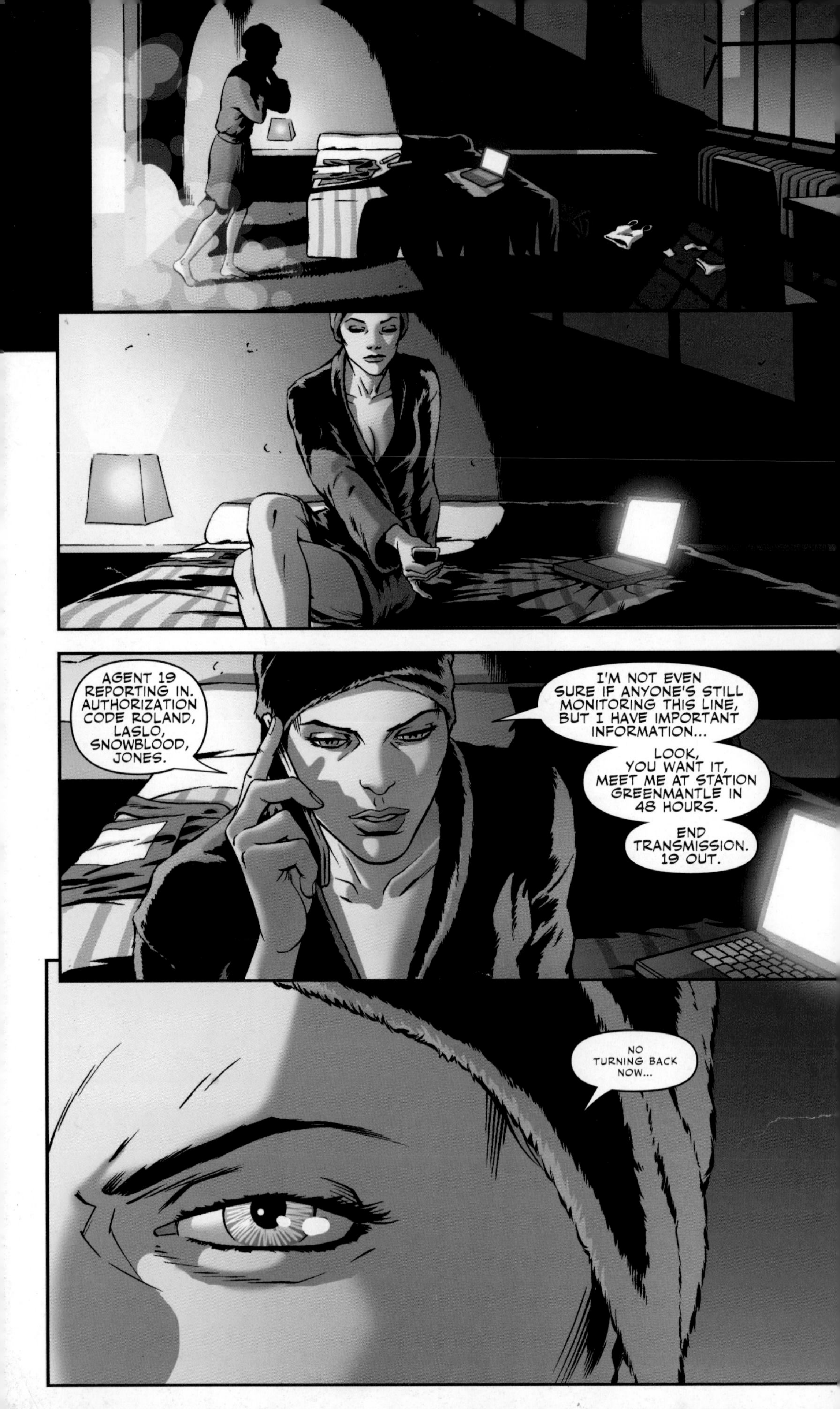
AGENT 19 REPORTING IN. AUTHORIZATION CODE ROLAND, LASLO, SNOWBLOOD, JONES.
I'M NOT EVEN SURE IF ANYONE'S STILL MONITORING THIS LINE, BUT I HAVE IMPORTANT INFORMATION...
LOOK, YOU WANT IT, MEET ME AT STATION GREENMANTLE IN 48 HOURS.
END TRANSMISSION. 19 OUT.
NO TURNING BACK NOW...

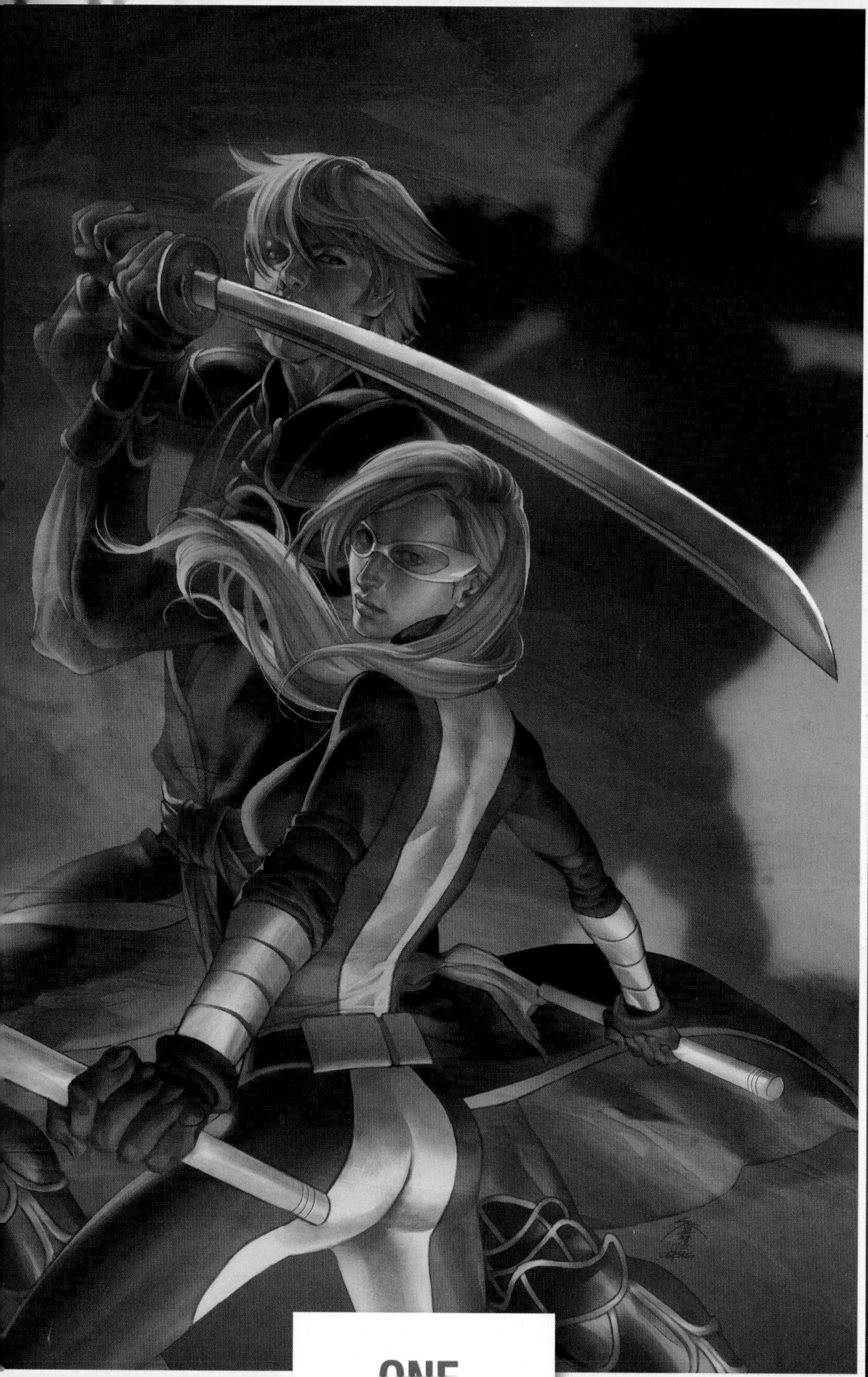

ONE

FROM THE DESK OF LEONARD SAMSON

Case File AT006197106
<u>Name:</u> Morse, Barbara "Bobbi"
<u>Codename:</u> MOCKINGBIRD
<u>Team Affiliation:</u> Avengers

In the wake of the recent Skrull Invasion, the humans that were abducted and replaced by Skrull agents were returned to us. Barbara "Bobbi" Morse was among them, proving that the Skrulls infiltrated the Earth much earlier than we thought. Long thought to be dead, she says she was abducted [redacted]

While on the Skrull planet, she [redacted] that has left her experiencing a series of Post Traumatic Stress Disorder-induced visions. It has also affected her relationship with her team, from whom she is keeping secret [redacted]

It has also had a profound effect on her relationship with her estranged—legally, ex-husband, Clint Barton (see case file TS057196410: RONIN).

The relationship between Mockingbird and Ronin has had a history of issues dating back to the early days of their union. Due to the Skrull abduction, [redacted] It is my assessment that this issue must be resolved sooner rather than later.

<u>STATUS:</u> Cleared for active duty as Mockingbird.

<u>RECOMMENDATIONS:</u>
1. Continuing therapy.
2. See update sent to Captain America, advising that a close eye be kept on her during this period of adjustment.

LEONARD SAMSON, M.D.

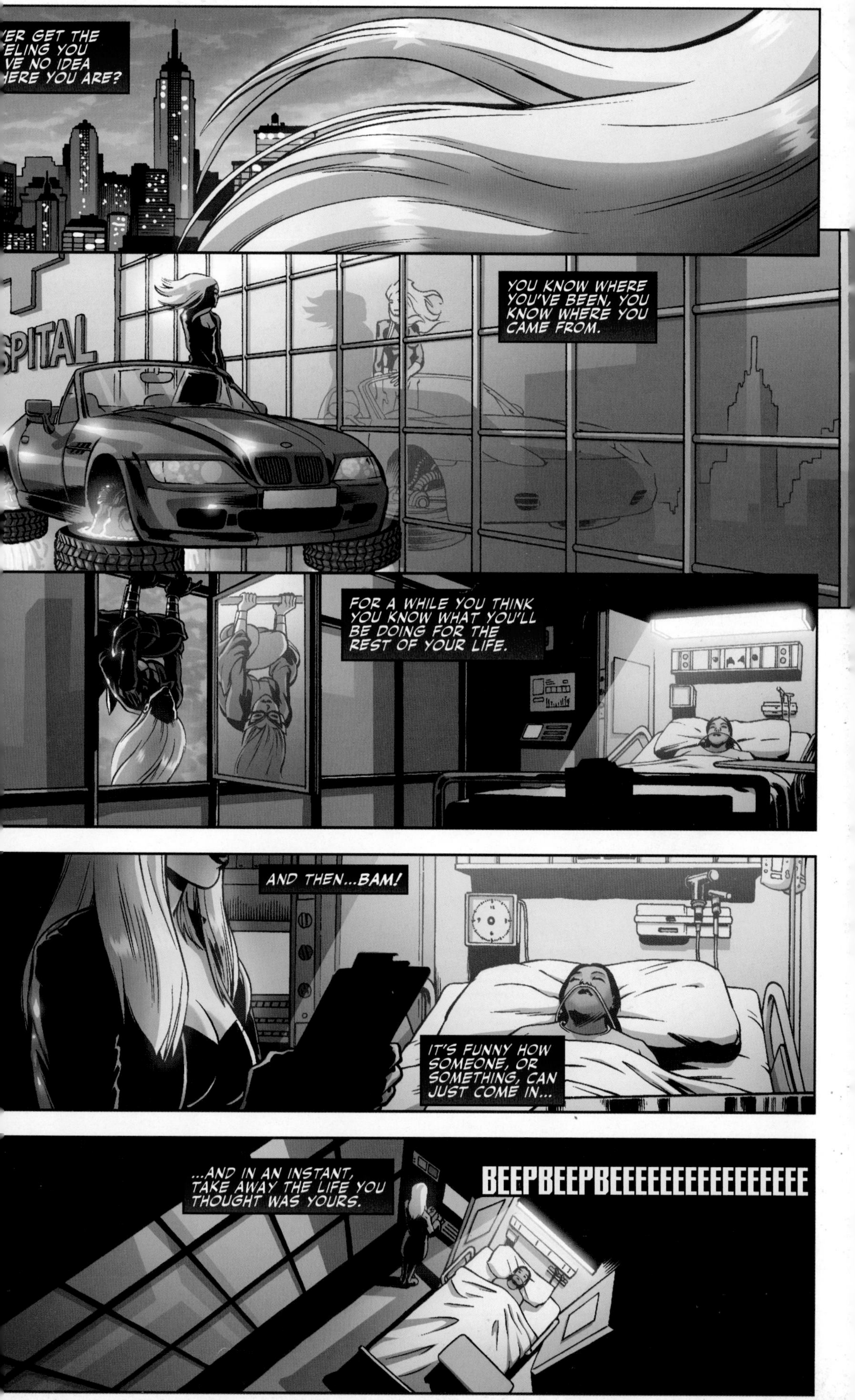

'ER GET THE
'ELING YOU
'VE NO IDEA
'HERE YOU ARE?
SPITAL
YOU KNOW WHERE YOU'VE BEEN, YOU KNOW WHERE YOU CAME FROM.
FOR A WHILE YOU THINK YOU KNOW WHAT YOU'LL BE DOING FOR THE REST OF YOUR LIFE.
AND THEN...BAM!
IT'S FUNNY HOW SOMEONE, OR SOMETHING, CAN JUST COME IN...
...AND IN AN INSTANT, TAKE AWAY THE LIFE YOU THOUGHT WAS YOURS.
BEEPBEEPBEEEEEEEEEEEEEEEE

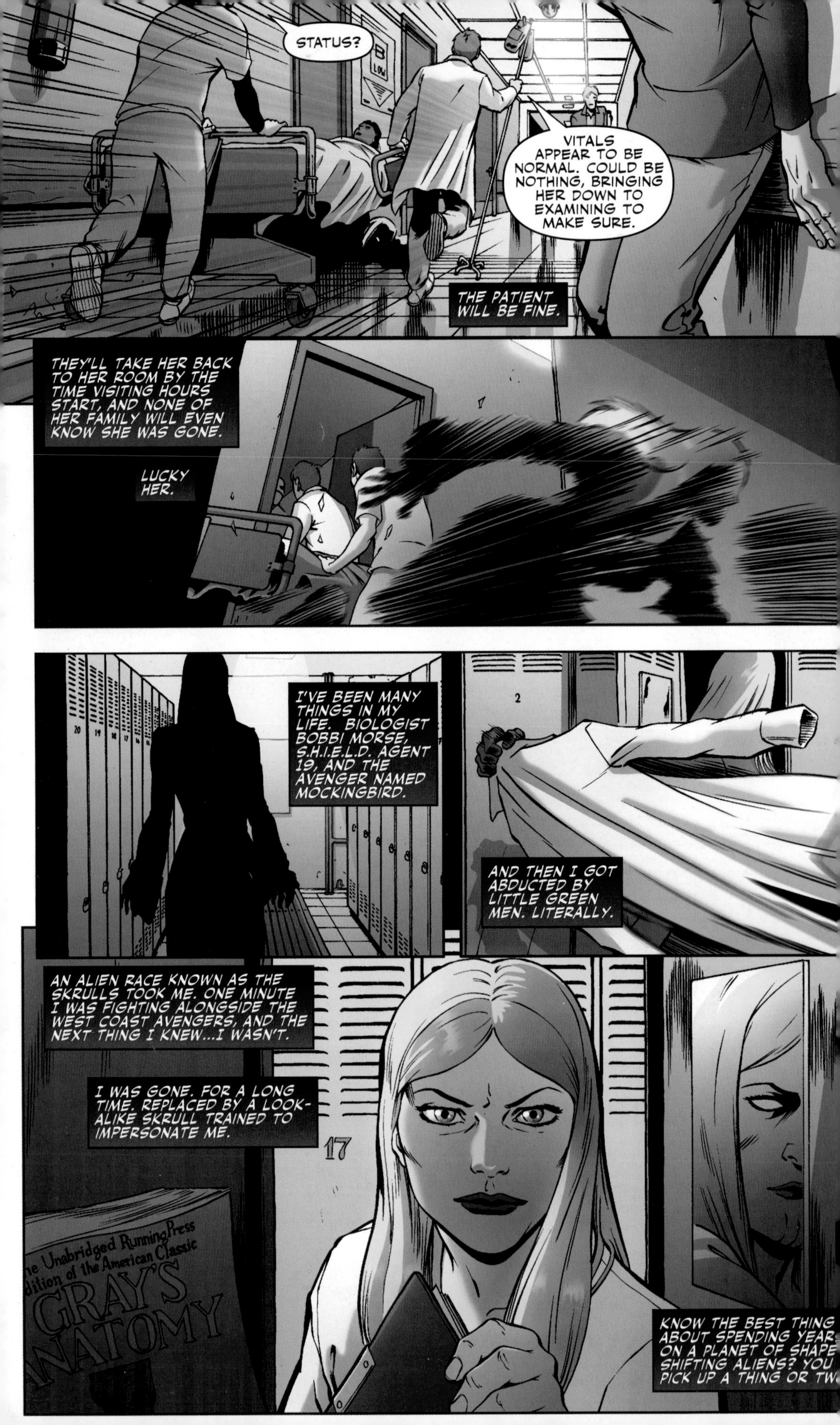
STATUS?
VITALS APPEAR TO BE NORMAL. COULD BE NOTHING, BRINGING HER DOWN TO EXAMINING TO MAKE SURE.
THE PATIENT WILL BE FINE.
THEY'LL TAKE HER BACK TO HER ROOM BY THE TIME VISITING HOURS START, AND NONE OF HER FAMILY WILL EVEN KNOW SHE WAS GONE.
LUCKY HER.
I'VE BEEN MANY THINGS IN MY LIFE. BIOLOGIST BOBBI MORSE, S.H.I.E.L.D. AGENT 19, AND THE AVENGER NAMED MOCKINGBIRD.
AND THEN I GOT ABDUCTED BY LITTLE GREEN MEN. LITERALLY.
AN ALIEN RACE KNOWN AS THE SKRULLS TOOK ME. ONE MINUTE I WAS FIGHTING ALONGSIDE THE WEST COAST AVENGERS, AND THE NEXT THING I KNEW...I WASN'T.
I WAS GONE. FOR A LONG TIME. REPLACED BY A LOOK-ALIKE SKRULL TRAINED TO IMPERSONATE ME.
17
The Unabridged Running Press
Edition of the American Classic
GRAY'S ANATOMY
KNOW THE BEST THING ABOUT SPENDING YEAR ON A PLANET OF SHAPE SHIFTING ALIENS? YOU PICK UP A THING OR TW

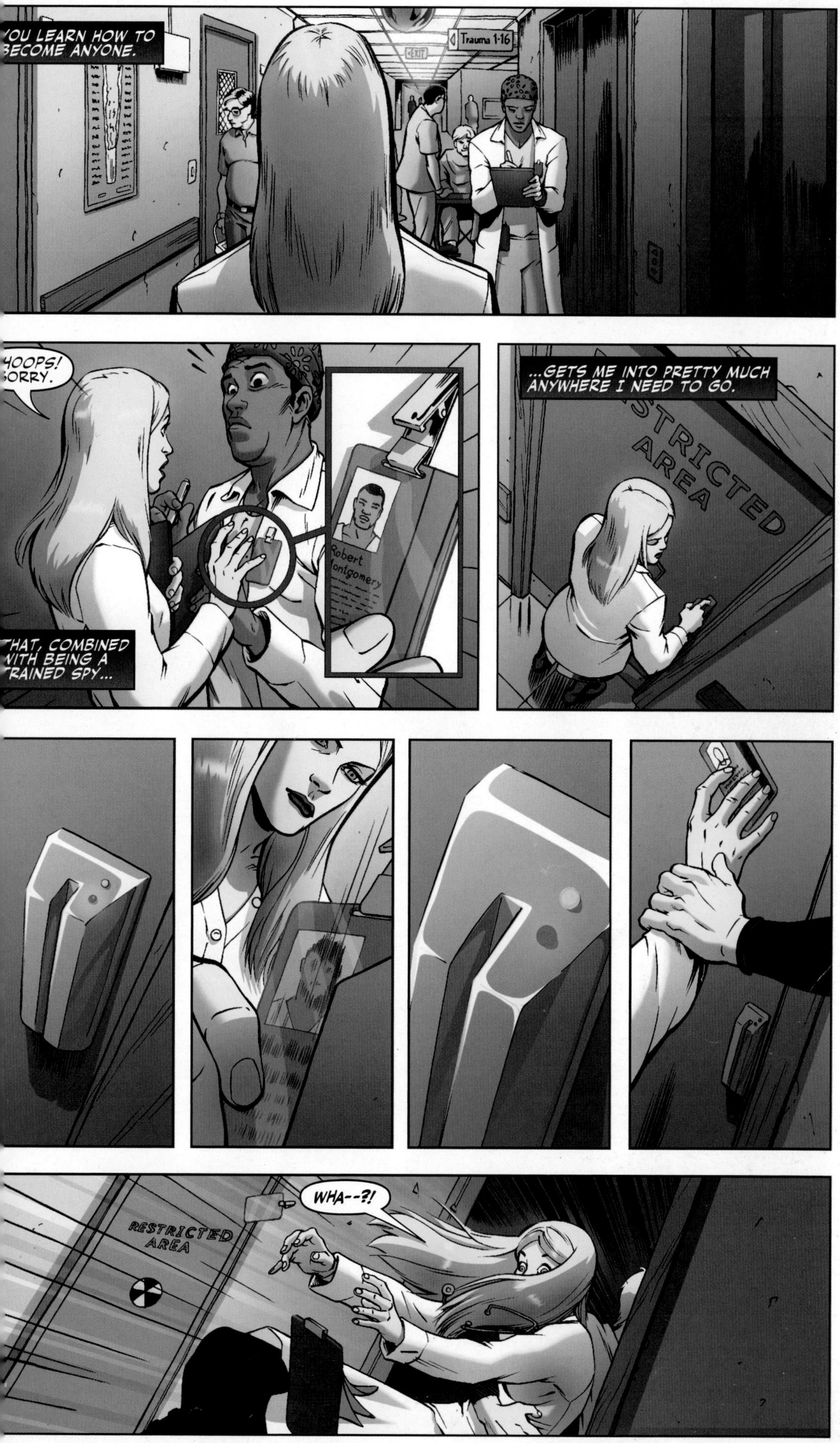
YOU LEARN HOW TO BECOME ANYONE.
Trauma 1-16
EXIT
HOOPS! SORRY.
Robert Montgomery
THAT, COMBINED WITH BEING A TRAINED SPY...
...GETS ME INTO PRETTY MUCH ANYWHERE I NEED TO GO.
RESTRICTED AREA
WHA--?!
RESTRICTED AREA

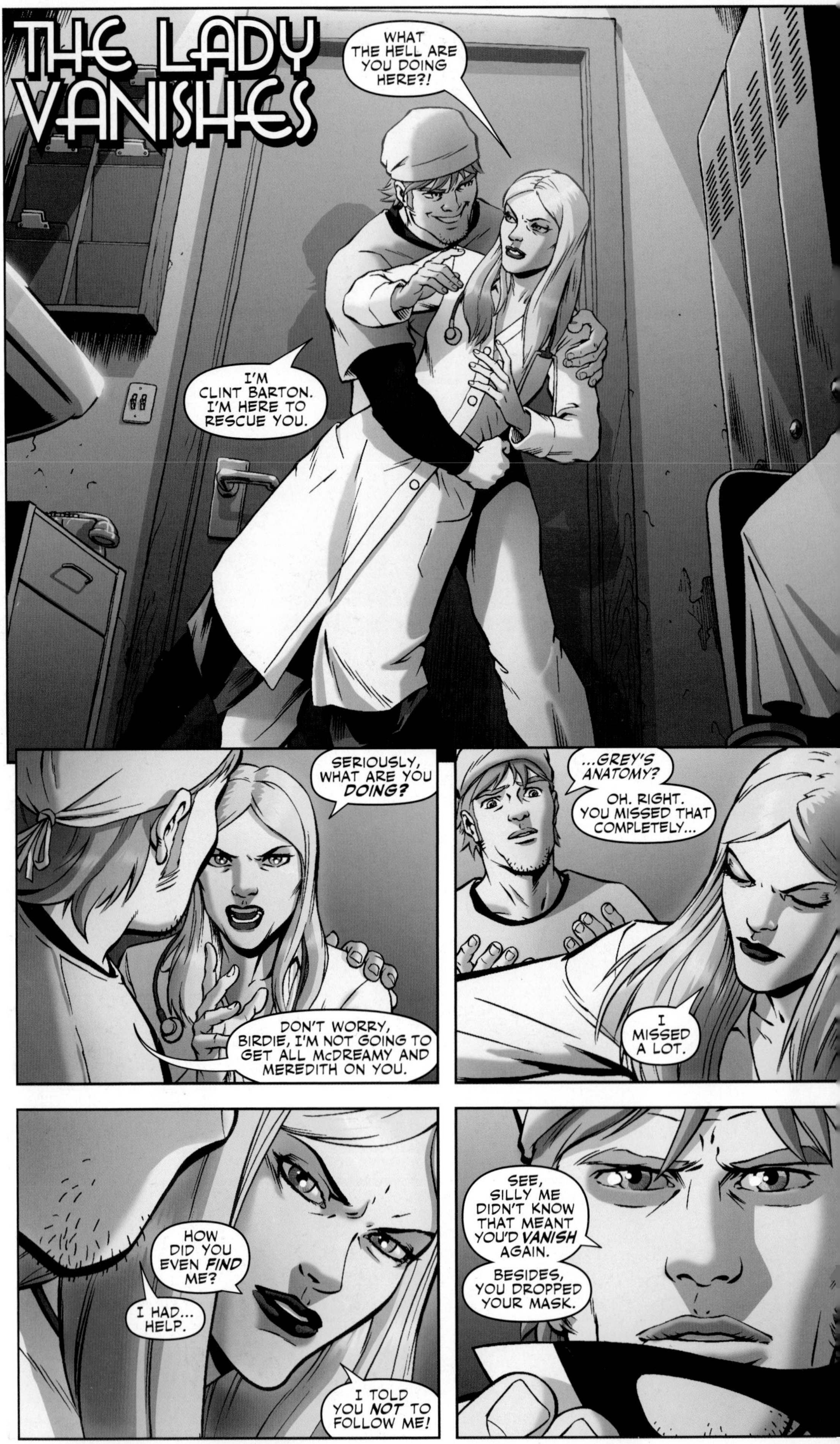
THE LADY VANISHES
WHAT THE HELL ARE YOU DOING HERE?!
I'M CLINT BARTON. I'M HERE TO RESCUE YOU.
SERIOUSLY, WHAT ARE YOU DOING?
DON'T WORRY, BIRDIE, I'M NOT GOING TO GET ALL McDREAMY AND MEREDITH ON YOU.
...GREY'S ANATOMY?
OH. RIGHT. YOU MISSED THAT COMPLETELY...
I MISSED A LOT.
HOW DID YOU EVEN FIND ME?
I HAD... HELP.
I TOLD YOU NOT TO FOLLOW ME!
SEE, SILLY ME DIDN'T KNOW THAT MEANT YOU'D VANISH AGAIN.
BESIDES, YOU DROPPED YOUR MASK.

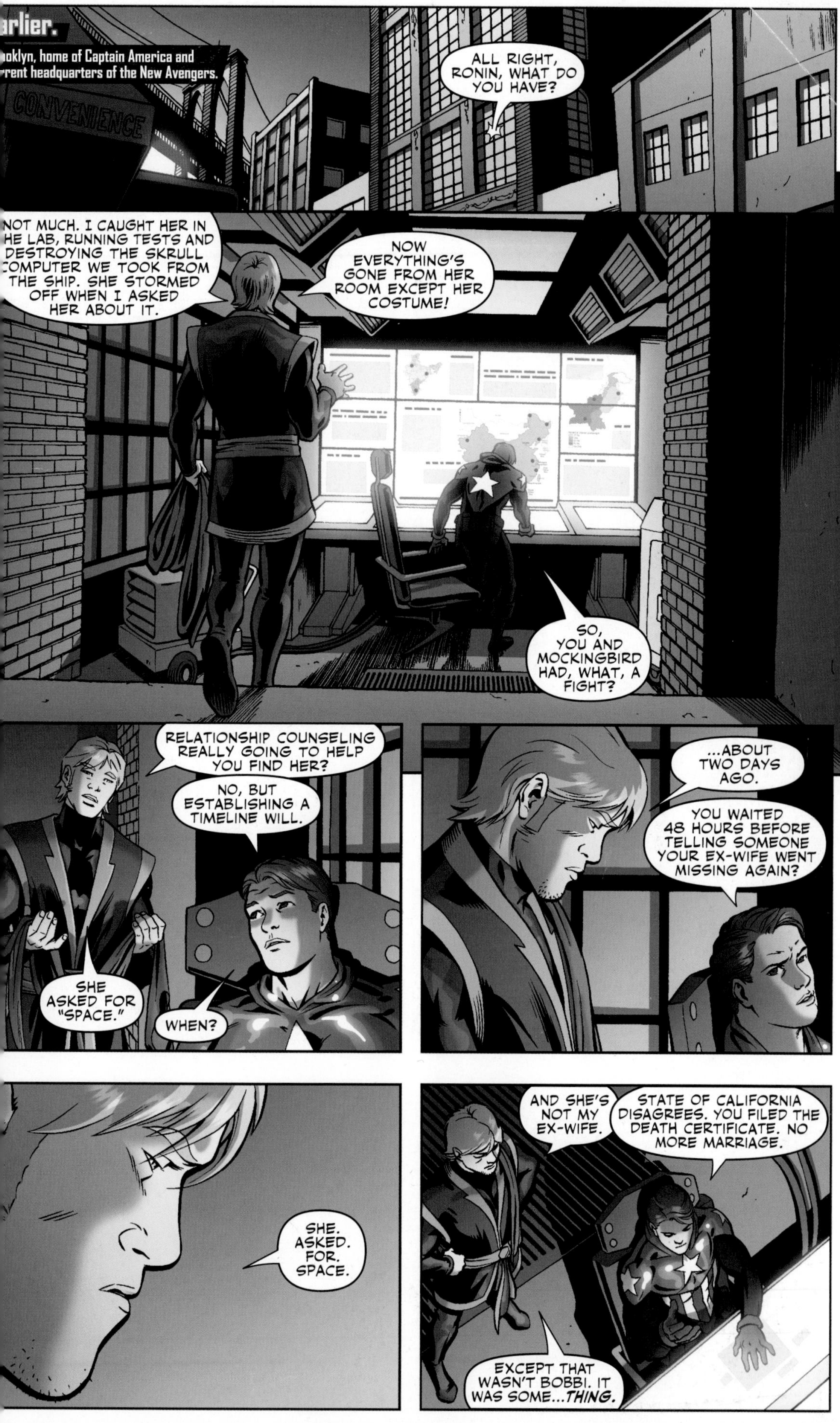
arlier.
ooklyn, home of Captain America and
rrent headquarters of the New Avengers.
CONVENIENCE
ALL RIGHT, RONIN, WHAT DO YOU HAVE?
NOT MUCH. I CAUGHT HER IN HE LAB, RUNNING TESTS AND DESTROYING THE SKRULL COMPUTER WE TOOK FROM THE SHIP. SHE STORMED OFF WHEN I ASKED HER ABOUT IT.
NOW EVERYTHING'S GONE FROM HER ROOM EXCEPT HER COSTUME!
SO, YOU AND MOCKINGBIRD HAD, WHAT, A FIGHT?
SHE ASKED FOR "SPACE."
RELATIONSHIP COUNSELING REALLY GOING TO HELP YOU FIND HER?
NO, BUT ESTABLISHING A TIMELINE WILL.
WHEN?
...ABOUT TWO DAYS AGO.
YOU WAITED 48 HOURS BEFORE TELLING SOMEONE YOUR EX-WIFE WENT MISSING AGAIN?
SHE. ASKED. FOR. SPACE.
AND SHE'S NOT MY EX-WIFE.
STATE OF CALIFORNIA DISAGREES. YOU FILED THE DEATH CERTIFICATE. NO MORE MARRIAGE.
EXCEPT THAT WASN'T BOBBI. IT WAS SOME...*THING*.

AND AFTER IT DIED, THE BODY TURNED TO DUST...NOT MUCH LEFT FOR AN AUTOPSY.

THE SKRULLS FOOLED *ALL* OF US, NOT JUST ME!

EASY. *YOU* CAME TO *ME* FOR HELP.

YEAH, STARTING TO REGRET THAT.

NO ONE IS LAYING BLAME ON *YOU*, BARTON.

AND IF BOBBI'S GONE, SHE'S A GROWN WOMAN...

DON'T EVEN *THINK* OF FINISHING THAT SENTENCE.

I CAN'T LOSE HER. NOT AGAIN.

YOU'VE BEEN ON ICE MOST'A YOUR LIFE, SO YOU HAVEN'T HAD TO LIVE EVERY DAY LOOKING BACK ON THE DECISIONS YOU'VE MADE.

PLAY THEM OVER AND OVER IN YOUR HEAD, THE "WHAT IF" GAME KEEPING YOU UP ALL NIGHT.

NO, KID, *YOU* GOT TO GO BACK TO SLEEP IN A RUSSIAN FREEZER.

ME, I'VE HAD YEARS TO GO OVER EVERYTHING I WOULD'VE DONE SHOULD'VE DONE DIFFERENT.

NOW I *CAN* DO IT, JUST AS SOON AS YOU GET BACK TO FINDING HER!

YOU KNOW, THEY OFFERED IT TO ME FIRST, RIGHT? THE SHIELD. AFTER HE DIED.

I COULD'A BEEN CAP.

HING DATA FILE

VERING...

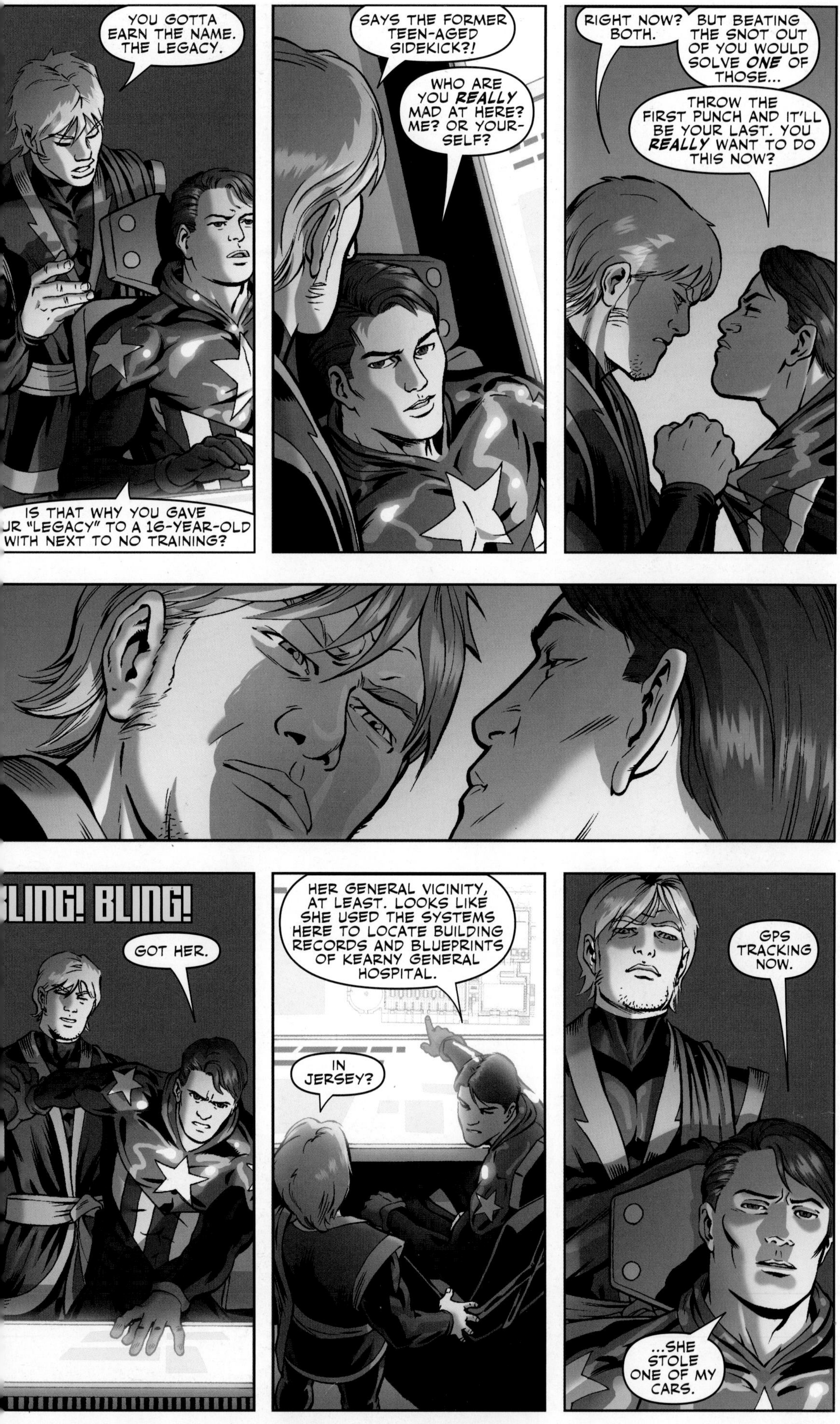
YOU GOTTA EARN THE NAME. THE LEGACY.
IS THAT WHY YOU GAVE UR "LEGACY" TO A 16-YEAR-OLD WITH NEXT TO NO TRAINING?
SAYS THE FORMER TEEN-AGED SIDEKICK?!
WHO ARE YOU REALLY MAD AT HERE? ME? OR YOURSELF?
RIGHT NOW? BOTH.
BUT BEATING THE SNOT OUT OF YOU WOULD SOLVE ONE OF THOSE...
THROW THE FIRST PUNCH AND IT'LL BE YOUR LAST. YOU REALLY WANT TO DO THIS NOW?
BLING! BLING!
GOT HER.
HER GENERAL VICINITY, AT LEAST. LOOKS LIKE SHE USED THE SYSTEMS HERE TO LOCATE BUILDING RECORDS AND BLUEPRINTS OF KEARNY GENERAL HOSPITAL.
IN JERSEY?
GPS TRACKING NOW.
...SHE STOLE ONE OF MY CARS.

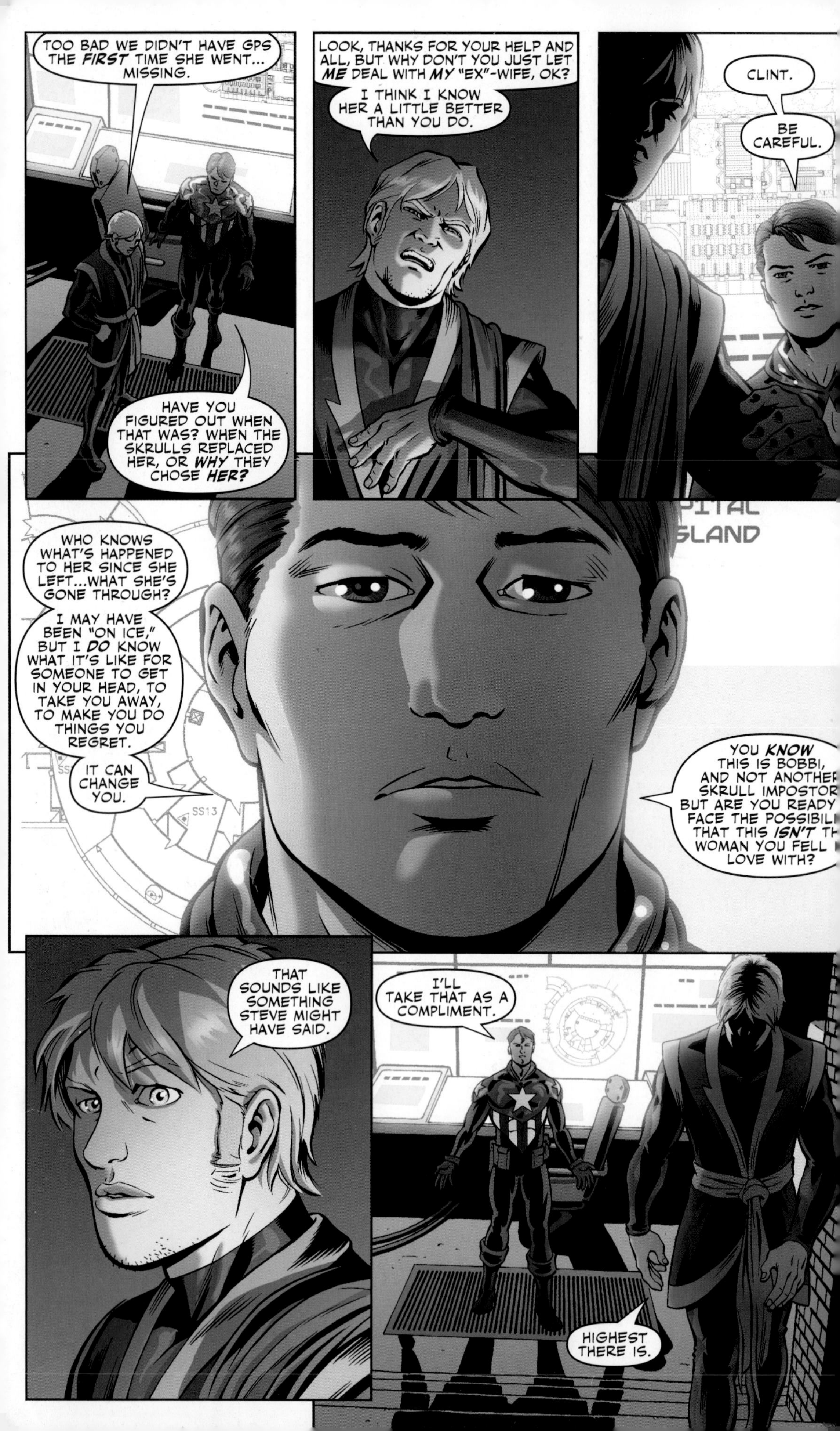
TOO BAD WE DIDN'T HAVE GPS THE FIRST TIME SHE WENT... MISSING.
HAVE YOU FIGURED OUT WHEN THAT WAS? WHEN THE SKRULLS REPLACED HER, OR WHY THEY CHOSE HER?
LOOK, THANKS FOR YOUR HELP AND ALL, BUT WHY DON'T YOU JUST LET ME DEAL WITH MY "EX"-WIFE, OK?
I THINK I KNOW HER A LITTLE BETTER THAN YOU DO.
CLINT.
BE CAREFUL.
WHO KNOWS WHAT'S HAPPENED TO HER SINCE SHE LEFT...WHAT SHE'S GONE THROUGH?
I MAY HAVE BEEN "ON ICE," BUT I DO KNOW WHAT IT'S LIKE FOR SOMEONE TO GET IN YOUR HEAD, TO TAKE YOU AWAY, TO MAKE YOU DO THINGS YOU REGRET.
IT CAN CHANGE YOU.
YOU KNOW THIS IS BOBBI, AND NOT ANOTHEI SKRULL IMPOSTOR BUT ARE YOU READY FACE THE POSSIBIL THAT THIS ISN'T TH WOMAN YOU FELL LOVE WITH?
THAT SOUNDS LIKE SOMETHING STEVE MIGHT HAVE SAID.
I'LL TAKE THAT AS A COMPLIMENT.
HIGHEST THERE IS.

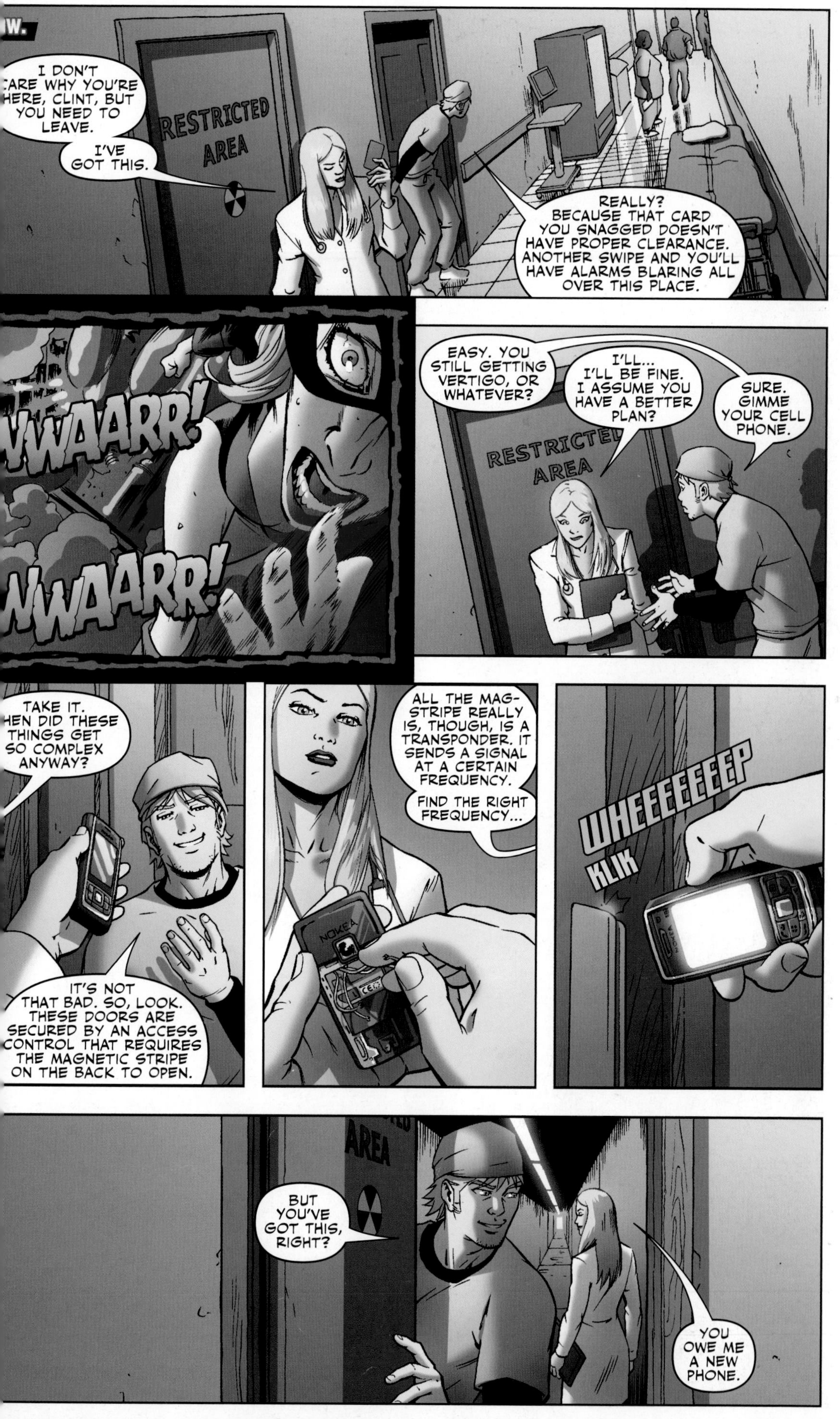
W.
I DON'T CARE WHY YOU'RE HERE, CLINT, BUT YOU NEED TO LEAVE.
I'VE GOT THIS.
RESTRICTED AREA
REALLY? BECAUSE THAT CARD YOU SNAGGED DOESN'T HAVE PROPER CLEARANCE. ANOTHER SWIPE AND YOU'LL HAVE ALARMS BLARING ALL OVER THIS PLACE.
WAARR!
WAARR!
EASY. YOU STILL GETTING VERTIGO, OR WHATEVER?
I'LL... I'LL BE FINE. I ASSUME YOU HAVE A BETTER PLAN?
SURE. GIMME YOUR CELL PHONE.
RESTRICTED AREA
TAKE IT. HEN DID THESE THINGS GET SO COMPLEX ANYWAY?
IT'S NOT THAT BAD. SO, LOOK. THESE DOORS ARE SECURED BY AN ACCESS CONTROL THAT REQUIRES THE MAGNETIC STRIPE ON THE BACK TO OPEN.
ALL THE MAG-STRIPE REALLY IS, THOUGH, IS A TRANSPONDER. IT SENDS A SIGNAL AT A CERTAIN FREQUENCY.
FIND THE RIGHT FREQUENCY...
NOKEA
WHEEEEEEEP
KLIK
AREA
BUT YOU'VE GOT THIS, RIGHT?
YOU OWE ME A NEW PHONE.

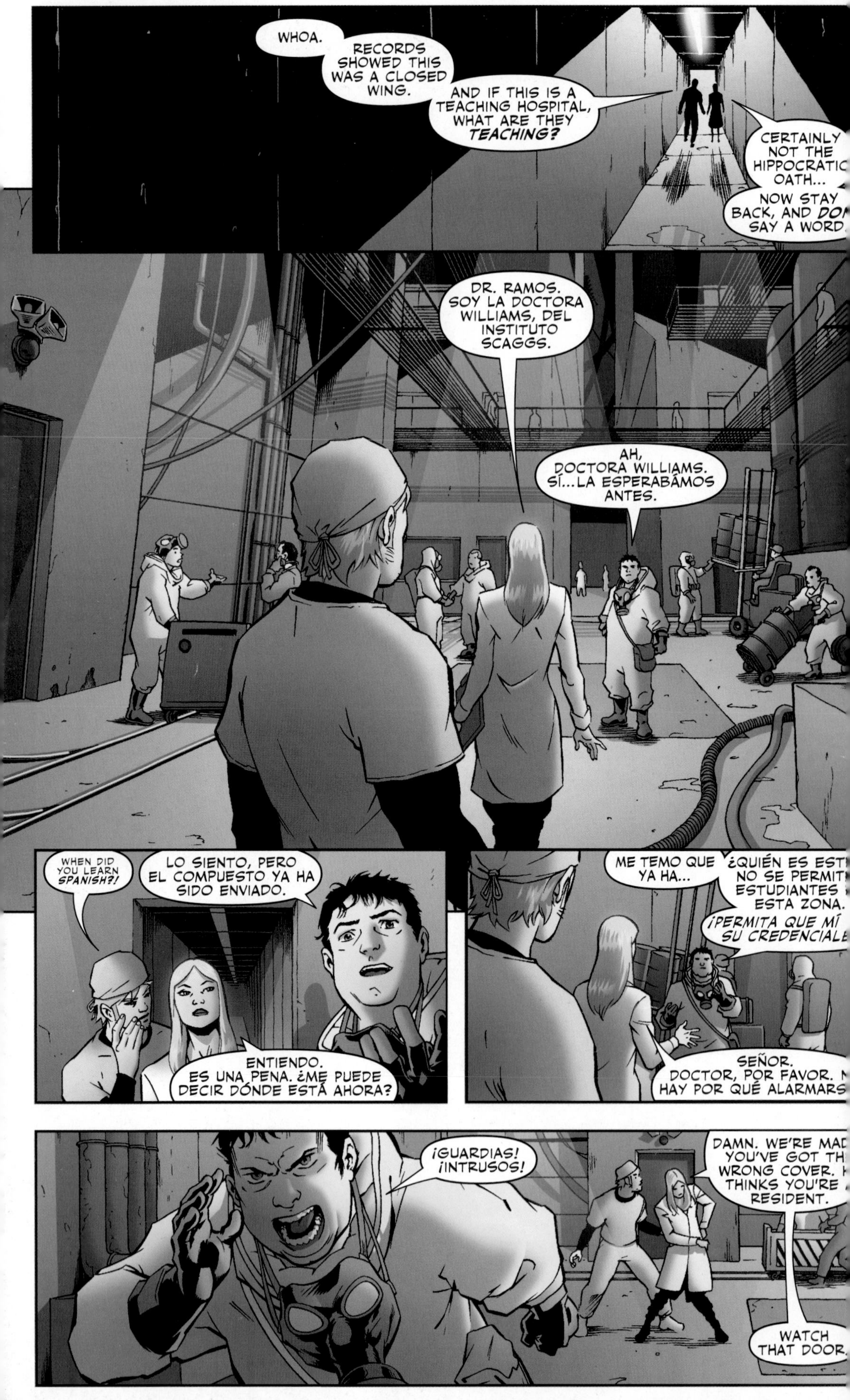
WHOA.
RECORDS SHOWED THIS WAS A CLOSED WING.
AND IF THIS IS A TEACHING HOSPITAL, WHAT ARE THEY *TEACHING?*
CERTAINLY NOT THE HIPPOCRATIC OATH...
NOW STAY BACK, AND *DO* SAY A WORD.
DR. RAMOS. SOY LA DOCTORA WILLIAMS, DEL INSTITUTO SCAGGS.
AH, DOCTORA WILLIAMS. SÍ...LA ESPERABÁMOS ANTES.
WHEN DID YOU LEARN *SPANISH?!*
LO SIENTO, PERO EL COMPUESTO YA HA SIDO ENVIADO.
ENTIENDO. ES UNA PENA. ¿ME PUEDE DECIR DÓNDE ESTÁ AHORA?
ME TEMO QUE YA HA...
¿QUIÉN ES EST NO SE PERMIT ESTUDIANTES ESTA ZONA.
¡PERMITA QUE MÍ SU CREDENCIALE
SEÑOR. DOCTOR, POR FAVOR. HAY POR QUÉ ALARMARS
¡GUARDIAS! ¡INTRUSOS!
DAMN. WE'RE MAD YOU'VE GOT TH WRONG COVER. THINKS YOU'RE RESIDENT.
WATCH THAT DOOR.

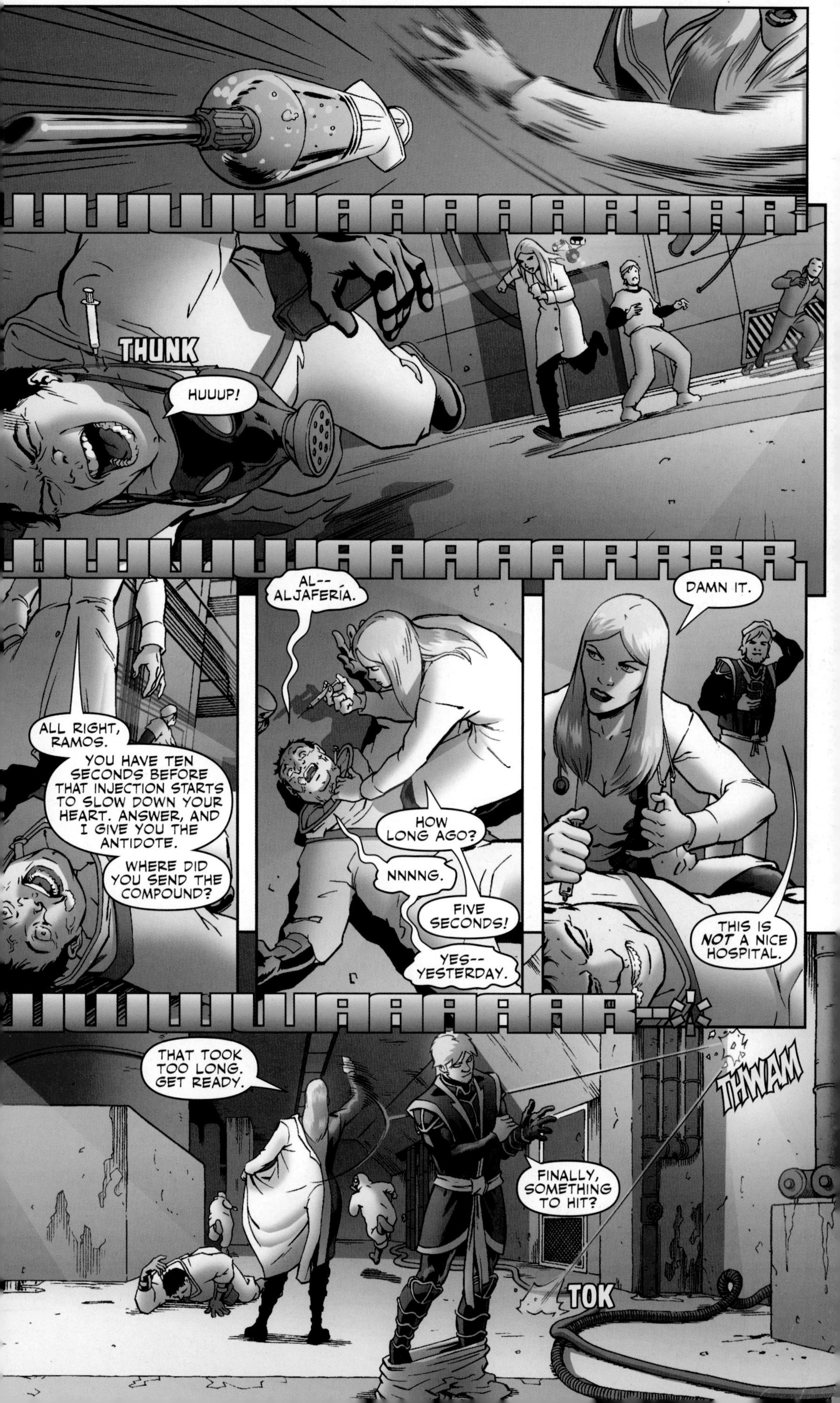
WWWWWAAAAAARRRR
THUNK
HUUUP!
WWWWWAAAAAARRRR
ALL RIGHT, RAMOS.
YOU HAVE TEN SECONDS BEFORE THAT INJECTION STARTS TO SLOW DOWN YOUR HEART. ANSWER, AND I GIVE YOU THE ANTIDOTE.
WHERE DID YOU SEND THE COMPOUND?
AL-- ALJAFERÍA.
HOW LONG AGO?
NNNNG.
FIVE SECONDS!
YES-- YESTERDAY.
DAMN IT.
THIS IS *NOT* A NICE HOSPITAL.
WWWWWAAAAAR--
THAT TOOK TOO LONG. GET READY.
THWAM
FINALLY, SOMETHING TO HIT?
TOK

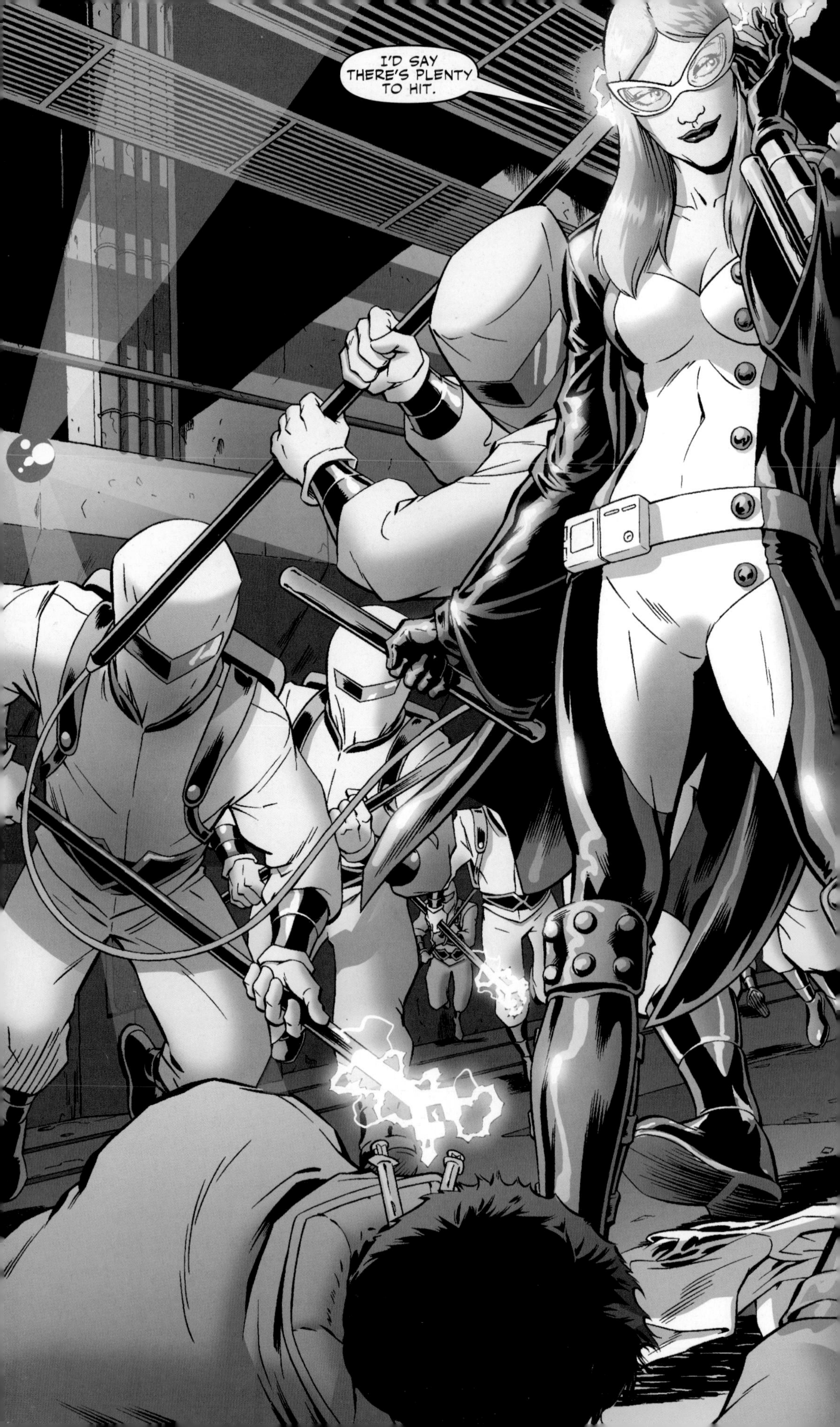
I'D SAY THERE'S PLENTY TO HIT.

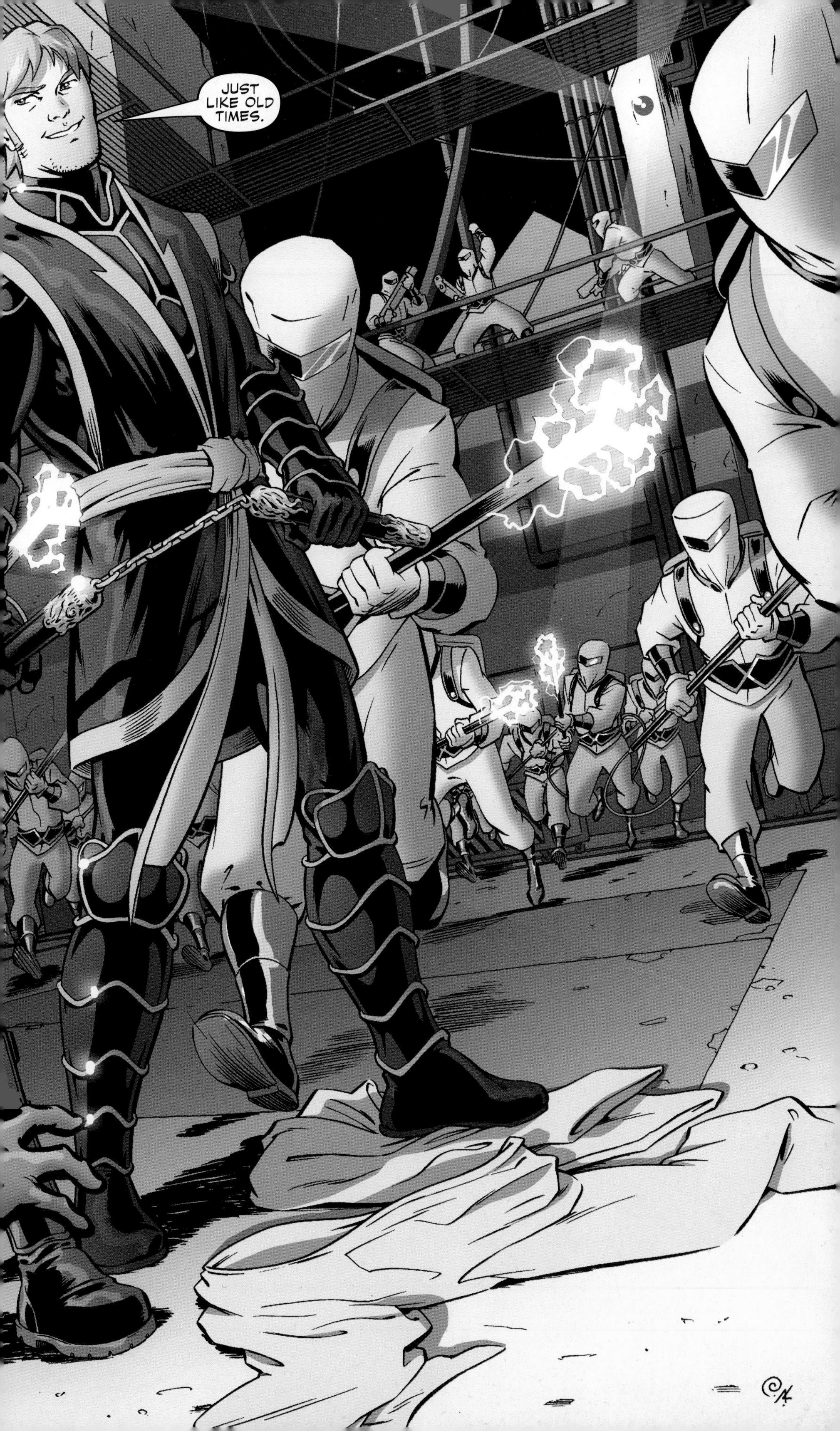
JUST LIKE OLD TIMES.

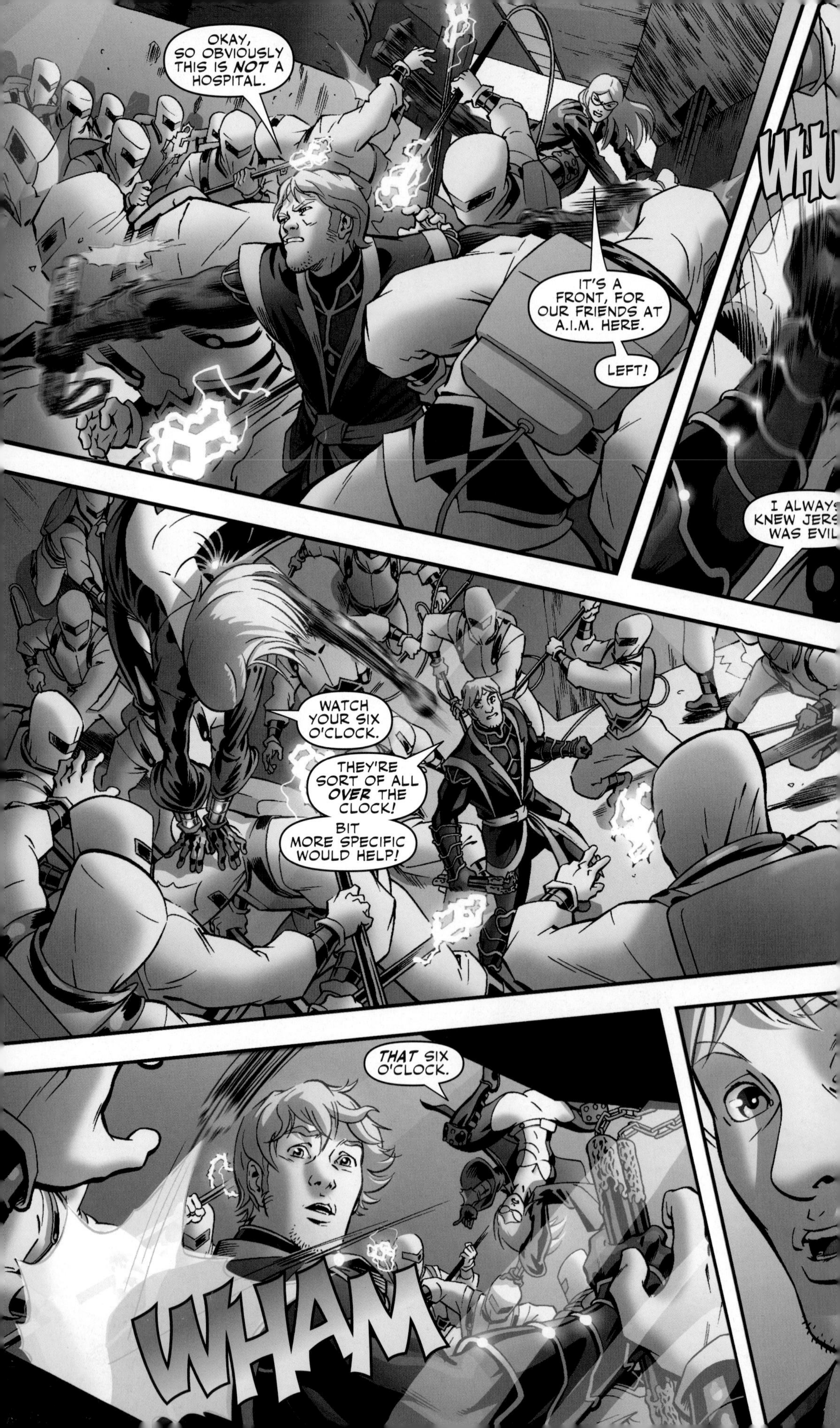
OKAY, SO OBVIOUSLY THIS IS *NOT* A HOSPITAL.
IT'S A FRONT, FOR OUR FRIENDS AT A.I.M. HERE.
LEFT!
WHU
I ALWAYS KNEW JERS WAS EVIL
WATCH YOUR SIX O'CLOCK.
THEY'RE SORT OF ALL *OVER* THE CLOCK!
BIT MORE SPECIFIC WOULD HELP!
THAT SIX O'CLOCK.
WHAM

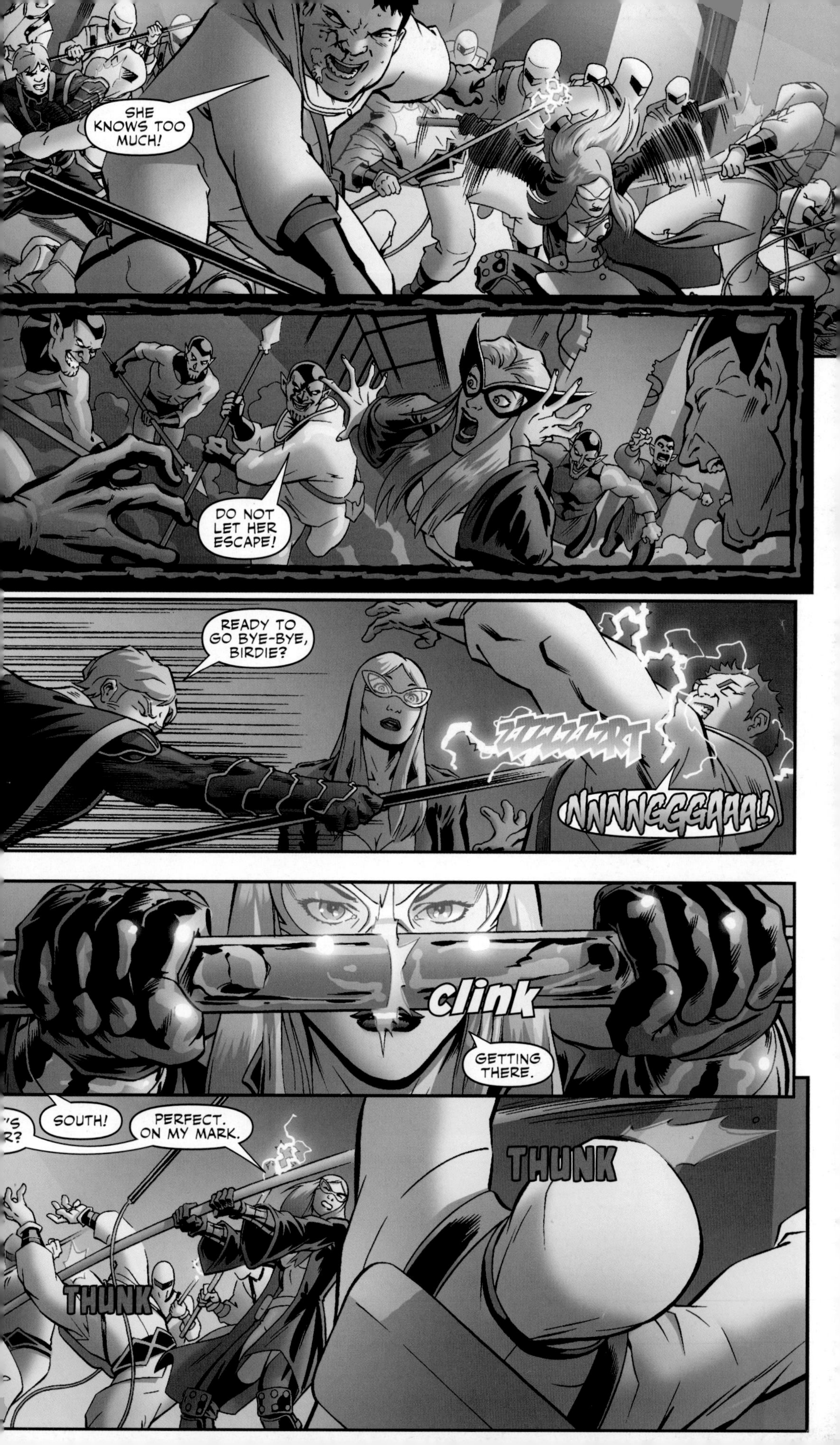
SHE KNOWS TOO MUCH!
DO NOT LET HER ESCAPE!
READY TO GO BYE-BYE, BIRDIE?
ZZZZZRT
NNNNGGGAAA!
clink
GETTING THERE.
SOUTH!
PERFECT. ON MY MARK.
THUNK
THUNK

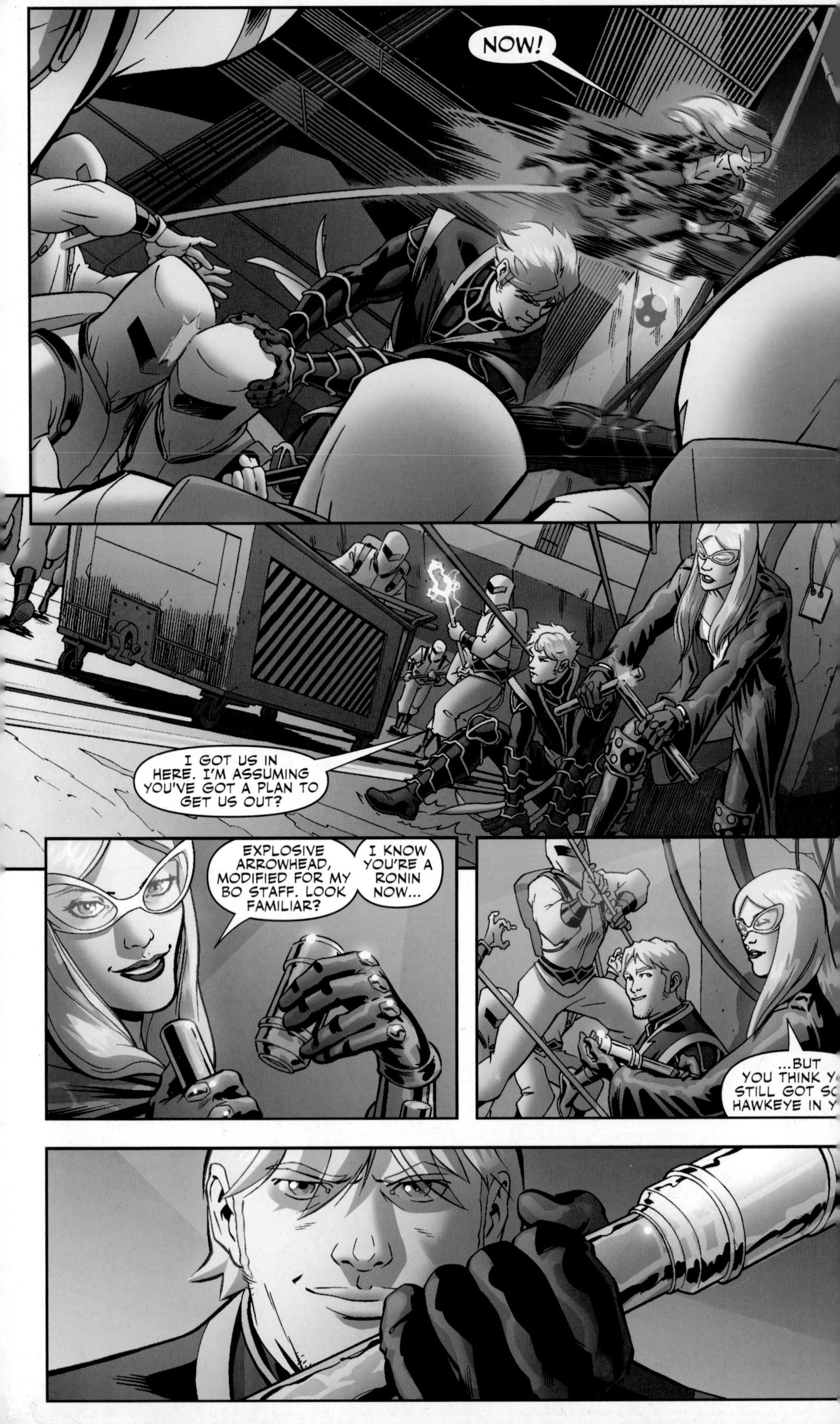
NOW!
I GOT US IN HERE. I'M ASSUMING YOU'VE GOT A PLAN TO GET US OUT?
EXPLOSIVE ARROWHEAD, MODIFIED FOR MY BO STAFF. LOOK FAMILIAR?
I KNOW YOU'RE A RONIN NOW...
...BUT YOU THINK Y STILL GOT S HAWKEYE IN Y

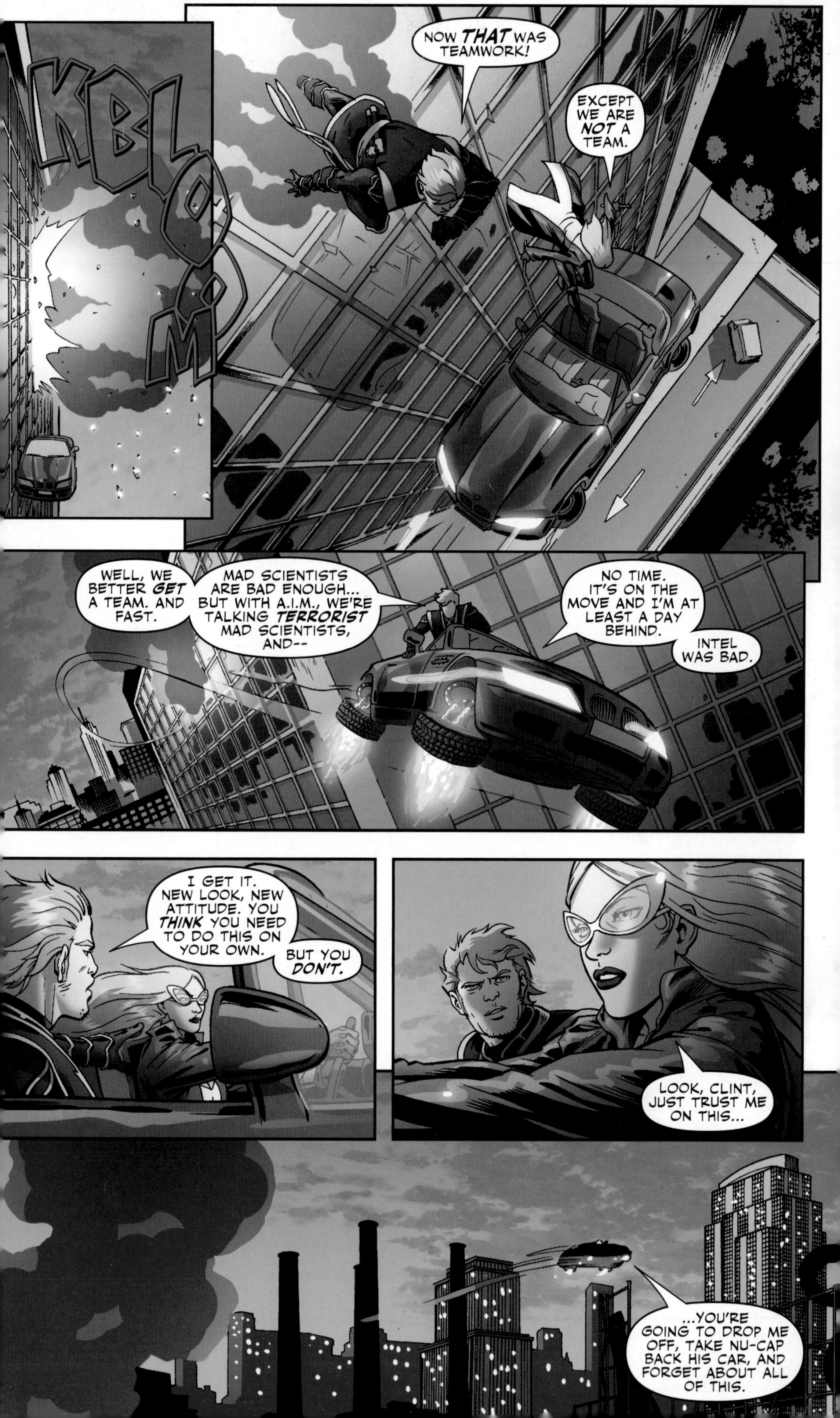

KBLOOM
NOW THAT WAS TEAMWORK!
EXCEPT WE ARE NOT A TEAM.
WELL, WE BETTER GET A TEAM. AND FAST.
MAD SCIENTISTS ARE BAD ENOUGH... BUT WITH A.I.M., WE'RE TALKING TERRORIST MAD SCIENTISTS, AND--
NO TIME. IT'S ON THE MOVE AND I'M AT LEAST A DAY BEHIND.
INTEL WAS BAD.
I GET IT. NEW LOOK, NEW ATTITUDE. YOU THINK YOU NEED TO DO THIS ON YOUR OWN.
BUT YOU DON'T.
LOOK, CLINT, JUST TRUST ME ON THIS...
...YOU'RE GOING TO DROP ME OFF, TAKE NU-CAP BACK HIS CAR, AND FORGET ABOUT ALL OF THIS.

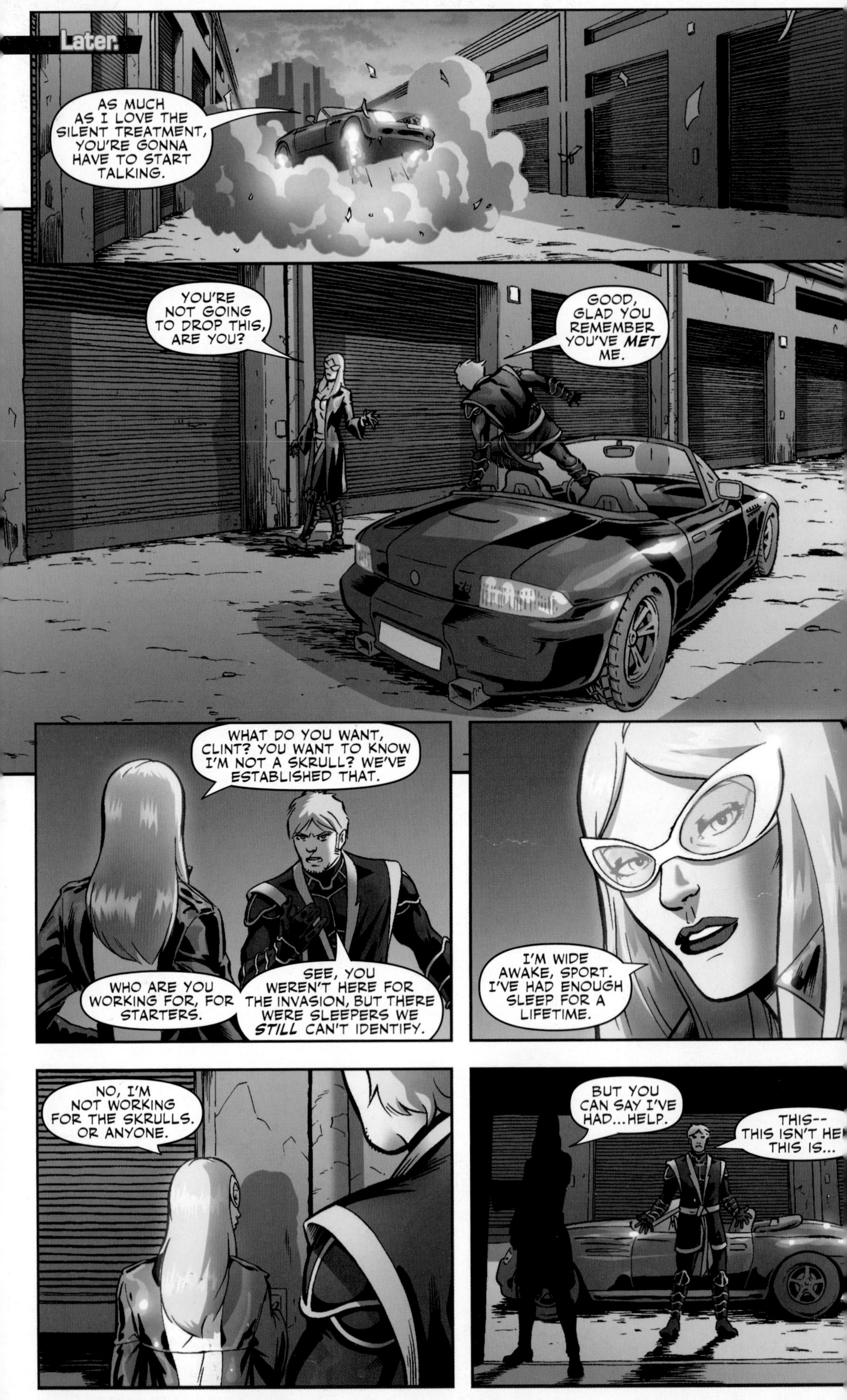
Later.
AS MUCH AS I LOVE THE SILENT TREATMENT, YOU'RE GONNA HAVE TO START TALKING.
YOU'RE NOT GOING TO DROP THIS, ARE YOU?
GOOD, GLAD YOU REMEMBER YOU'VE MET ME.
WHAT DO YOU WANT, CLINT? YOU WANT TO KNOW I'M NOT A SKRULL? WE'VE ESTABLISHED THAT.
WHO ARE YOU WORKING FOR, FOR STARTERS.
SEE, YOU WEREN'T HERE FOR THE INVASION, BUT THERE WERE SLEEPERS WE STILL CAN'T IDENTIFY.
I'M WIDE AWAKE, SPORT. I'VE HAD ENOUGH SLEEP FOR A LIFETIME.
NO, I'M NOT WORKING FOR THE SKRULLS. OR ANYONE.
BUT YOU CAN SAY I'VE HAD...HELP.
THIS-- THIS ISN'T HE THIS IS...

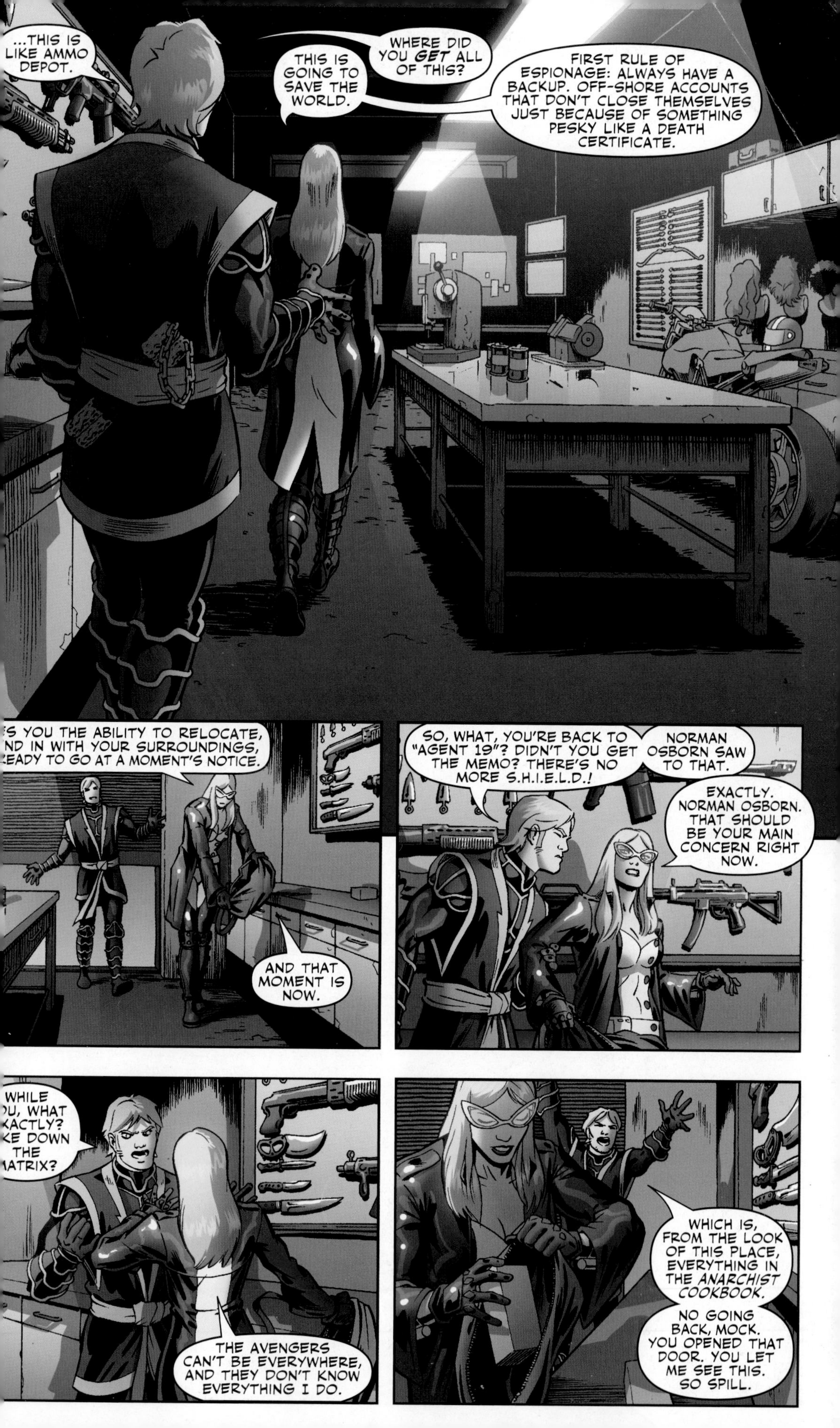

...THIS IS LIKE AMMO DEPOT.
WHERE DID YOU *GET* ALL OF THIS?
THIS IS GOING TO SAVE THE WORLD.
FIRST RULE OF ESPIONAGE: ALWAYS HAVE A BACKUP. OFF-SHORE ACCOUNTS THAT DON'T CLOSE THEMSELVES JUST BECAUSE OF SOMETHING PESKY LIKE A DEATH CERTIFICATE.
'S YOU THE ABILITY TO RELOCATE, ND IN WITH YOUR SURROUNDINGS, EADY TO GO AT A MOMENT'S NOTICE.
AND THAT MOMENT IS NOW.
SO, WHAT, YOU'RE BACK TO "AGENT 19"? DIDN'T YOU GET THE MEMO? THERE'S NO MORE S.H.I.E.L.D.!
NORMAN OSBORN SAW TO THAT.
EXACTLY. NORMAN OSBORN. THAT SHOULD BE YOUR MAIN CONCERN RIGHT NOW.
WHILE U, WHAT XACTLY? KE DOWN THE ATRIX?
THE AVENGERS CAN'T BE EVERYWHERE, AND THEY DON'T KNOW EVERYTHING I DO.
WHICH IS, FROM THE LOOK OF THIS PLACE, EVERYTHING IN THE *ANARCHIST COOKBOOK*.
NO GOING BACK, MOCK. YOU OPENED THAT DOOR. YOU LET ME SEE THIS. SO SPILL.

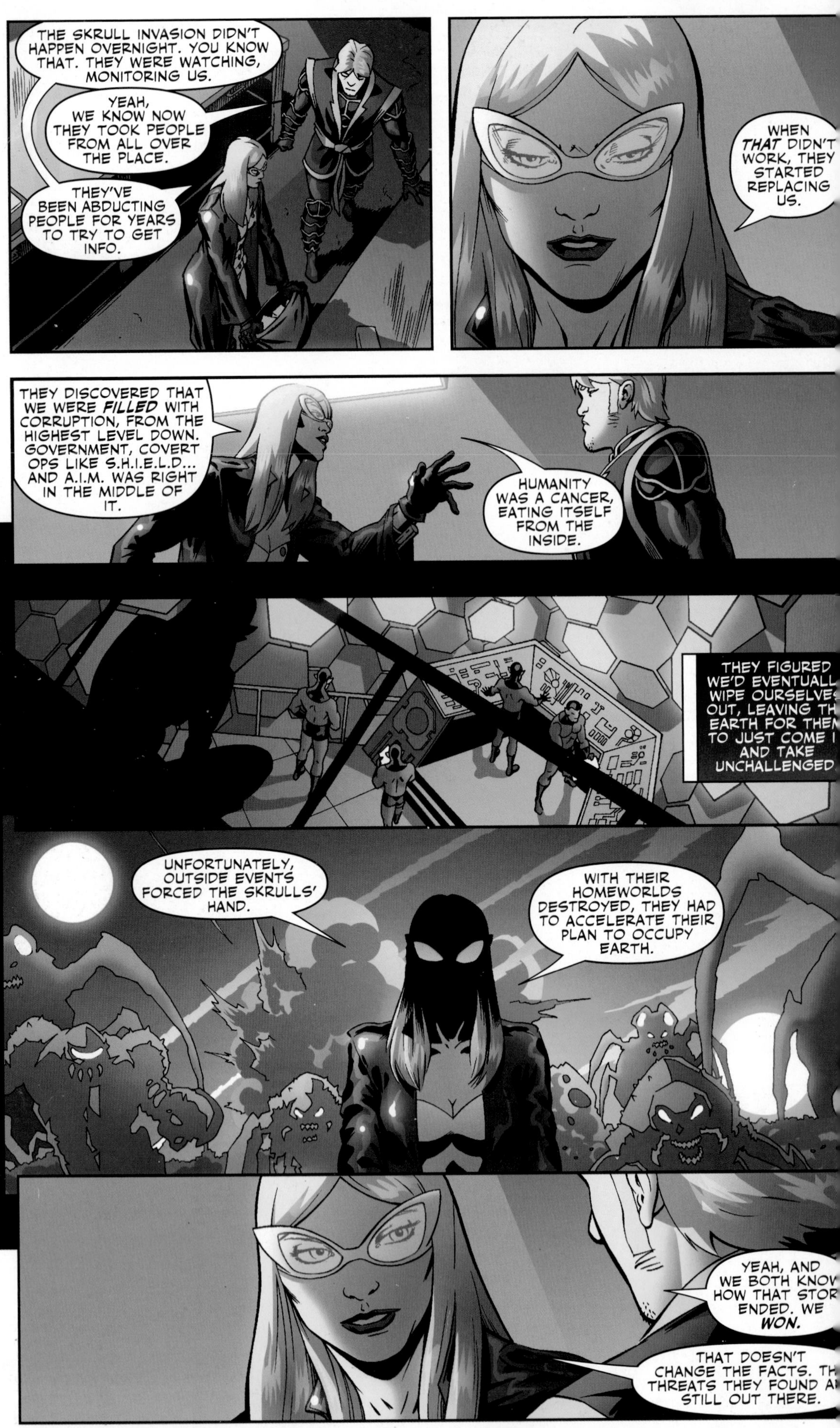
THE SKRULL INVASION DIDN'T HAPPEN OVERNIGHT. YOU KNOW THAT. THEY WERE WATCHING, MONITORING US.
YEAH, WE KNOW NOW THEY TOOK PEOPLE FROM ALL OVER THE PLACE.
THEY'VE BEEN ABDUCTING PEOPLE FOR YEARS TO TRY TO GET INFO.
WHEN THAT DIDN'T WORK, THEY STARTED REPLACING US.
THEY DISCOVERED THAT WE WERE FILLED WITH CORRUPTION, FROM THE HIGHEST LEVEL DOWN. GOVERNMENT, COVERT OPS LIKE S.H.I.E.L.D... AND A.I.M. WAS RIGHT IN THE MIDDLE OF IT.
HUMANITY WAS A CANCER, EATING ITSELF FROM THE INSIDE.
THEY FIGURED WE'D EVENTUALL WIPE OURSELVES OUT, LEAVING TH EARTH FOR THEM TO JUST COME I AND TAKE UNCHALLENGED
UNFORTUNATELY, OUTSIDE EVENTS FORCED THE SKRULLS' HAND.
WITH THEIR HOMEWORLDS DESTROYED, THEY HAD TO ACCELERATE THEIR PLAN TO OCCUPY EARTH.
YEAH, AND WE BOTH KNOW HOW THAT STOR ENDED. WE WON.
THAT DOESN'T CHANGE THE FACTS. TH THREATS THEY FOUND A STILL OUT THERE.

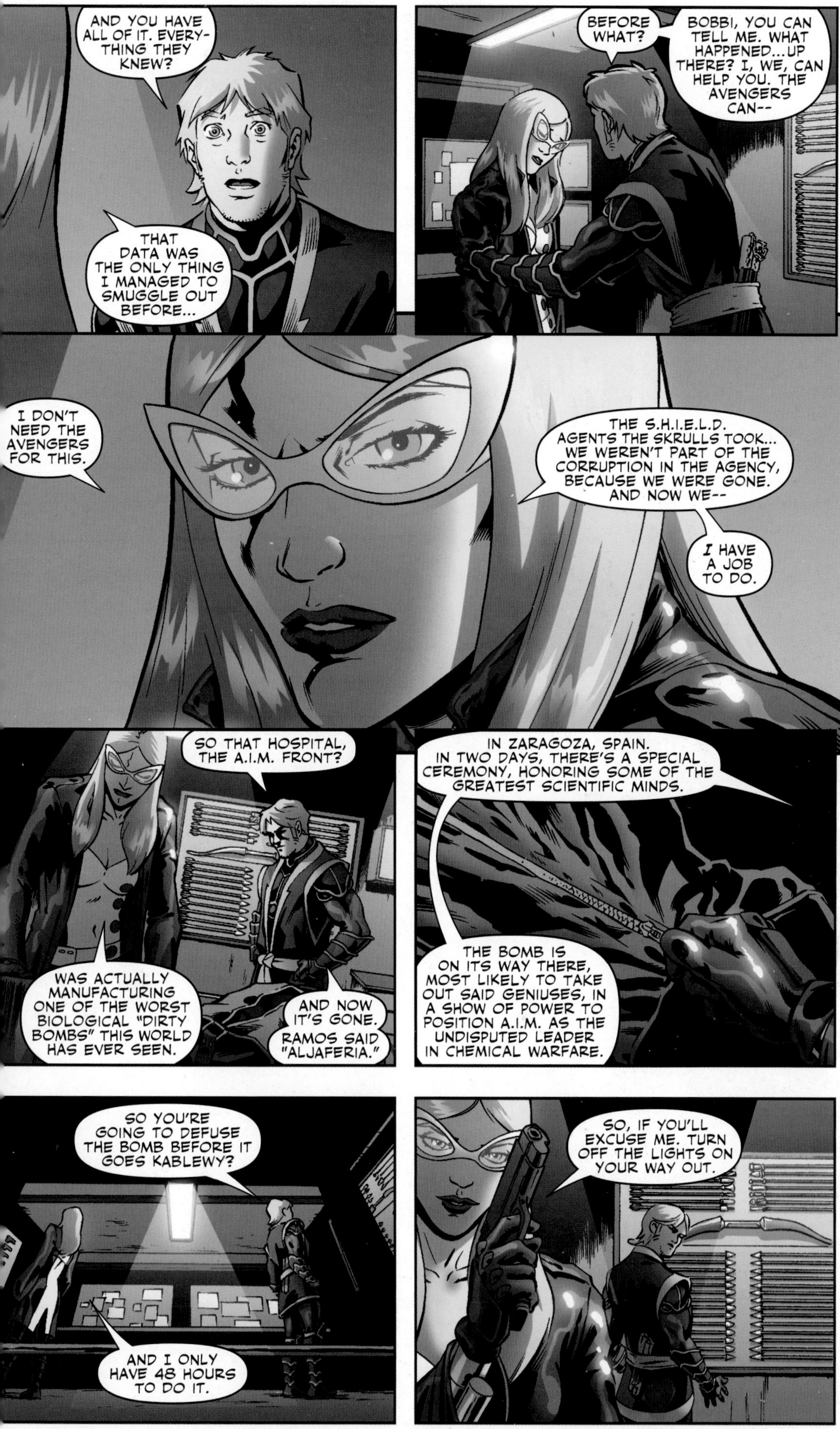
AND YOU HAVE ALL OF IT. EVERYTHING THEY KNEW?
THAT DATA WAS THE ONLY THING I MANAGED TO SMUGGLE OUT BEFORE...
BEFORE WHAT?
BOBBI, YOU CAN TELL ME. WHAT HAPPENED...UP THERE? I, WE, CAN HELP YOU. THE AVENGERS CAN--
I DON'T NEED THE AVENGERS FOR THIS.
THE S.H.I.E.L.D. AGENTS THE SKRULLS TOOK... WE WEREN'T PART OF THE CORRUPTION IN THE AGENCY, BECAUSE WE WERE GONE. AND NOW WE--
I HAVE A JOB TO DO.
SO THAT HOSPITAL, THE A.I.M. FRONT?
WAS ACTUALLY MANUFACTURING ONE OF THE WORST BIOLOGICAL "DIRTY BOMBS" THIS WORLD HAS EVER SEEN.
AND NOW IT'S GONE. RAMOS SAID "ALJAFERIA."
IN ZARAGOZA, SPAIN. IN TWO DAYS, THERE'S A SPECIAL CEREMONY, HONORING SOME OF THE GREATEST SCIENTIFIC MINDS.
THE BOMB IS ON ITS WAY THERE, MOST LIKELY TO TAKE OUT SAID GENIUSES, IN A SHOW OF POWER TO POSITION A.I.M. AS THE UNDISPUTED LEADER IN CHEMICAL WARFARE.
SO YOU'RE GOING TO DEFUSE THE BOMB BEFORE IT GOES KABLEWY?
AND I ONLY HAVE 48 HOURS TO DO IT.
SO, IF YOU'LL EXCUSE ME. TURN OFF THE LIGHTS ON YOUR WAY OUT.

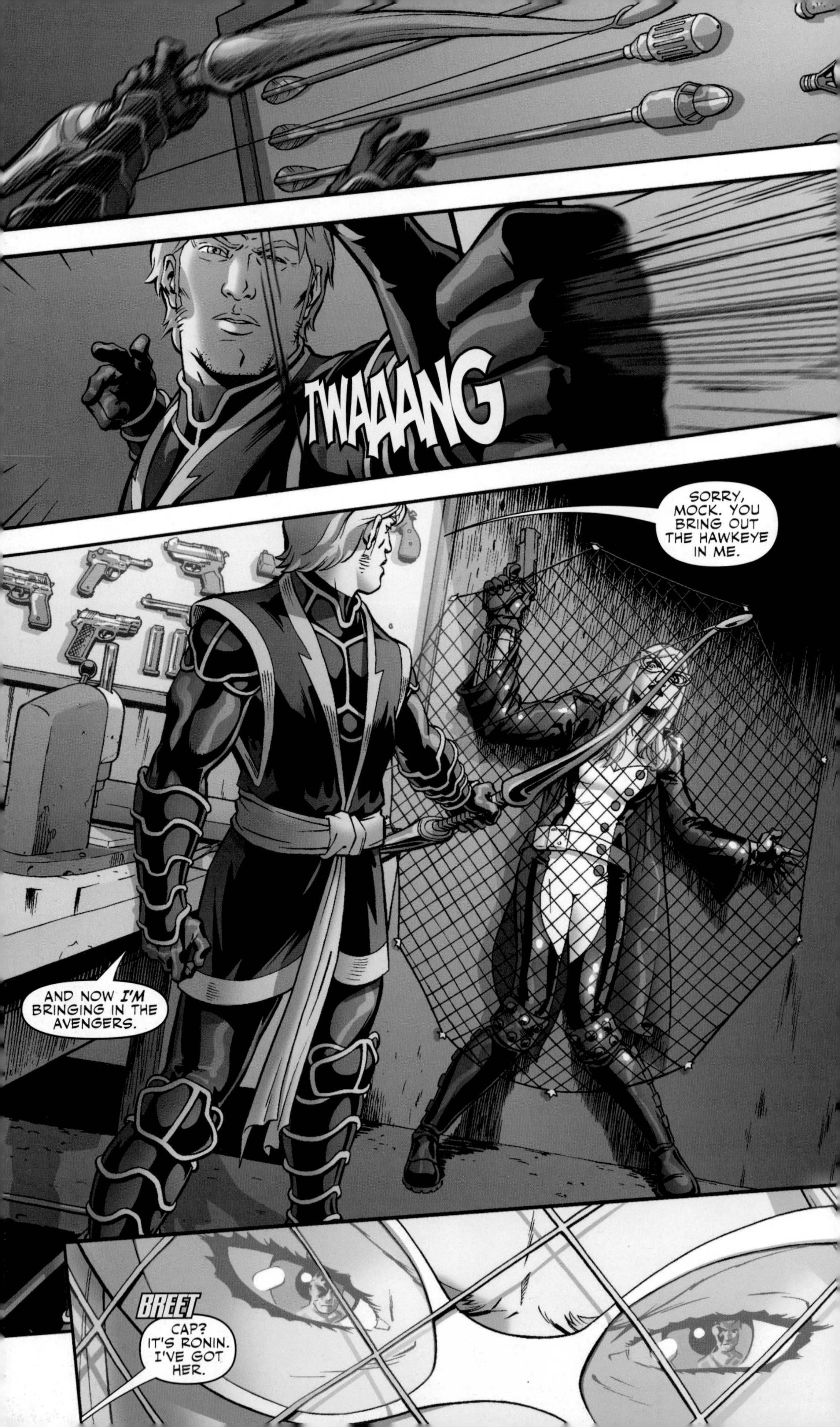
TWAAANG
SORRY, MOCK. YOU BRING OUT THE HAWKEYE IN ME.
AND NOW I'M BRINGING IN THE AVENGERS.
BREET
CAP? IT'S RONIN. I'VE GOT HER.

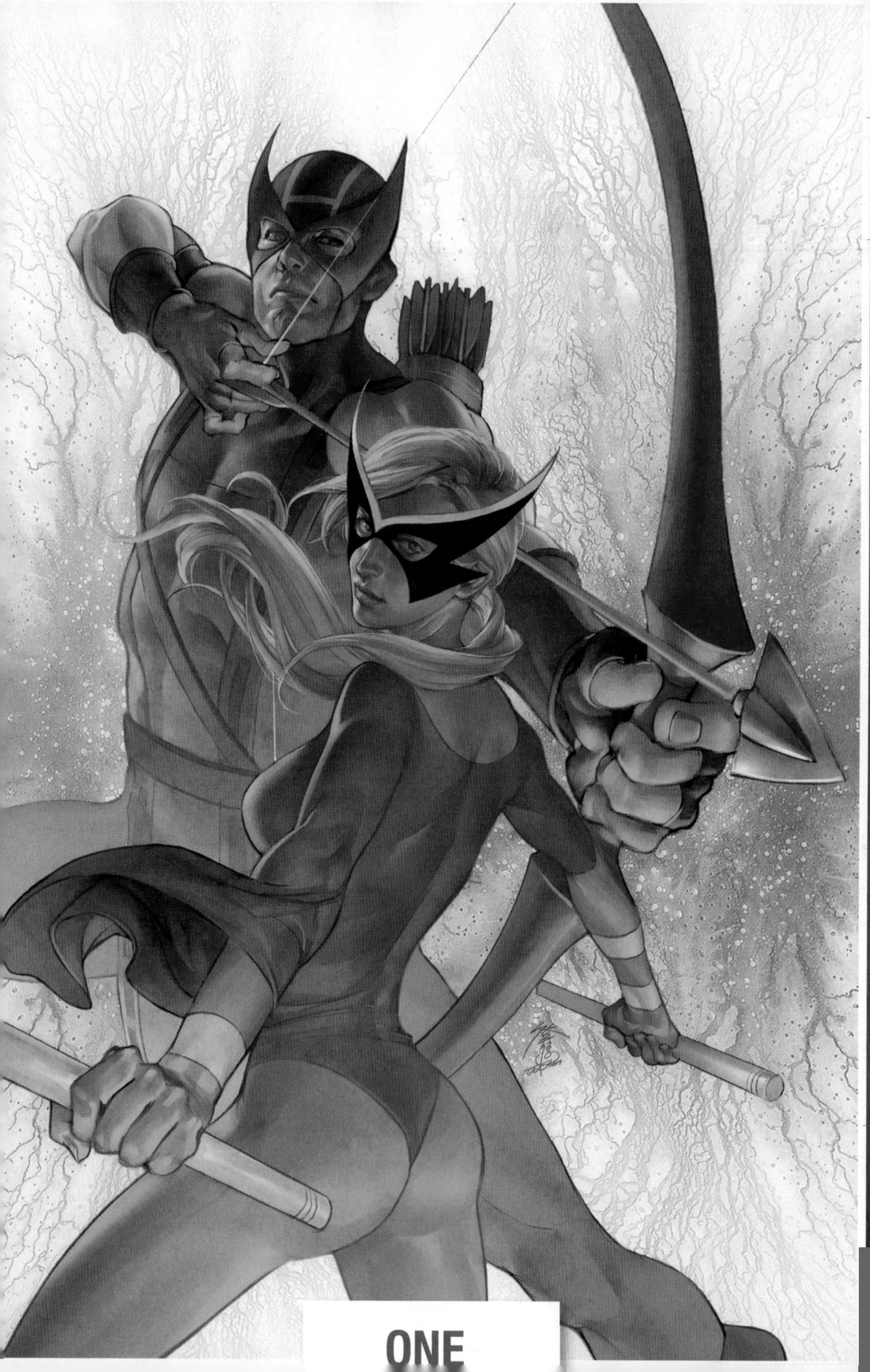

ONE

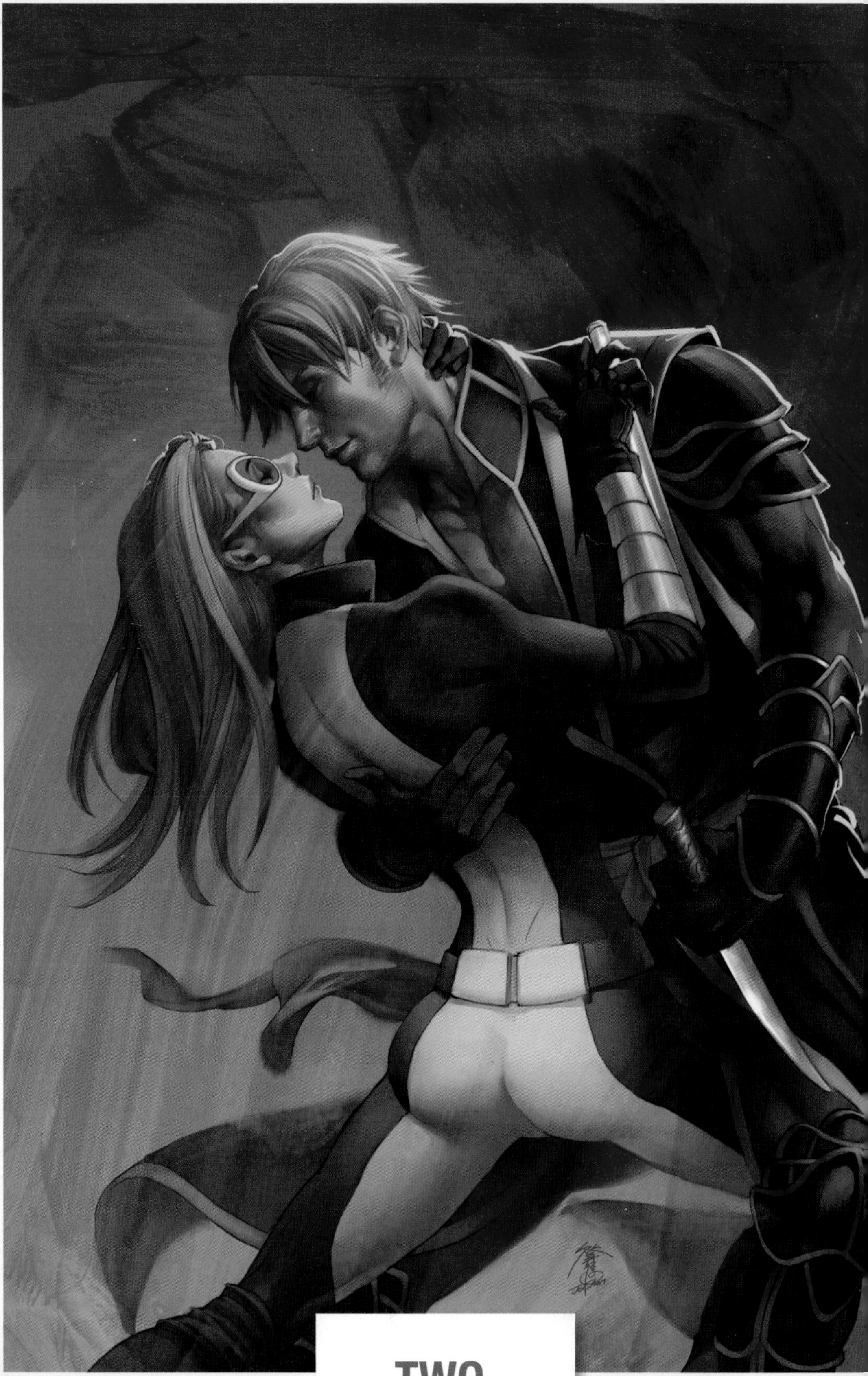

TWO

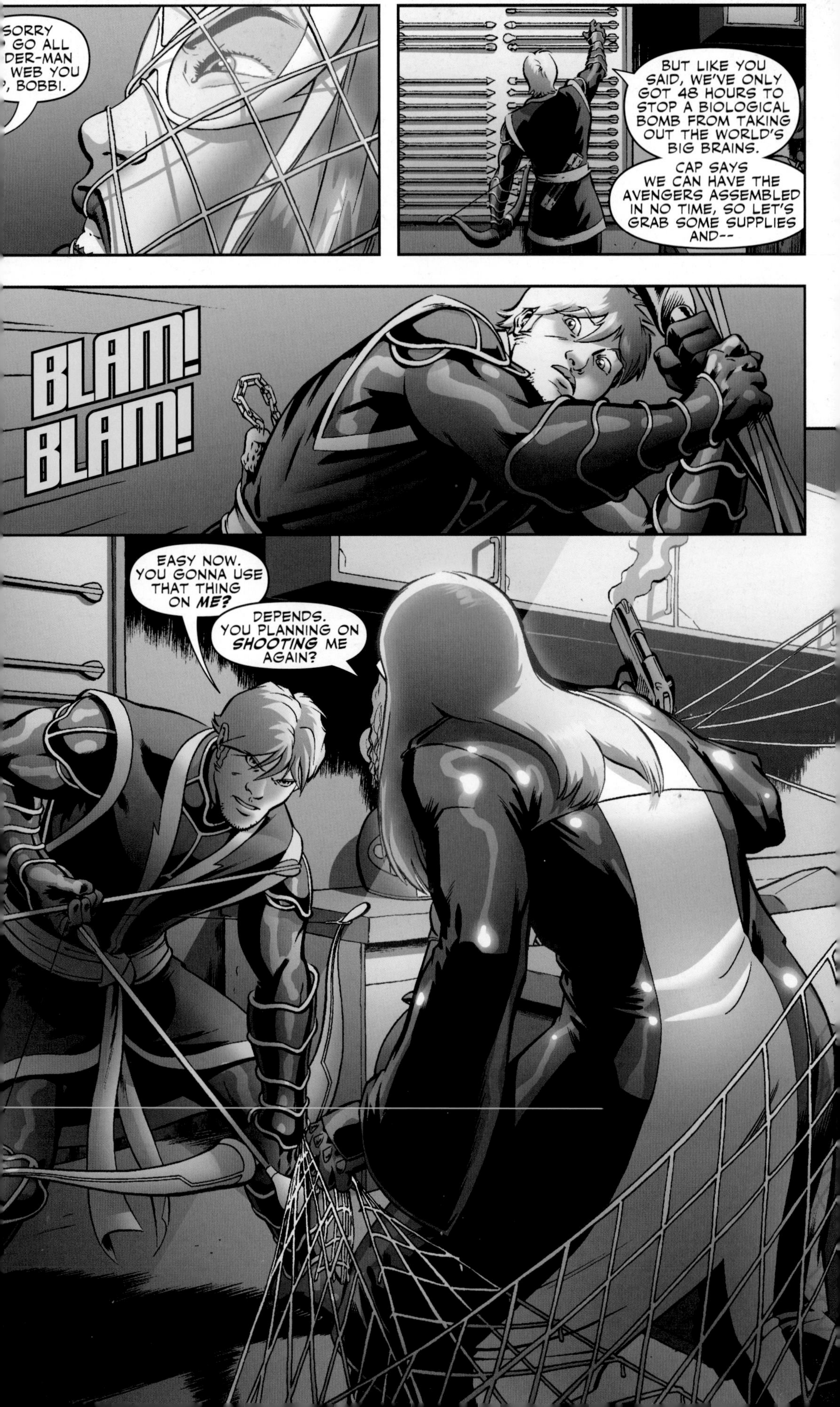

SORRY
GO ALL
DER-MAN
WEB YOU
, BOBBI.
BUT LIKE YOU SAID, WE'VE ONLY GOT 48 HOURS TO STOP A BIOLOGICAL BOMB FROM TAKING OUT THE WORLD'S BIG BRAINS.
CAP SAYS WE CAN HAVE THE AVENGERS ASSEMBLED IN NO TIME, SO LET'S GRAB SOME SUPPLIES AND--
BLAM! BLAM!
EASY NOW. YOU GONNA USE THAT THING ON ME?
DEPENDS. YOU PLANNING ON SHOOTING ME AGAIN?

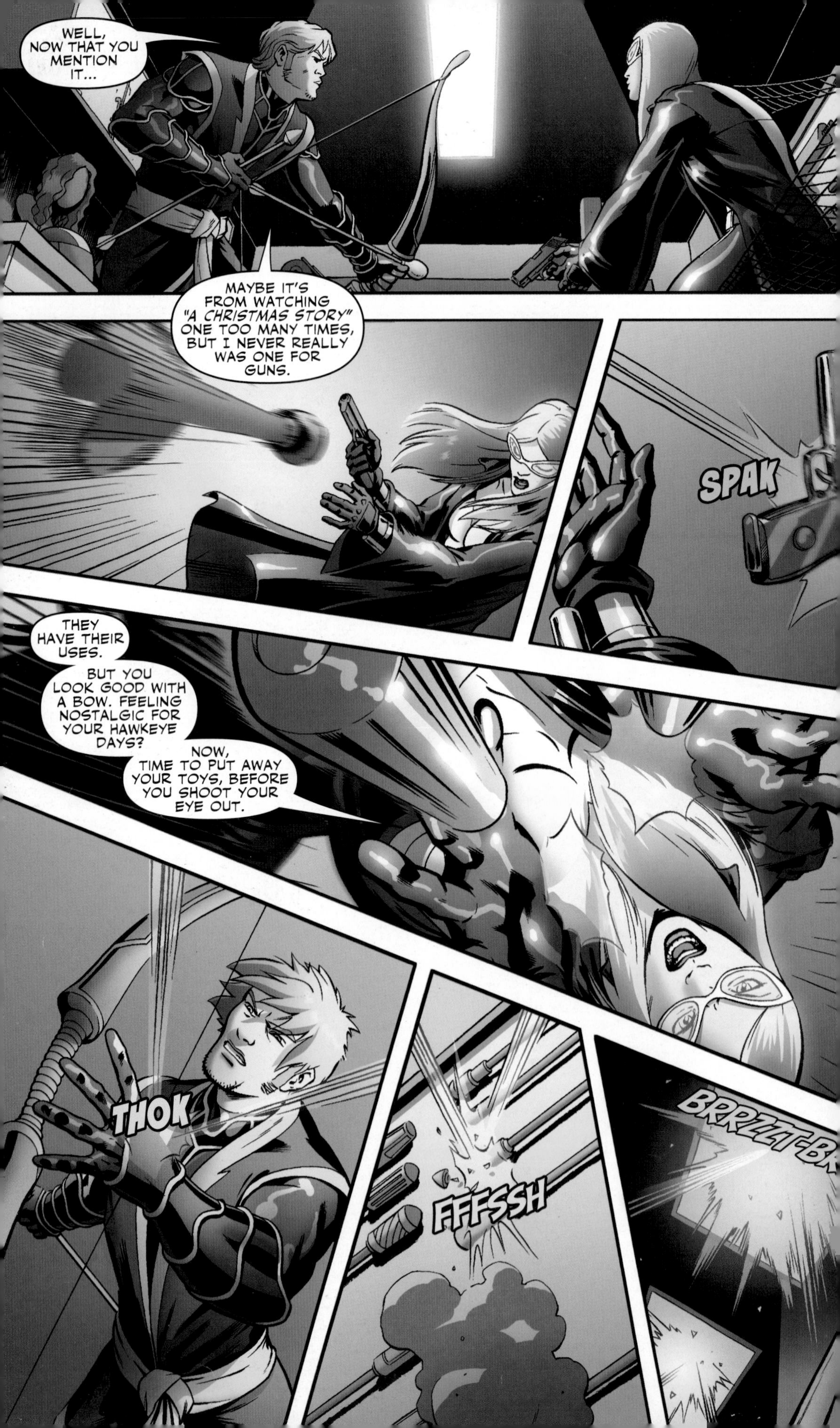
WELL, NOW THAT YOU MENTION IT...
MAYBE IT'S FROM WATCHING "A CHRISTMAS STORY" ONE TOO MANY TIMES, BUT I NEVER REALLY WAS ONE FOR GUNS.
SPAK
THEY HAVE THEIR USES.
BUT YOU LOOK GOOD WITH A BOW. FEELING NOSTALGIC FOR YOUR HAWKEYE DAYS?
NOW, TIME TO PUT AWAY YOUR TOYS, BEFORE YOU SHOOT YOUR EYE OUT.
THOK
FFFSSH
BRRZZZT-BR

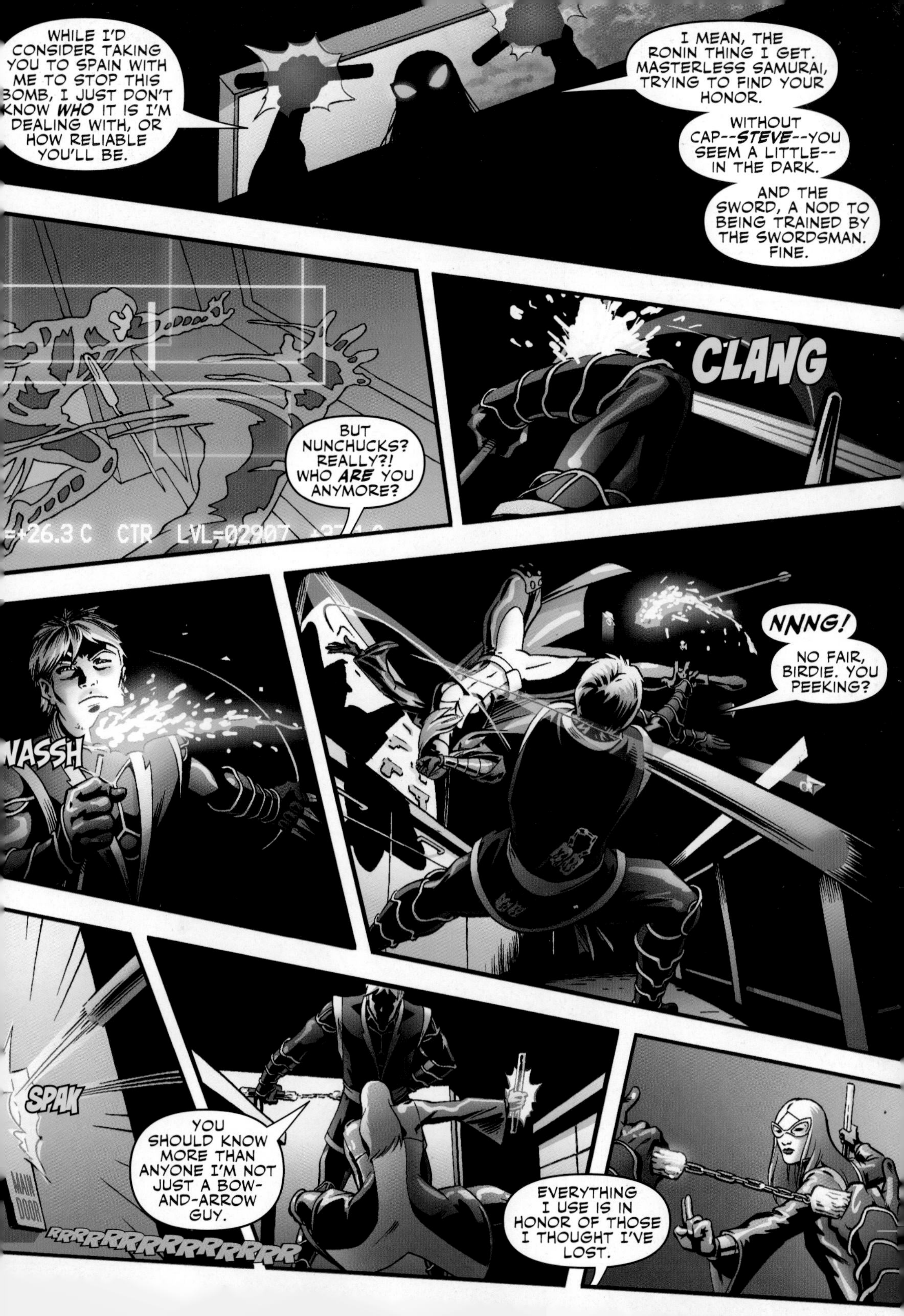
WHILE I'D CONSIDER TAKING YOU TO SPAIN WITH ME TO STOP THIS BOMB, I JUST DON'T KNOW *WHO* IT IS I'M DEALING WITH, OR HOW RELIABLE YOU'LL BE.
I MEAN, THE RONIN THING I GET. MASTERLESS SAMURAI, TRYING TO FIND YOUR HONOR.
WITHOUT CAP--*STEVE*--YOU SEEM A LITTLE--IN THE DARK.
AND THE SWORD, A NOD TO BEING TRAINED BY THE SWORDSMAN. FINE.
CLANG
BUT NUNCHUCKS? REALLY?! WHO *ARE* YOU ANYMORE?
=+26.3 C CTR LVL=02907
NASSH
NNNG!
NO FAIR, BIRDIE. YOU PEEKING?
SPAK
MAIN DOOR
YOU SHOULD KNOW MORE THAN ANYONE I'M NOT JUST A BOW-AND-ARROW GUY.
RRRRRRRRRRRRRRRR
EVERYTHING I USE IS IN HONOR OF THOSE I THOUGHT I'VE LOST.

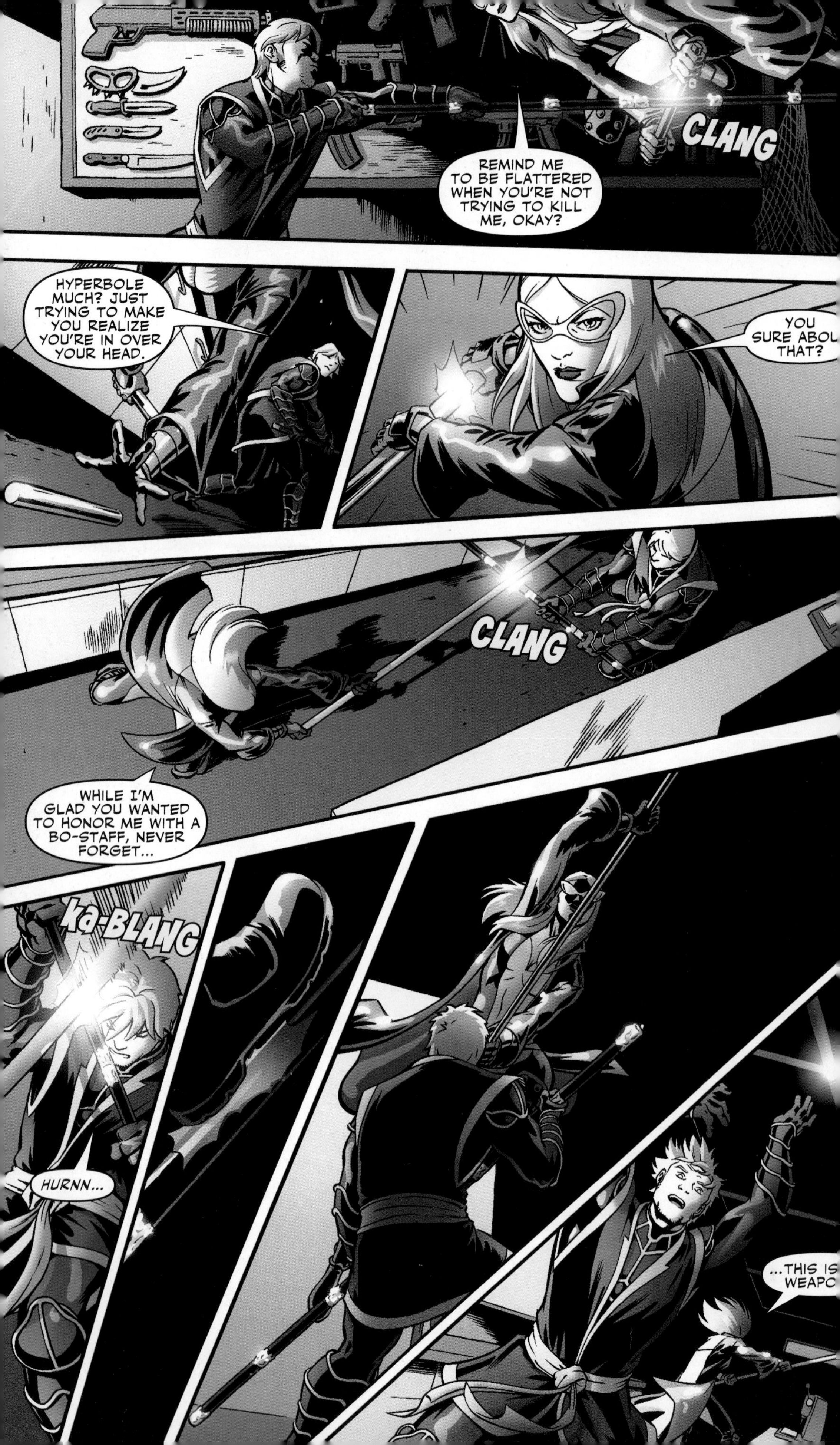
CLANG
REMIND ME TO BE FLATTERED WHEN YOU'RE NOT TRYING TO KILL ME, OKAY?
HYPERBOLE MUCH? JUST TRYING TO MAKE YOU REALIZE YOU'RE IN OVER YOUR HEAD.
YOU SURE ABOU THAT?
CLANG
WHILE I'M GLAD YOU WANTED TO HONOR ME WITH A BO-STAFF, NEVER FORGET...
ka-BLANG
HURNN...
...THIS IS WEAPO

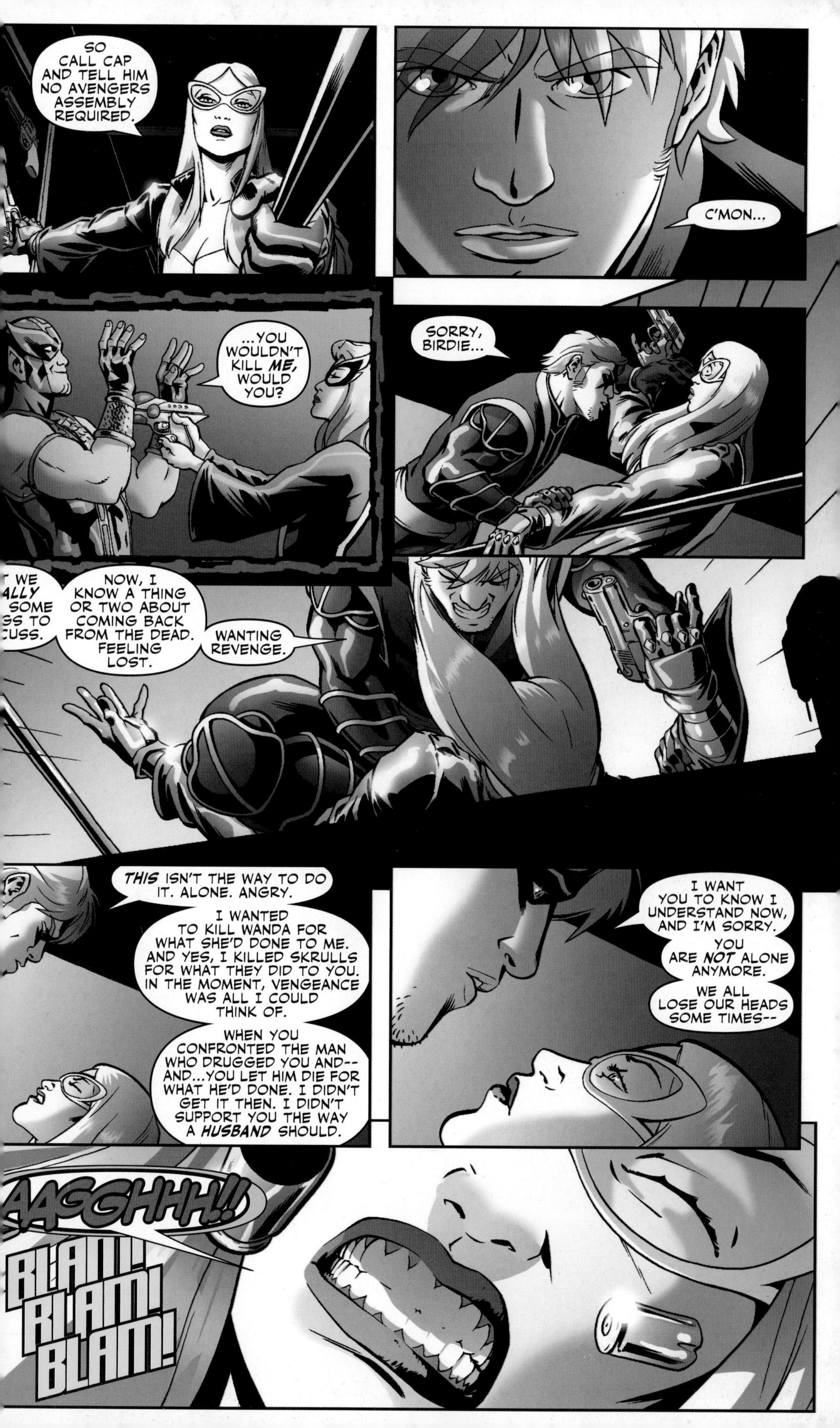
SO CALL CAP AND TELL HIM NO AVENGERS ASSEMBLY REQUIRED.
C'MON...
...YOU WOULDN'T KILL *ME*, WOULD YOU?
SORRY, BIRDIE...
NOW, I KNOW A THING OR TWO ABOUT COMING BACK FROM THE DEAD. FEELING LOST.
WANTING REVENGE.
THIS ISN'T THE WAY TO DO IT. ALONE. ANGRY.
I WANTED TO KILL WANDA FOR WHAT SHE'D DONE TO ME. AND YES, I KILLED SKRULLS FOR WHAT THEY DID TO YOU. IN THE MOMENT, VENGEANCE WAS ALL I COULD THINK OF.
WHEN YOU CONFRONTED THE MAN WHO DRUGGED YOU AND-- AND...YOU LET HIM DIE FOR WHAT HE'D DONE. I DIDN'T GET IT THEN. I DIDN'T SUPPORT YOU THE WAY A *HUSBAND* SHOULD.
I WANT YOU TO KNOW I UNDERSTAND NOW, AND I'M SORRY.
YOU ARE *NOT* ALONE ANYMORE.
WE ALL LOSE OUR HEADS SOME TIMES--
AAGGHHH!!
BLAM! BLAM! BLAM!

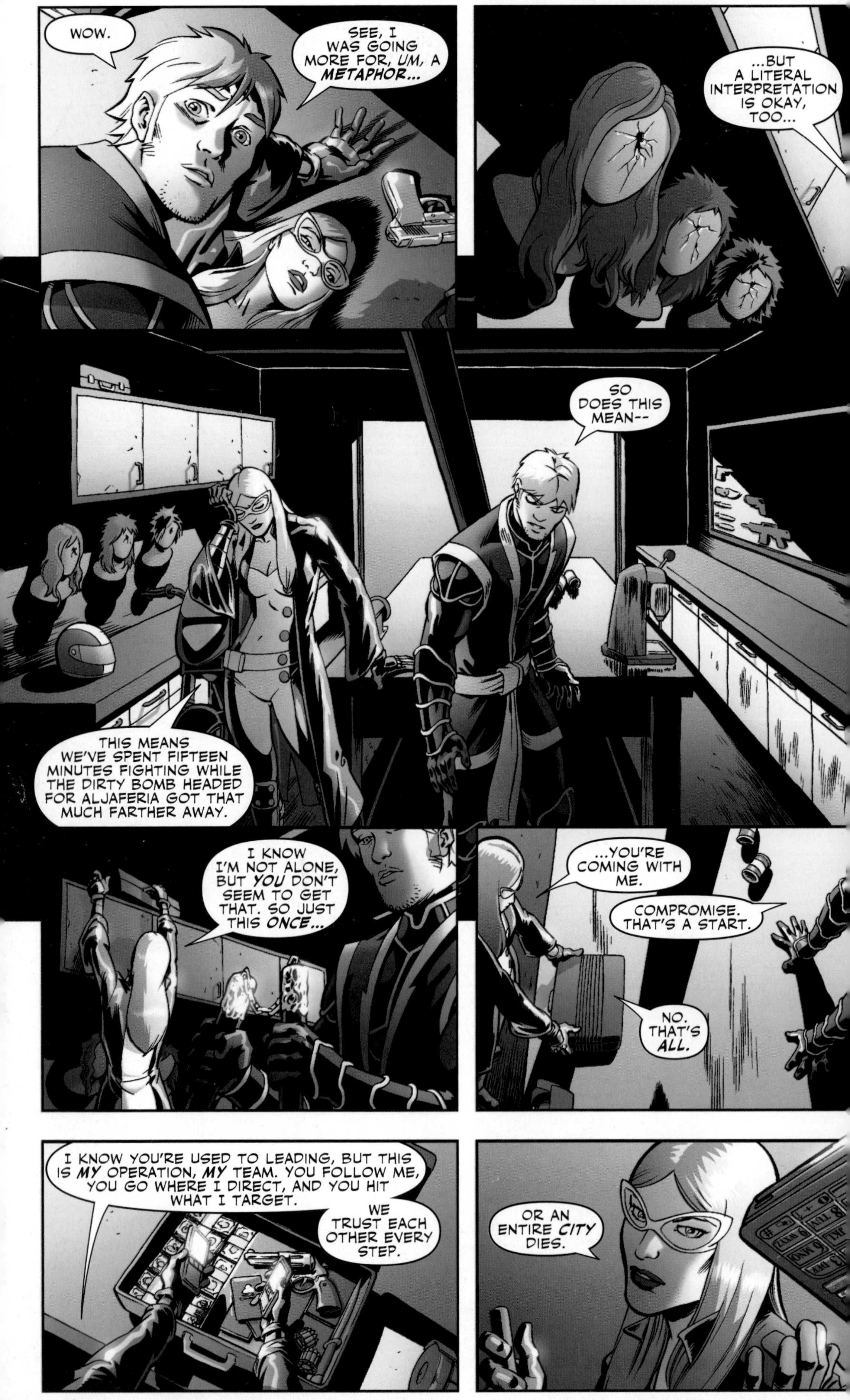
WOW.
SEE, I WAS GOING MORE FOR, UM, A *METAPHOR*...
...BUT A LITERAL INTERPRETATION IS OKAY, TOO...
SO DOES THIS MEAN--
THIS MEANS WE'VE SPENT FIFTEEN MINUTES FIGHTING WHILE THE DIRTY BOMB HEADED FOR ALJAFERIA GOT THAT MUCH FARTHER AWAY.
I KNOW I'M NOT ALONE, BUT *YOU* DON'T SEEM TO GET THAT. SO JUST THIS *ONCE*...
...YOU'RE COMING WITH ME.
COMPROMISE. THAT'S A START.
NO. THAT'S *ALL*.
I KNOW YOU'RE USED TO LEADING, BUT THIS IS *MY* OPERATION, *MY* TEAM. YOU FOLLOW ME, YOU GO WHERE I DIRECT, AND YOU HIT WHAT I TARGET.
WE TRUST EACH OTHER EVERY STEP.
OR AN ENTIRE *CITY* DIES.

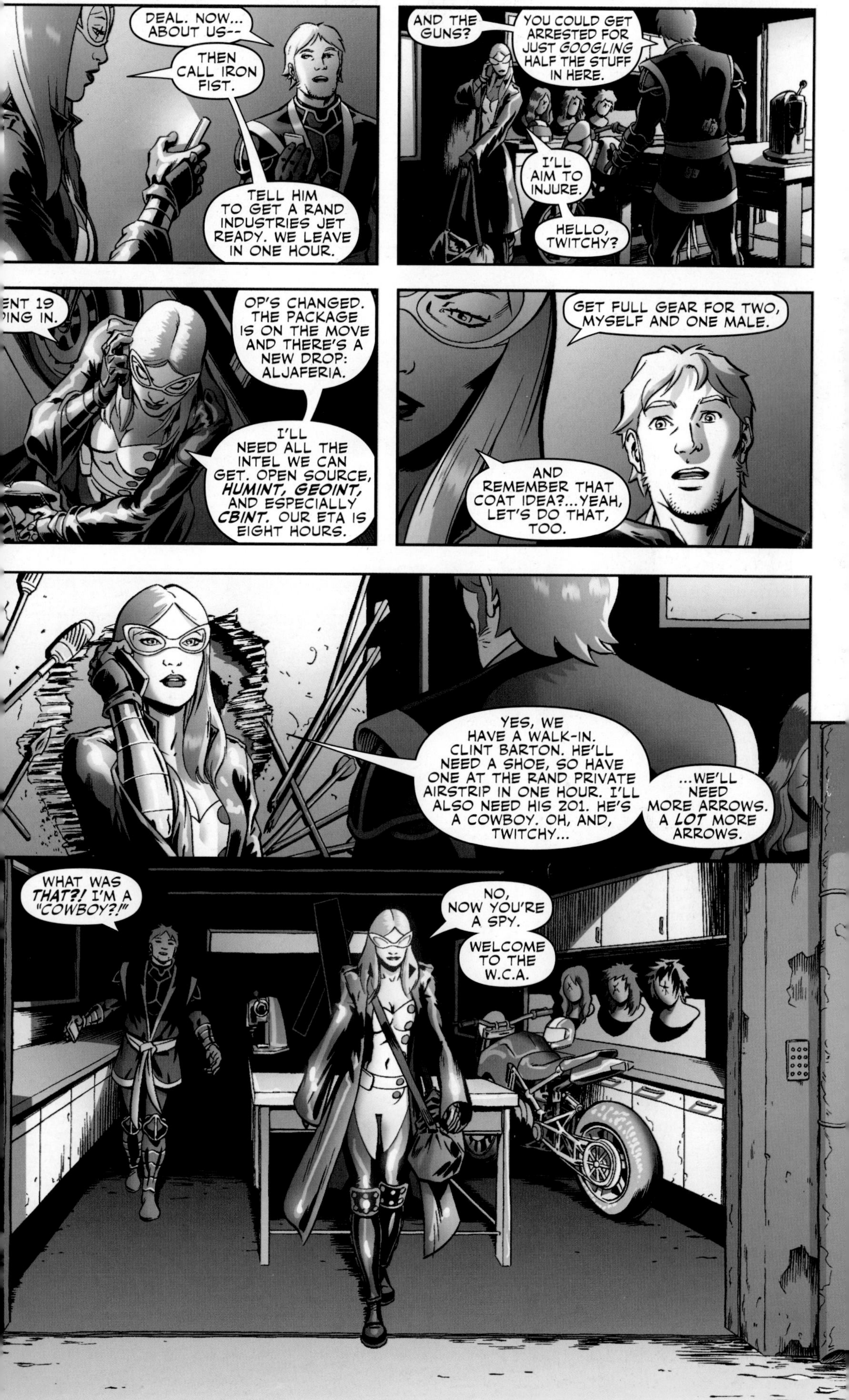
DEAL. NOW... ABOUT US--
THEN CALL IRON FIST.
TELL HIM TO GET A RAND INDUSTRIES JET READY. WE LEAVE IN ONE HOUR.
AND THE GUNS?
YOU COULD GET ARRESTED FOR JUST *GOOGLING* HALF THE STUFF IN HERE.
I'LL AIM TO INJURE.
HELLO, TWITCHY?
ENT 19 PING IN.
OP'S CHANGED. THE PACKAGE IS ON THE MOVE AND THERE'S A NEW DROP: ALJAFERIA.
I'LL NEED ALL THE INTEL WE CAN GET. OPEN SOURCE, ***HUMINT, GEOINT,*** AND ESPECIALLY ***CBINT.*** OUR ETA IS EIGHT HOURS.
GET FULL GEAR FOR TWO, MYSELF AND ONE MALE.
AND REMEMBER THAT COAT IDEA?...YEAH, LET'S DO THAT, TOO.
YES, WE HAVE A WALK-IN. CLINT BARTON. HE'LL NEED A SHOE, SO HAVE ONE AT THE RAND PRIVATE AIRSTRIP IN ONE HOUR. I'LL ALSO NEED HIS 201. HE'S A COWBOY. OH, AND, TWITCHY...
...WE'LL NEED MORE ARROWS. A *LOT* MORE ARROWS.
WHAT WAS *THAT?!* I'M A *"COWBOY?!"*
NO, NOW YOU'RE A SPY.
WELCOME TO THE W.C.A.

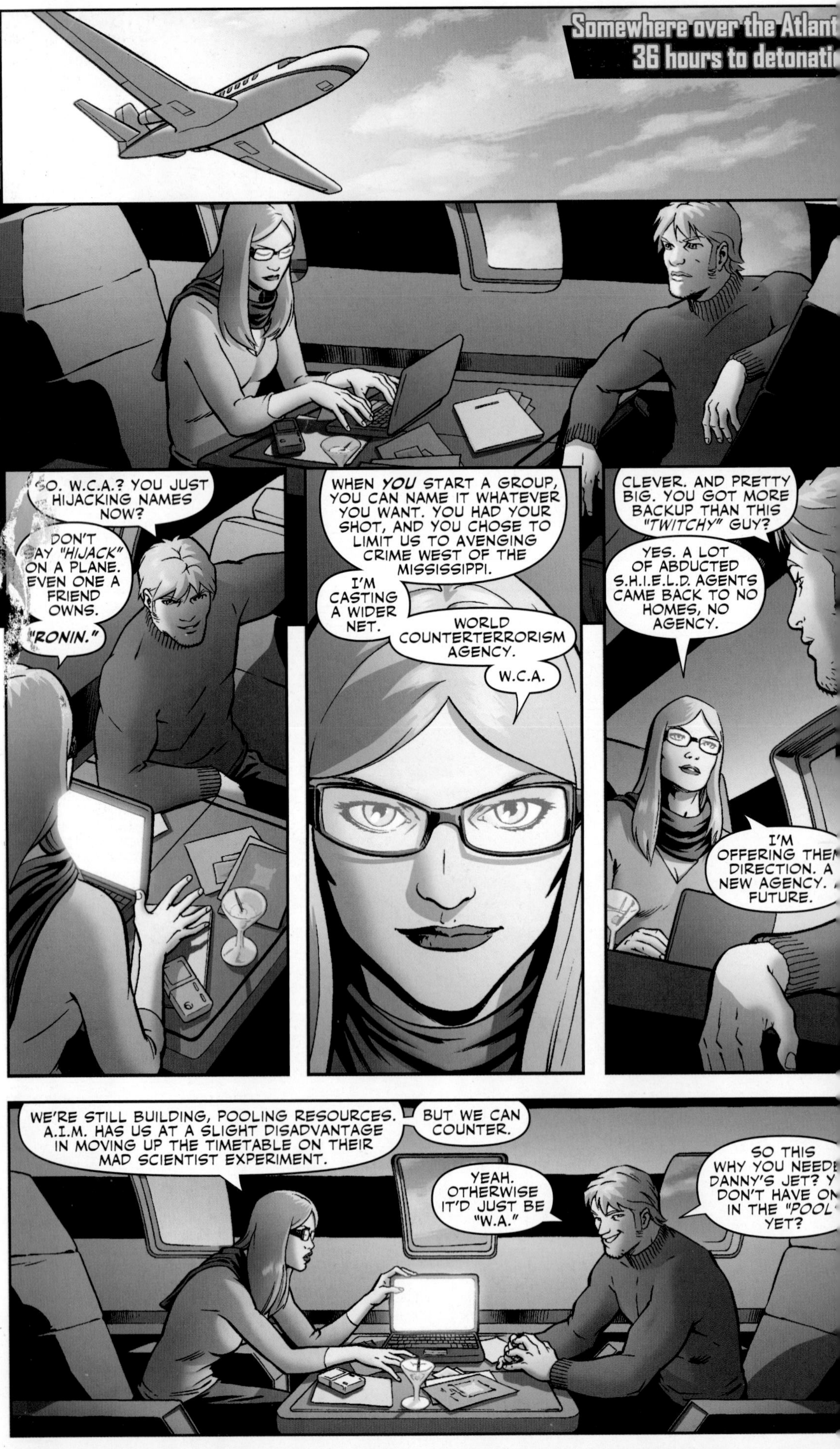

Somewhere over the Atlant
36 hours to detonati
SO. W.C.A.? YOU JUST HIJACKING NAMES NOW?
DON'T SAY "HIJACK" ON A PLANE. EVEN ONE A FRIEND OWNS.
"RONIN."
WHEN YOU START A GROUP, YOU CAN NAME IT WHATEVER YOU WANT. YOU HAD YOUR SHOT, AND YOU CHOSE TO LIMIT US TO AVENGING CRIME WEST OF THE MISSISSIPPI.
I'M CASTING A WIDER NET.
WORLD COUNTERTERRORISM AGENCY.
W.C.A.
CLEVER. AND PRETTY BIG. YOU GOT MORE BACKUP THAN THIS "TWITCHY" GUY?
YES. A LOT OF ABDUCTED S.H.I.E.L.D. AGENTS CAME BACK TO NO HOMES, NO AGENCY.
I'M OFFERING THE DIRECTION. A NEW AGENCY. FUTURE.
WE'RE STILL BUILDING, POOLING RESOURCES. A.I.M. HAS US AT A SLIGHT DISADVANTAGE IN MOVING UP THE TIMETABLE ON THEIR MAD SCIENTIST EXPERIMENT.
BUT WE CAN COUNTER.
YEAH. OTHERWISE IT'D JUST BE "W.A."
SO THIS WHY YOU NEED DANNY'S JET? Y DON'T HAVE ON IN THE "POOL" YET?

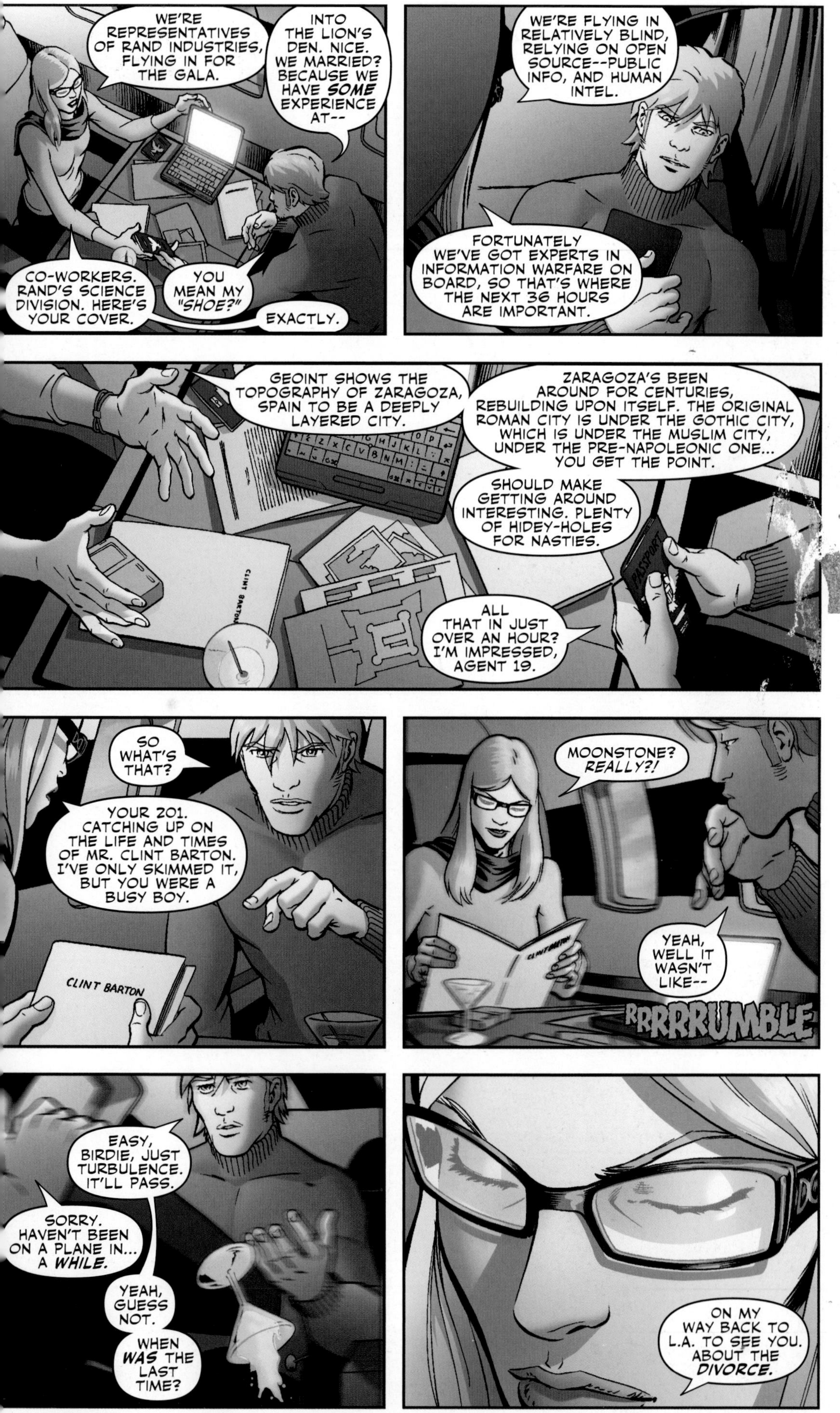
WE'RE REPRESENTATIVES OF RAND INDUSTRIES, FLYING IN FOR THE GALA.
INTO THE LION'S DEN. NICE. WE MARRIED? BECAUSE WE HAVE *SOME* EXPERIENCE AT--
CO-WORKERS. RAND'S SCIENCE DIVISION. HERE'S YOUR COVER.
YOU MEAN MY *"SHOE?"*
EXACTLY.
WE'RE FLYING IN RELATIVELY BLIND, RELYING ON OPEN SOURCE--PUBLIC INFO, AND HUMAN INTEL.
FORTUNATELY WE'VE GOT EXPERTS IN INFORMATION WARFARE ON BOARD, SO THAT'S WHERE THE NEXT 36 HOURS ARE IMPORTANT.
GEOINT SHOWS THE TOPOGRAPHY OF ZARAGOZA, SPAIN TO BE A DEEPLY LAYERED CITY.
ZARAGOZA'S BEEN AROUND FOR CENTURIES, REBUILDING UPON ITSELF. THE ORIGINAL ROMAN CITY IS UNDER THE GOTHIC CITY, WHICH IS UNDER THE MUSLIM CITY, UNDER THE PRE-NAPOLEONIC ONE... YOU GET THE POINT.
SHOULD MAKE GETTING AROUND INTERESTING. PLENTY OF HIDEY-HOLES FOR NASTIES.
CLINT BARTON
PASSPORT
ALL THAT IN JUST OVER AN HOUR? I'M IMPRESSED, AGENT 19.
SO WHAT'S THAT?
YOUR 201. CATCHING UP ON THE LIFE AND TIMES OF MR. CLINT BARTON. I'VE ONLY SKIMMED IT, BUT YOU WERE A BUSY BOY.
CLINT BARTON
MOONSTONE? *REALLY?!*
YEAH, WELL IT WASN'T LIKE--
RRRRRUMBLE
EASY, BIRDIE, JUST TURBULENCE. IT'LL PASS.
SORRY. HAVEN'T BEEN ON A PLANE IN... A *WHILE.*
YEAH, GUESS NOT.
WHEN *WAS* THE LAST TIME?
ON MY WAY BACK TO L.A. TO SEE YOU. ABOUT THE *DIVORCE.*

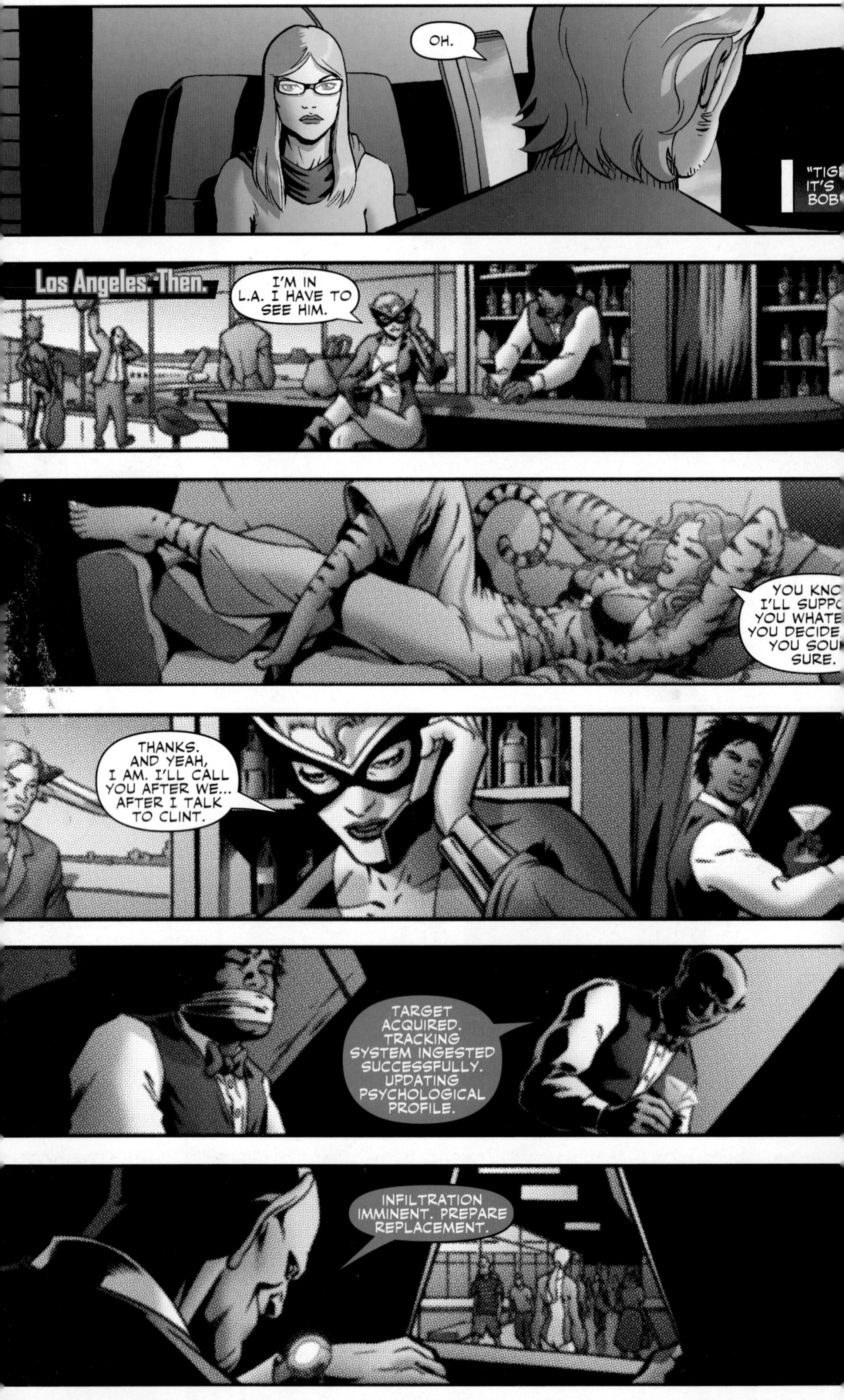
OH.
"TIG
IT'S
BOB
Los Angeles. Then.
I'M IN L.A. I HAVE TO SEE HIM.
YOU KNO
I'LL SUPPO
YOU WHATE
YOU DECIDE
YOU SOU
SURE.
THANKS. AND YEAH, I AM. I'LL CALL YOU AFTER WE... AFTER I TALK TO CLINT.
TARGET ACQUIRED. TRACKING SYSTEM INGESTED SUCCESSFULLY. UPDATING PSYCHOLOGICAL PROFILE.
INFILTRATION IMMINENT. PREPARE REPLACEMENT.

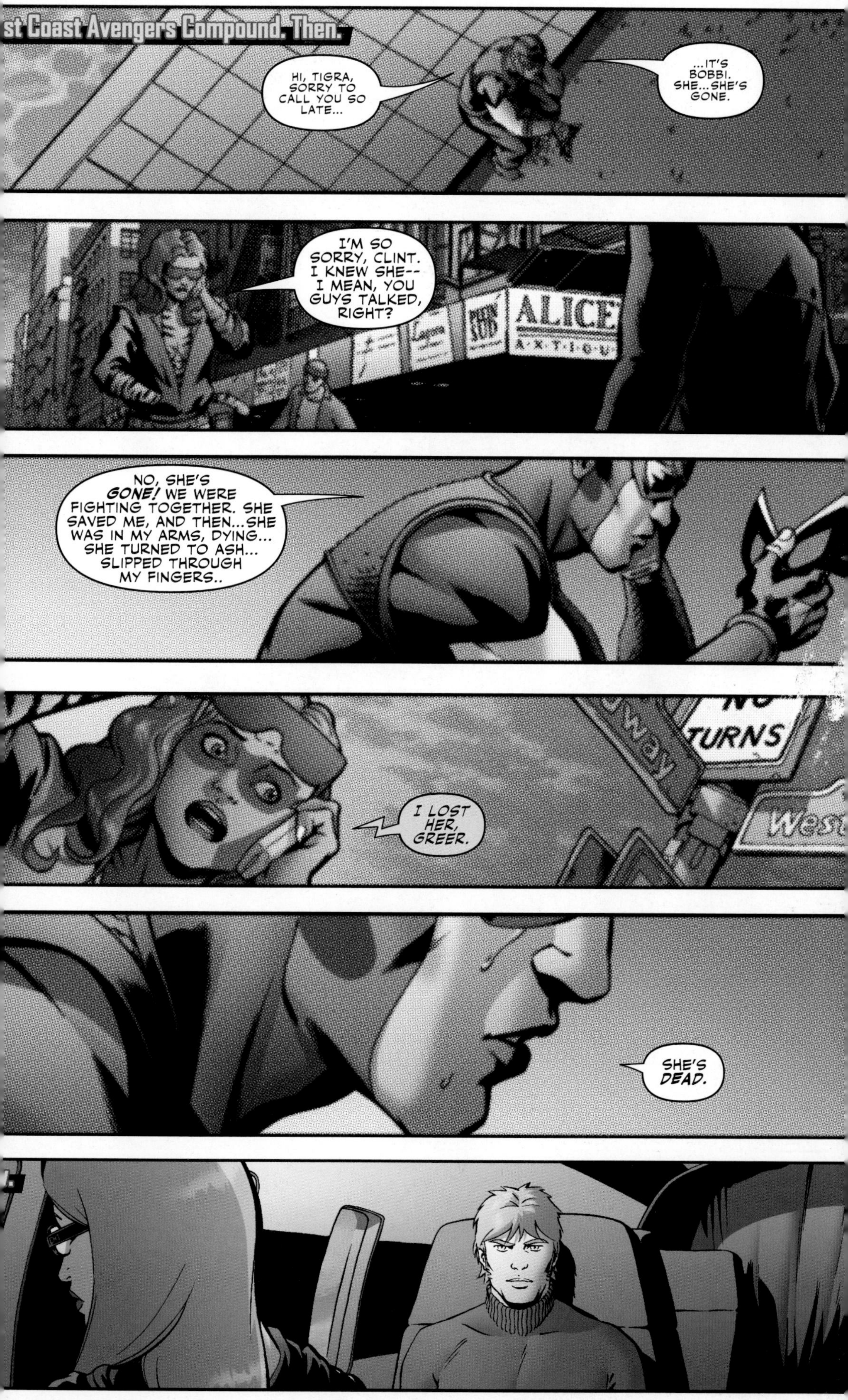
st Coast Avengers Compound. Then.
HI, TIGRA, SORRY TO CALL YOU SO LATE...
...IT'S BOBBI. SHE...SHE'S GONE.
I'M SO SORRY, CLINT. I KNEW SHE-- I MEAN, YOU GUYS TALKED, RIGHT?
ALICE
NO, SHE'S GONE! WE WERE FIGHTING TOGETHER. SHE SAVED ME, AND THEN...SHE WAS IN MY ARMS, DYING... SHE TURNED TO ASH... SLIPPED THROUGH MY FINGERS..
TURNS
I LOST HER, GREER.
SHE'S DEAD.

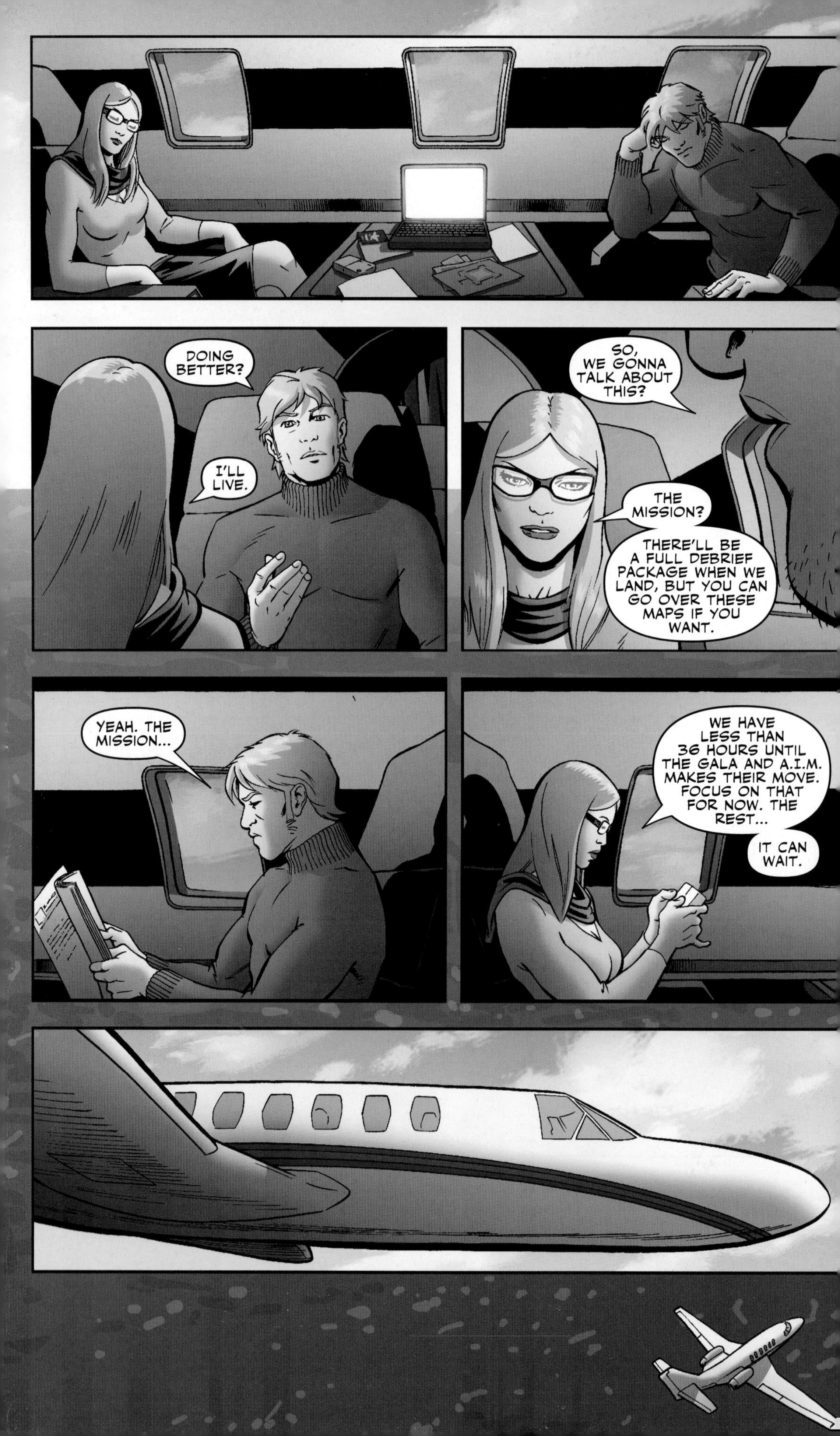
DOING BETTER?
I'LL LIVE.
SO, WE GONNA TALK ABOUT THIS?
THE MISSION?
THERE'LL BE A FULL DEBRIEF PACKAGE WHEN WE LAND, BUT YOU CAN GO OVER THESE MAPS IF YOU WANT.
YEAH. THE MISSION...
WE HAVE LESS THAN 36 HOURS UNTIL THE GALA AND A.I.M. MAKES THEIR MOVE. FOCUS ON THAT FOR NOW. THE REST...
IT CAN WAIT.

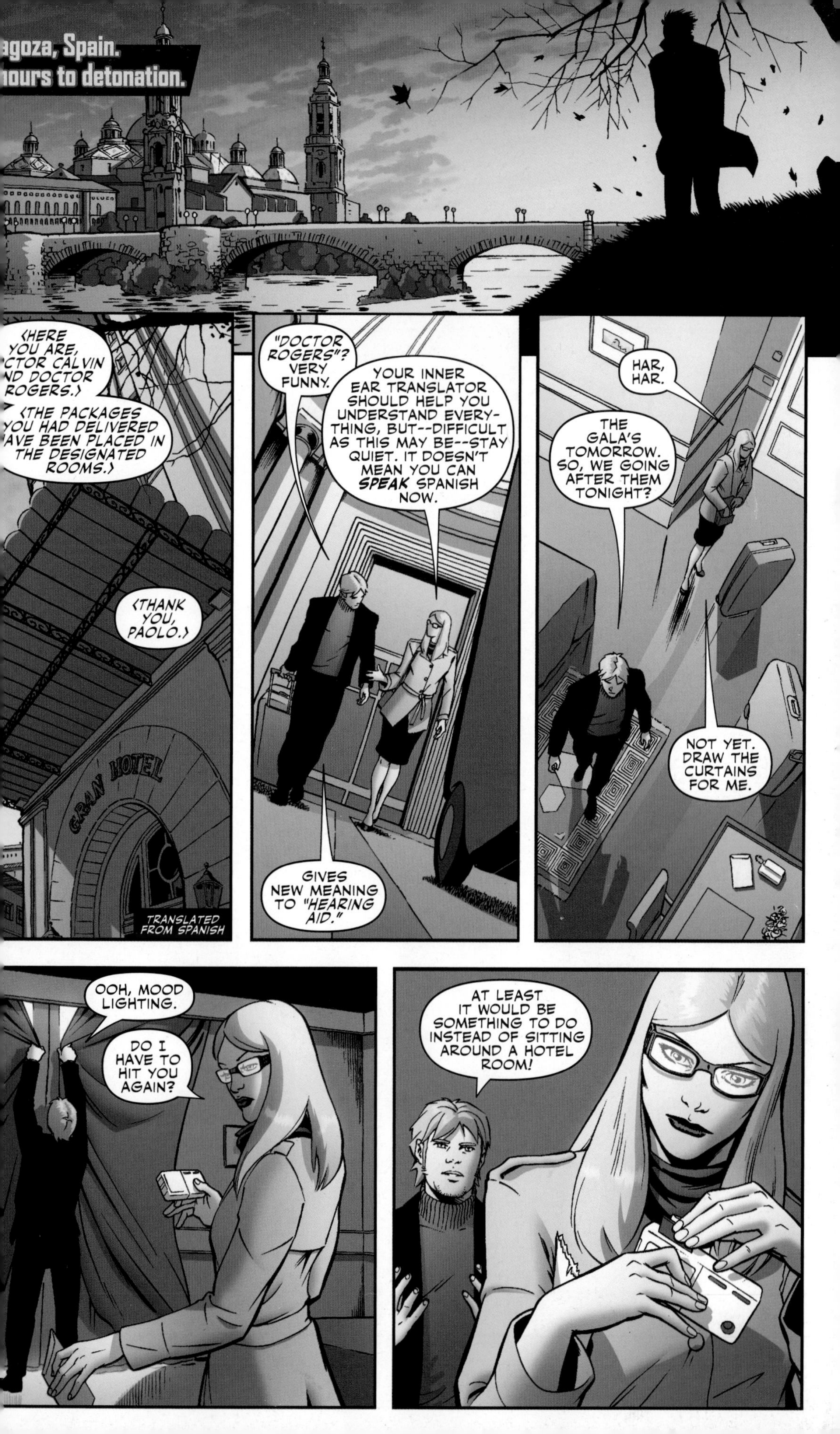

agoza, Spain.
hours to detonation.
<HERE YOU ARE, CTOR CALVIN ND DOCTOR ROGERS.>
<THE PACKAGES YOU HAD DELIVERED AVE BEEN PLACED IN THE DESIGNATED ROOMS.>
<THANK YOU, PAOLO.>
GRAN HOTEL
TRANSLATED FROM SPANISH
"DOCTOR ROGERS"? VERY FUNNY.
YOUR INNER EAR TRANSLATOR SHOULD HELP YOU UNDERSTAND EVERYTHING, BUT--DIFFICULT AS THIS MAY BE--STAY QUIET. IT DOESN'T MEAN YOU CAN SPEAK SPANISH NOW.
GIVES NEW MEANING TO "HEARING AID."
HAR, HAR.
THE GALA'S TOMORROW. SO, WE GOING AFTER THEM TONIGHT?
NOT YET. DRAW THE CURTAINS FOR ME.
OOH, MOOD LIGHTING.
DO I HAVE TO HIT YOU AGAIN?
AT LEAST IT WOULD BE SOMETHING TO DO INSTEAD OF SITTING AROUND A HOTEL ROOM!

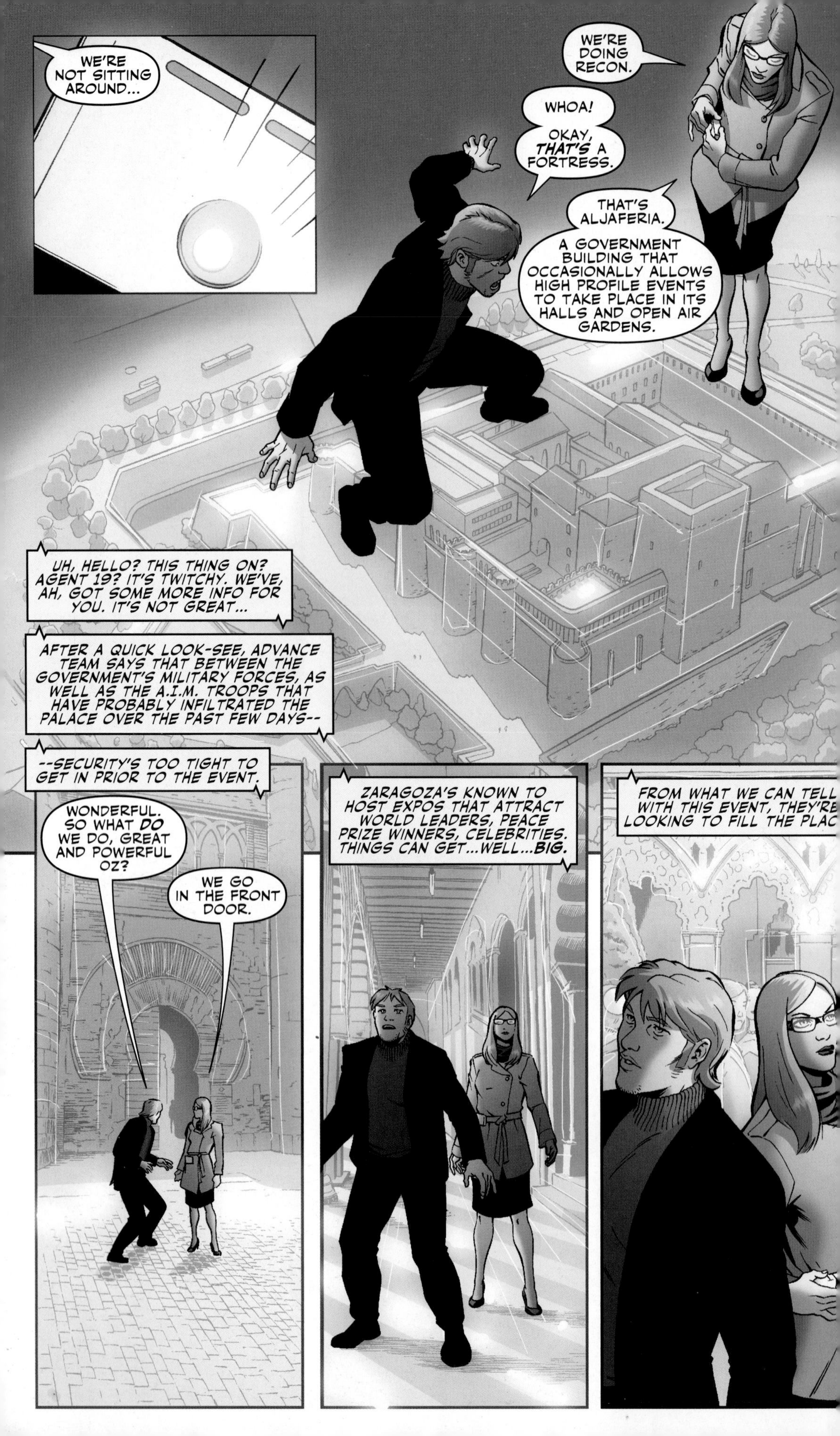
WE'RE NOT SITTING AROUND...
WE'RE DOING RECON.
WHOA!
OKAY, THAT'S A FORTRESS.
THAT'S ALJAFERIA.
A GOVERNMENT BUILDING THAT OCCASIONALLY ALLOWS HIGH PROFILE EVENTS TO TAKE PLACE IN ITS HALLS AND OPEN AIR GARDENS.
UH, HELLO? THIS THING ON? AGENT 19? IT'S TWITCHY. WE'VE, AH, GOT SOME MORE INFO FOR YOU. IT'S NOT GREAT...
AFTER A QUICK LOOK-SEE, ADVANCE TEAM SAYS THAT BETWEEN THE GOVERNMENT'S MILITARY FORCES, AS WELL AS THE A.I.M. TROOPS THAT HAVE PROBABLY INFILTRATED THE PALACE OVER THE PAST FEW DAYS--
--SECURITY'S TOO TIGHT TO GET IN PRIOR TO THE EVENT.
WONDERFUL. SO WHAT DO WE DO, GREAT AND POWERFUL OZ?
WE GO IN THE FRONT DOOR.
ZARAGOZA'S KNOWN TO HOST EXPOS THAT ATTRACT WORLD LEADERS, PEACE PRIZE WINNERS, CELEBRITIES. THINGS CAN GET...WELL...BIG.
FROM WHAT WE CAN TELL WITH THIS EVENT, THEY'RE LOOKING TO FILL THE PLAC

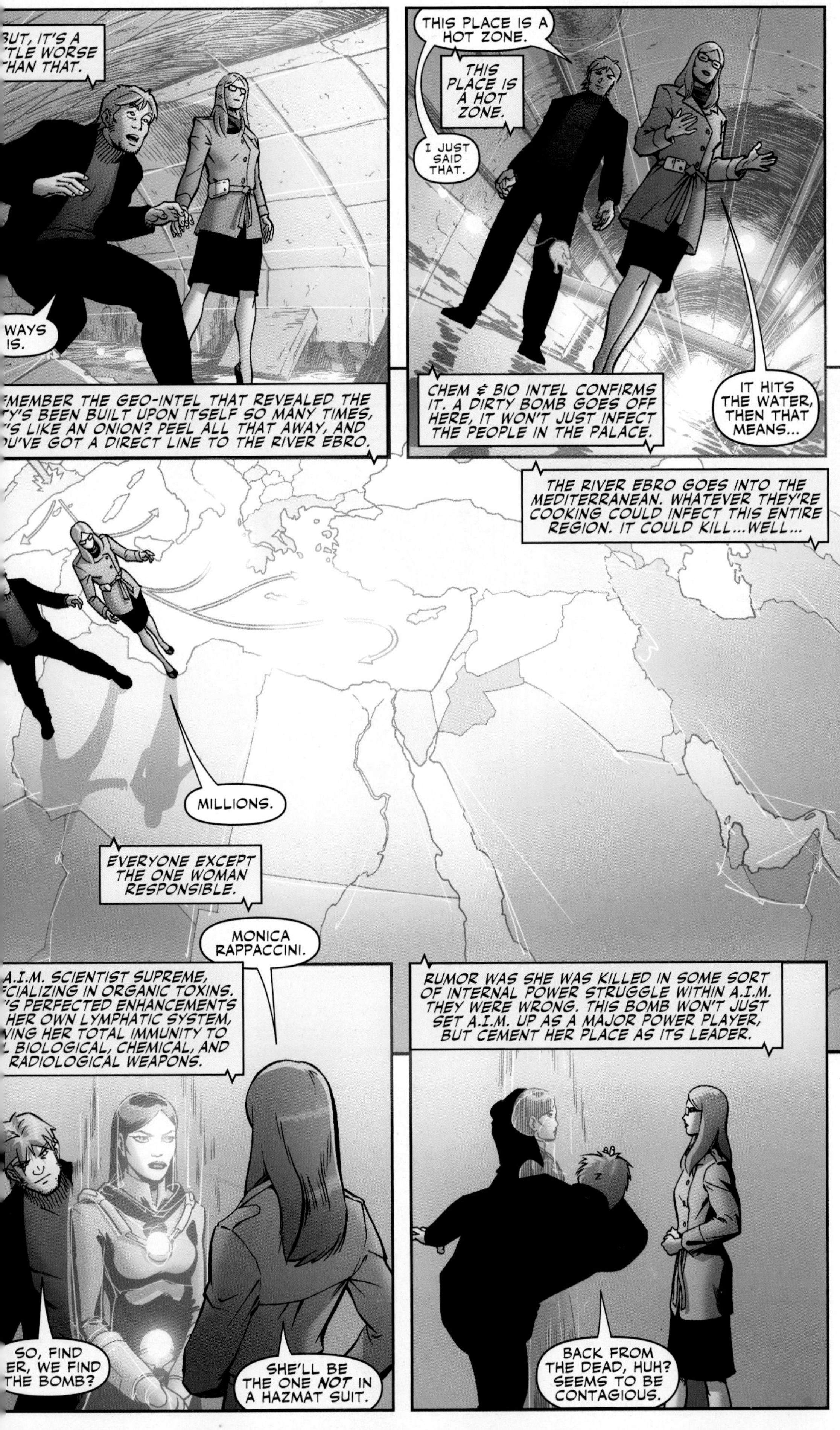
BUT, IT'S A
TTLE WORSE
THAN THAT.
WAYS
IS.
EMEMBER THE GEO-INTEL THAT REVEALED THE TY'S BEEN BUILT UPON ITSELF SO MANY TIMES, 'S LIKE AN ONION? PEEL ALL THAT AWAY, AND OU'VE GOT A DIRECT LINE TO THE RIVER EBRO.
THIS PLACE IS A HOT ZONE.
THIS PLACE IS A HOT ZONE.
I JUST SAID THAT.
CHEM & BIO INTEL CONFIRMS IT. A DIRTY BOMB GOES OFF HERE, IT WON'T JUST INFECT THE PEOPLE IN THE PALACE.
IT HITS THE WATER, THEN THAT MEANS...
THE RIVER EBRO GOES INTO THE MEDITERRANEAN. WHATEVER THEY'RE COOKING COULD INFECT THIS ENTIRE REGION. IT COULD KILL...WELL...
MILLIONS.
EVERYONE EXCEPT THE ONE WOMAN RESPONSIBLE.
MONICA RAPPACCINI.
A.I.M. SCIENTIST SUPREME, ECIALIZING IN ORGANIC TOXINS. 'S PERFECTED ENHANCEMENTS HER OWN LYMPHATIC SYSTEM, VING HER TOTAL IMMUNITY TO L BIOLOGICAL, CHEMICAL, AND RADIOLOGICAL WEAPONS.
SO, FIND ER, WE FIND THE BOMB?
SHE'LL BE THE ONE NOT IN A HAZMAT SUIT.
RUMOR WAS SHE WAS KILLED IN SOME SORT OF INTERNAL POWER STRUGGLE WITHIN A.I.M. THEY WERE WRONG. THIS BOMB WON'T JUST SET A.I.M. UP AS A MAJOR POWER PLAYER, BUT CEMENT HER PLACE AS ITS LEADER.
BACK FROM THE DEAD, HUH? SEEMS TO BE CONTAGIOUS.

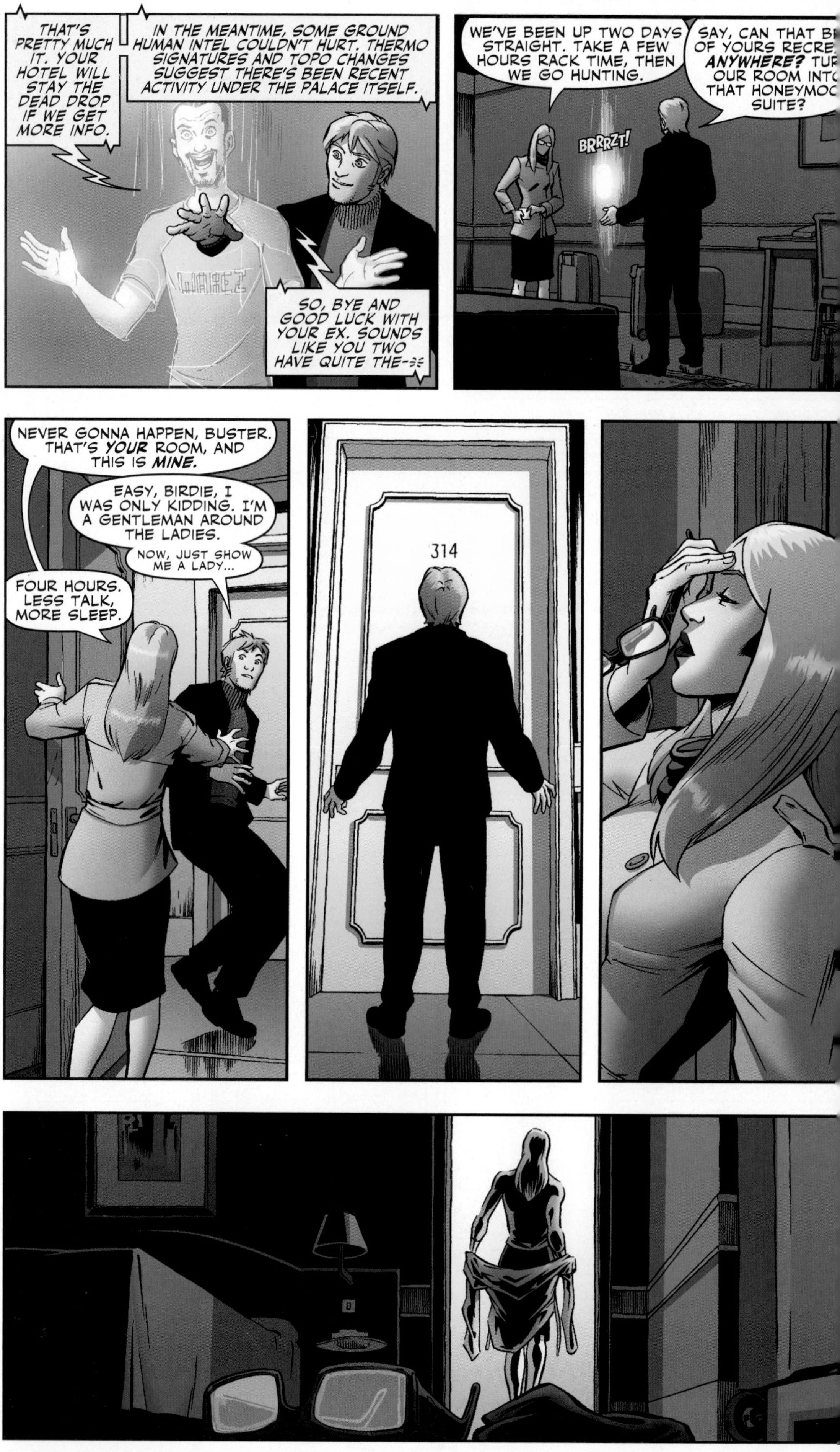

THAT'S PRETTY MUCH IT. YOUR HOTEL WILL STAY THE DEAD DROP IF WE GET MORE INFO.
IN THE MEANTIME, SOME GROUND HUMAN INTEL COULDN'T HURT. THERMO SIGNATURES AND TOPO CHANGES SUGGEST THERE'S BEEN RECENT ACTIVITY UNDER THE PALACE ITSELF.
WAREZ
SO, BYE AND GOOD LUCK WITH YOUR EX. SOUNDS LIKE YOU TWO HAVE QUITE THE--
WE'VE BEEN UP TWO DAYS STRAIGHT. TAKE A FEW HOURS RACK TIME, THEN WE GO HUNTING.
BRRRZT!
SAY, CAN THAT B OF YOURS RECRE ANYWHERE? TU OUR ROOM INT THAT HONEYMOO SUITE?
NEVER GONNA HAPPEN, BUSTER. THAT'S *YOUR* ROOM, AND THIS IS *MINE.*
EASY, BIRDIE, I WAS ONLY KIDDING. I'M A GENTLEMAN AROUND THE LADIES.
NOW, JUST SHOW ME A LADY...
FOUR HOURS. LESS TALK, MORE SLEEP.
314

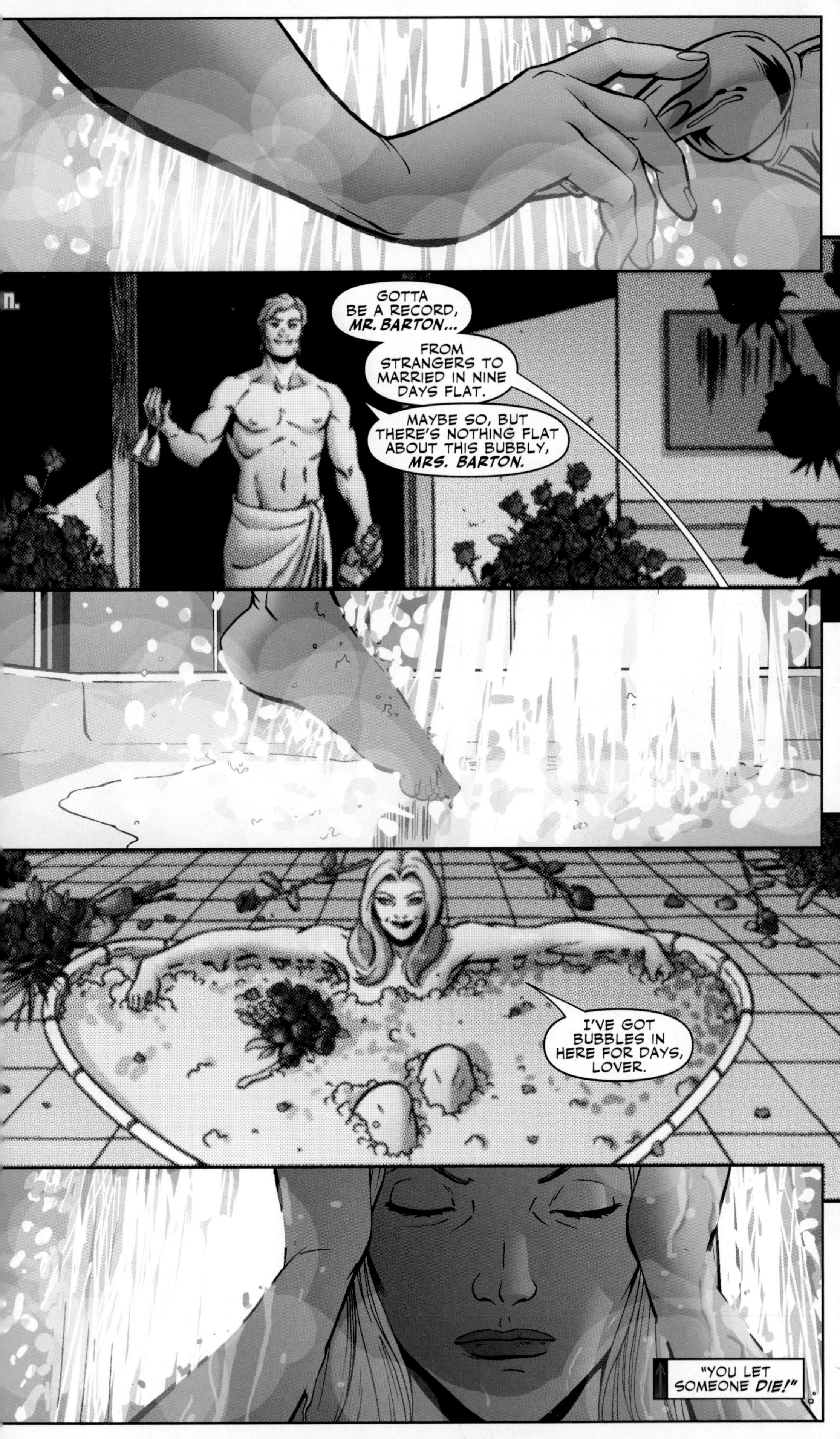

n.
GOTTA BE A RECORD, MR. BARTON...
FROM STRANGERS TO MARRIED IN NINE DAYS FLAT.
MAYBE SO, BUT THERE'S NOTHING FLAT ABOUT THIS BUBBLY, MRS. BARTON.
I'VE GOT BUBBLES IN HERE FOR DAYS, LOVER.
"YOU LET SOMEONE DIE!"

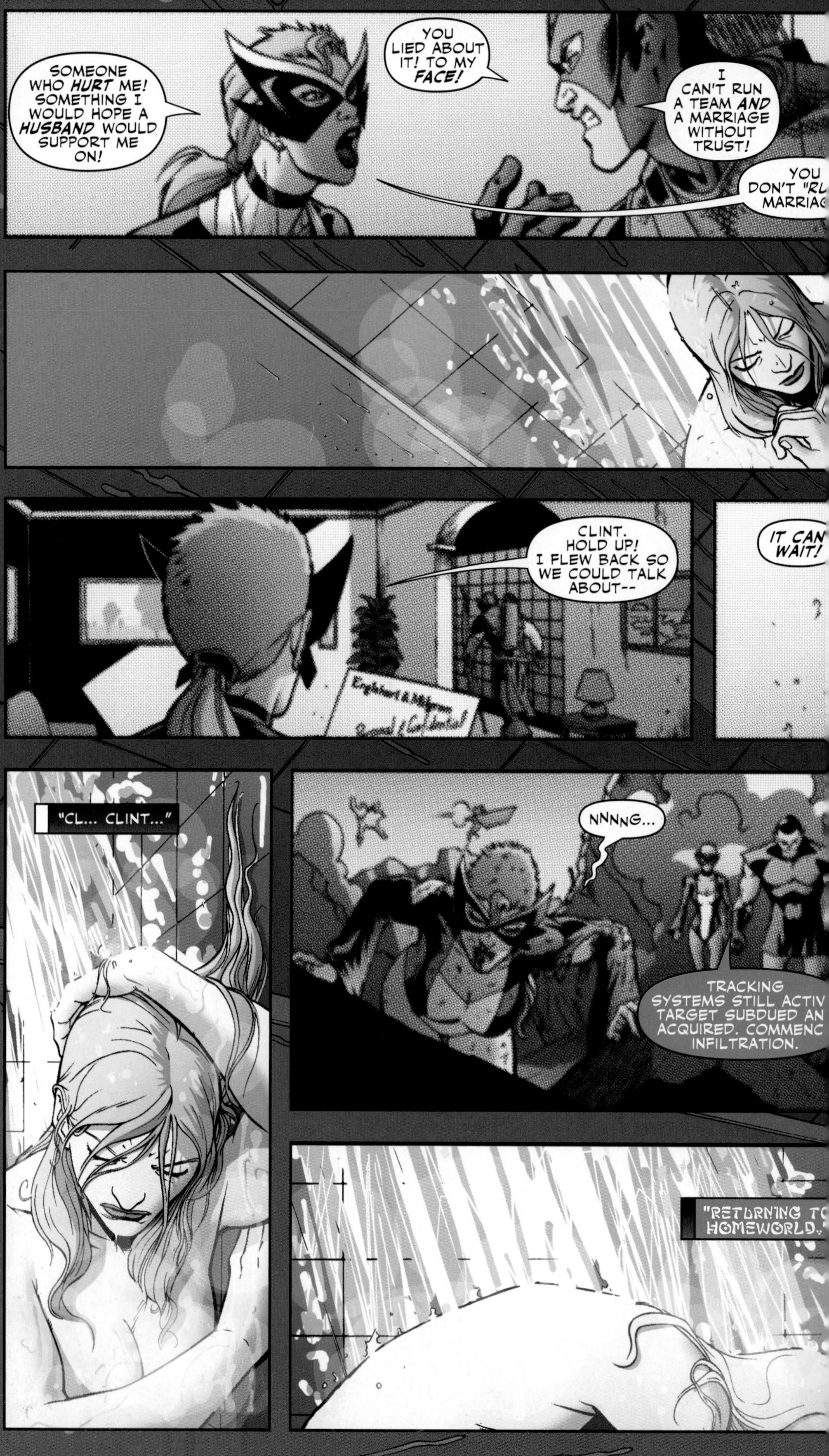
SOMEONE WHO *HURT* ME! SOMETHING I WOULD HOPE A *HUSBAND* WOULD SUPPORT ME ON!
YOU LIED ABOUT IT! TO MY *FACE!*
I CAN'T RUN A TEAM *AND* A MARRIAGE WITHOUT TRUST!
YOU DON'T "RU MARRIAG
CLINT. HOLD UP! I FLEW BACK SO WE COULD TALK ABOUT--
IT CAN WAIT!
"CL... CLINT..."
NNNNG...
TRACKING SYSTEMS STILL ACTIV TARGET SUBDUED AN ACQUIRED. COMMENC INFILTRATION.
"RETURNING T HOMEWORLD.."

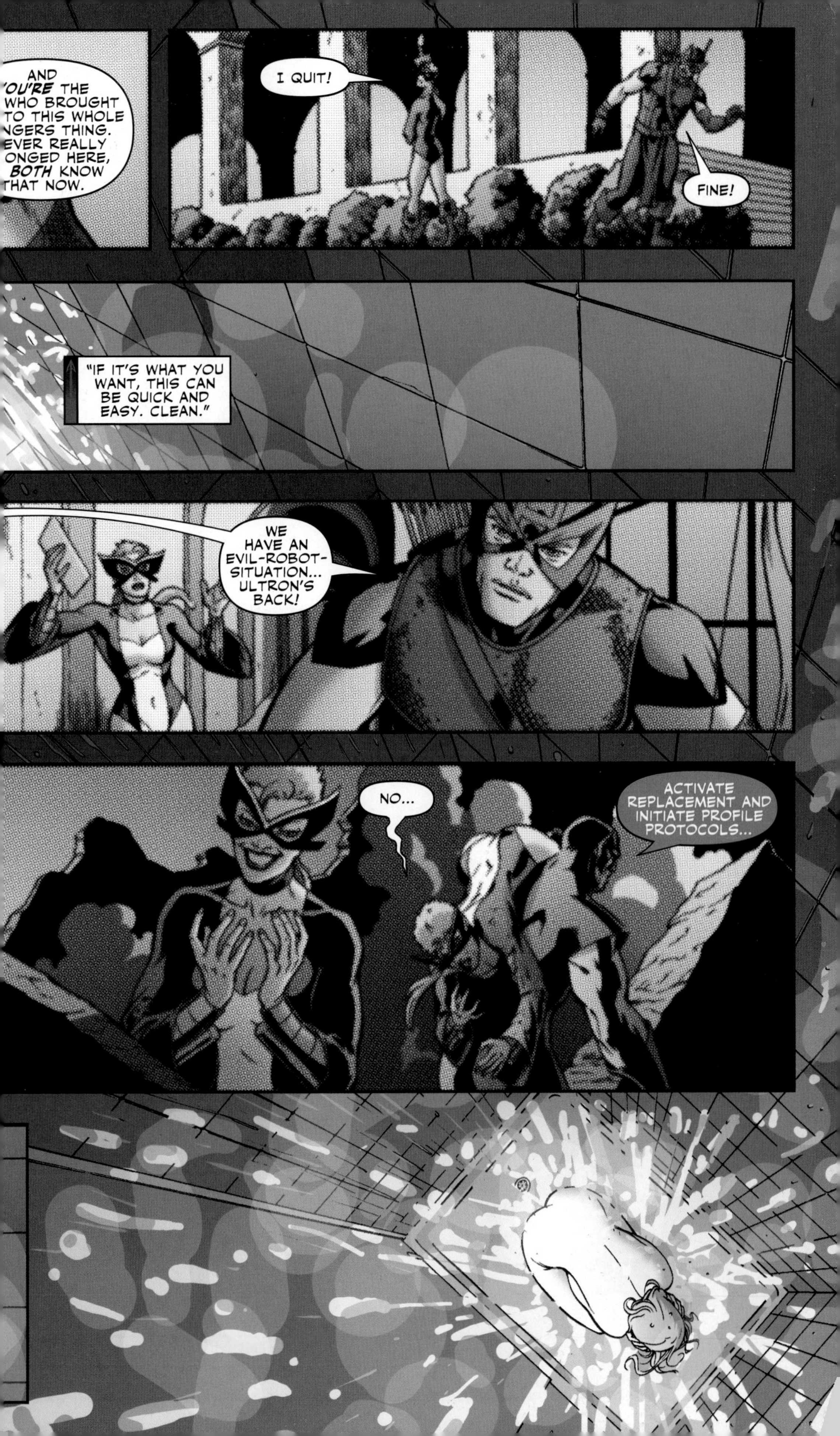
AND
OU'RE THE
WHO BROUGHT
TO THIS WHOLE
NGERS THING.
EVER REALLY
ONGED HERE,
BOTH KNOW
THAT NOW.
I QUIT!
FINE!
"IF IT'S WHAT YOU WANT, THIS CAN BE QUICK AND EASY. CLEAN."
WE HAVE AN EVIL-ROBOT-SITUATION... ULTRON'S BACK!
NO...
ACTIVATE REPLACEMENT AND INITIATE PROFILE PROTOCOLS...

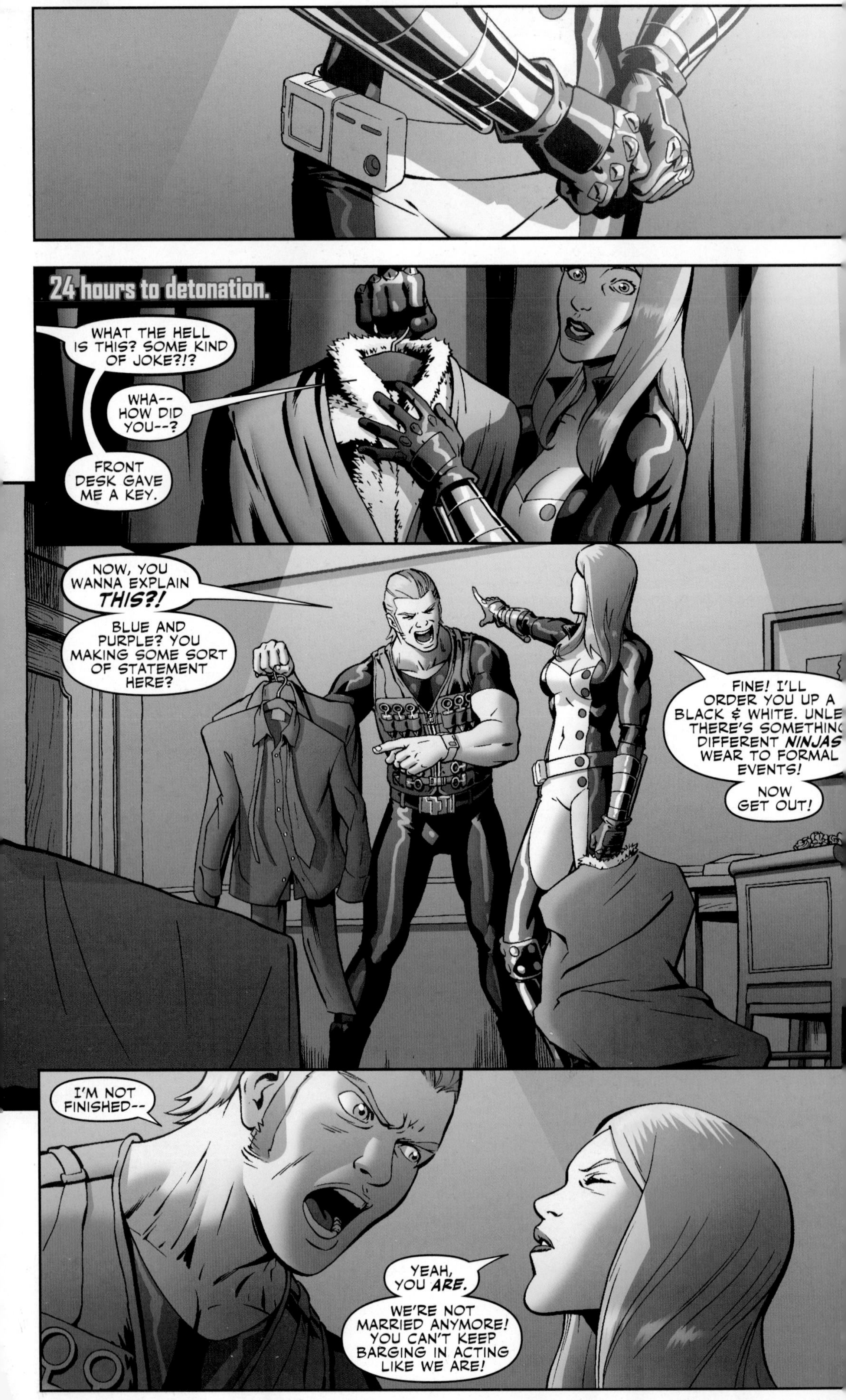
24 hours to detonation.
WHAT THE HELL IS THIS? SOME KIND OF JOKE?!?
WHA-- HOW DID YOU--?
FRONT DESK GAVE ME A KEY.
NOW, YOU WANNA EXPLAIN THIS?!
BLUE AND PURPLE? YOU MAKING SOME SORT OF STATEMENT HERE?
FINE! I'LL ORDER YOU UP A BLACK & WHITE. UNLE THERE'S SOMETHING DIFFERENT NINJAS WEAR TO FORMAL EVENTS!
NOW GET OUT!
I'M NOT FINISHED--
YEAH, YOU ARE.
WE'RE NOT MARRIED ANYMORE! YOU CAN'T KEEP BARGING IN ACTING LIKE WE ARE!

I'M **NOT** WALKING INTO POSSIBLE DEATH--**AGAIN**--UNTIL WE CLEAR UP ONE THING!

CAN'T YOU JUST LEAVE IT **ALONE!**

...OT ...N A ...TLE.

...NT TO ...W WHO, ...HAT I'M ...G INTO ... WITH. ...OSS? ...X? OR ...WIFE?

DOES IT MATTER?

YES!

I NEED TO KNOW I CAN TRUST YOU WITH MY LIFE, AND RIGHT NOW, I CAN'T EVEN TELL IF WE'RE ON THE SAME **SIDE** HALF THE TIME!

WE'RE TEAMING UP AGAIN. ISN'T THAT WHAT YOU WANTED?

NO! I WANT **US!!**

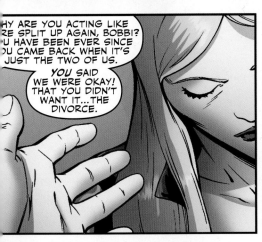

...HY ARE YOU ACTING LIKE ...RE SPLIT UP AGAIN, BOBBI? ...U HAVE BEEN EVER SINCE ...U CAME BACK WHEN IT'S ...JUST THE TWO OF US.

YOU SAID WE WERE OKAY! THAT YOU DIDN'T WANT IT...THE DIVORCE.

WHAT?! WHEN?

WHEN YOU FLEW BACK TO L.A.... AFTER ULTRON. JUST BEFORE YOU...

...BEFORE...

OH GOD.

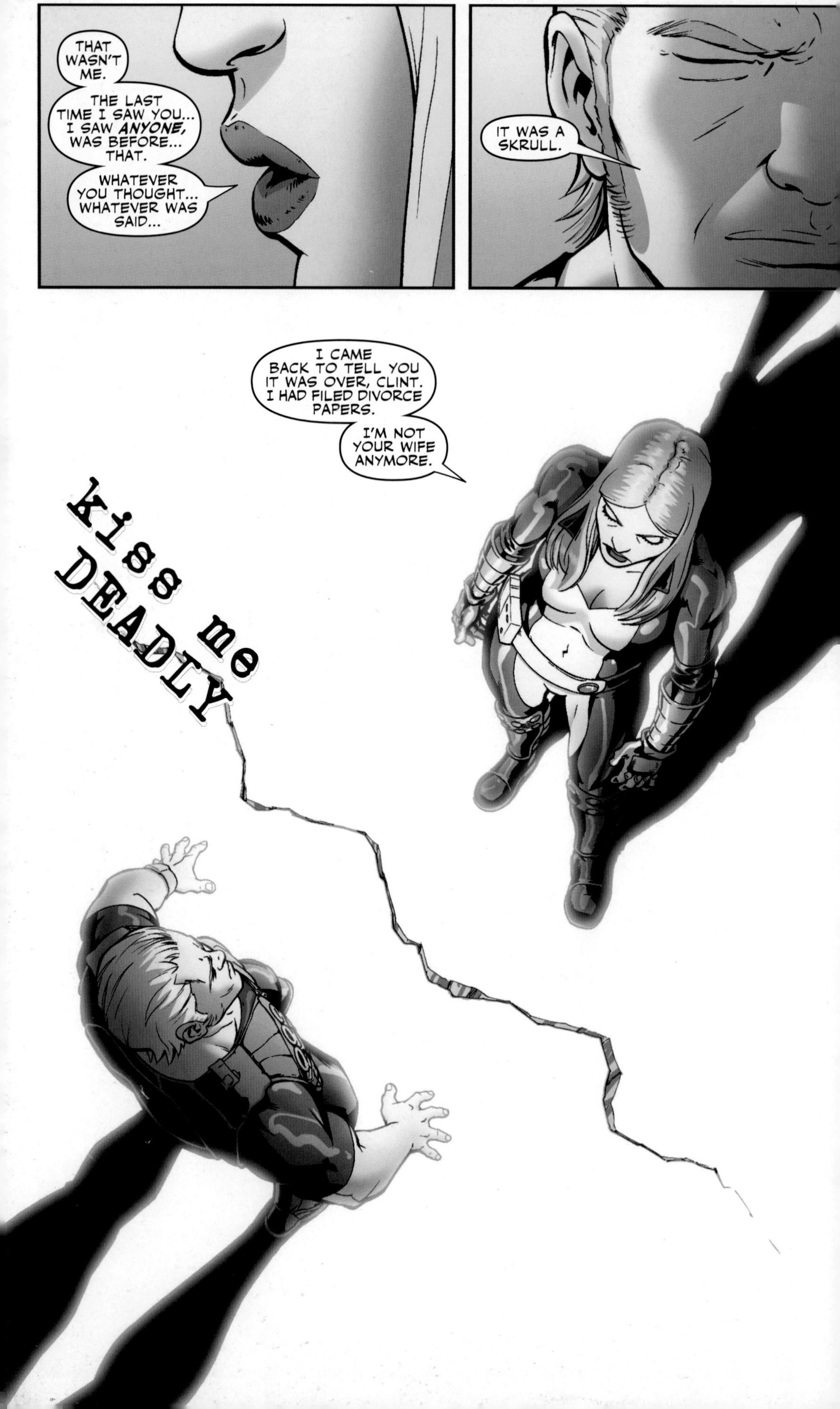
THAT WASN'T ME.
THE LAST TIME I SAW YOU... I SAW ANYONE, WAS BEFORE... THAT.
WHATEVER YOU THOUGHT... WHATEVER WAS SAID...
IT WAS A SKRULL.
I CAME BACK TO TELL YOU IT WAS OVER, CLINT. I HAD FILED DIVORCE PAPERS.
I'M NOT YOUR WIFE ANYMORE.
Kiss me DEADLY

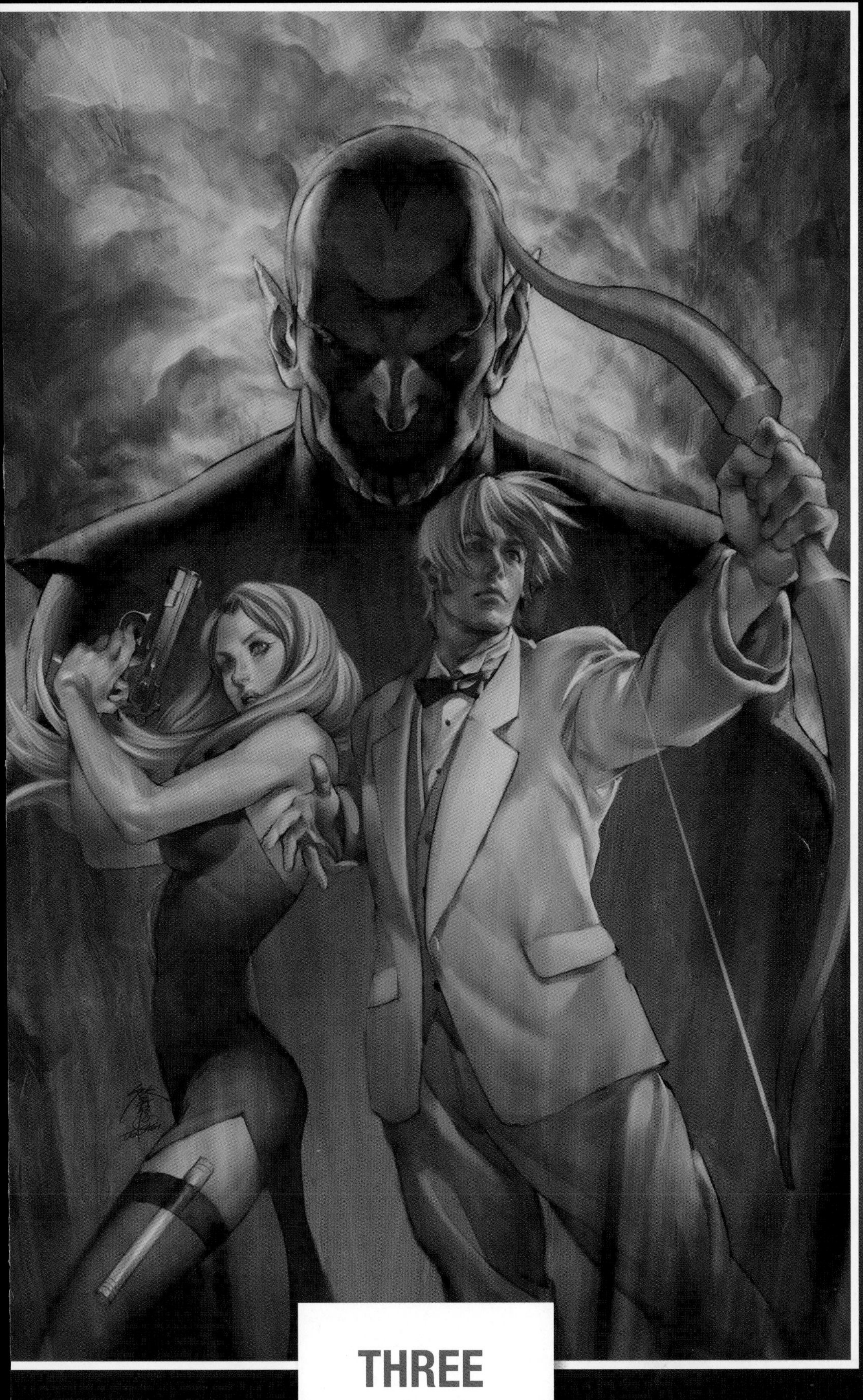

THREE

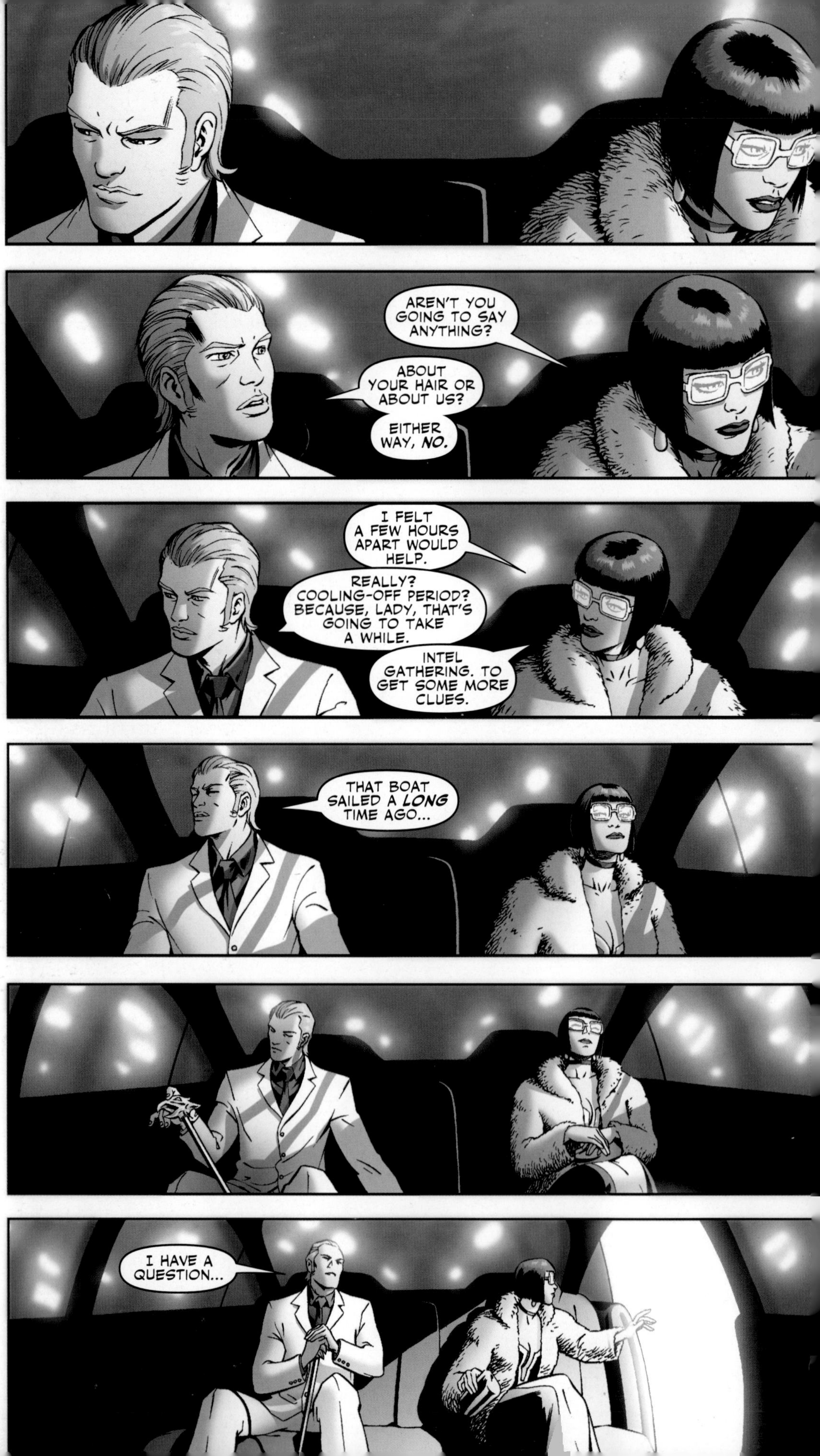

AREN'T YOU GOING TO SAY ANYTHING?
ABOUT YOUR HAIR OR ABOUT US?
EITHER WAY, *NO.*
I FELT A FEW HOURS APART WOULD HELP.
REALLY? COOLING-OFF PERIOD? BECAUSE, LADY, THAT'S GOING TO TAKE A WHILE.
INTEL GATHERING. TO GET SOME MORE CLUES.
THAT BOAT SAILED A *LONG* TIME AGO...
I HAVE A QUESTION...

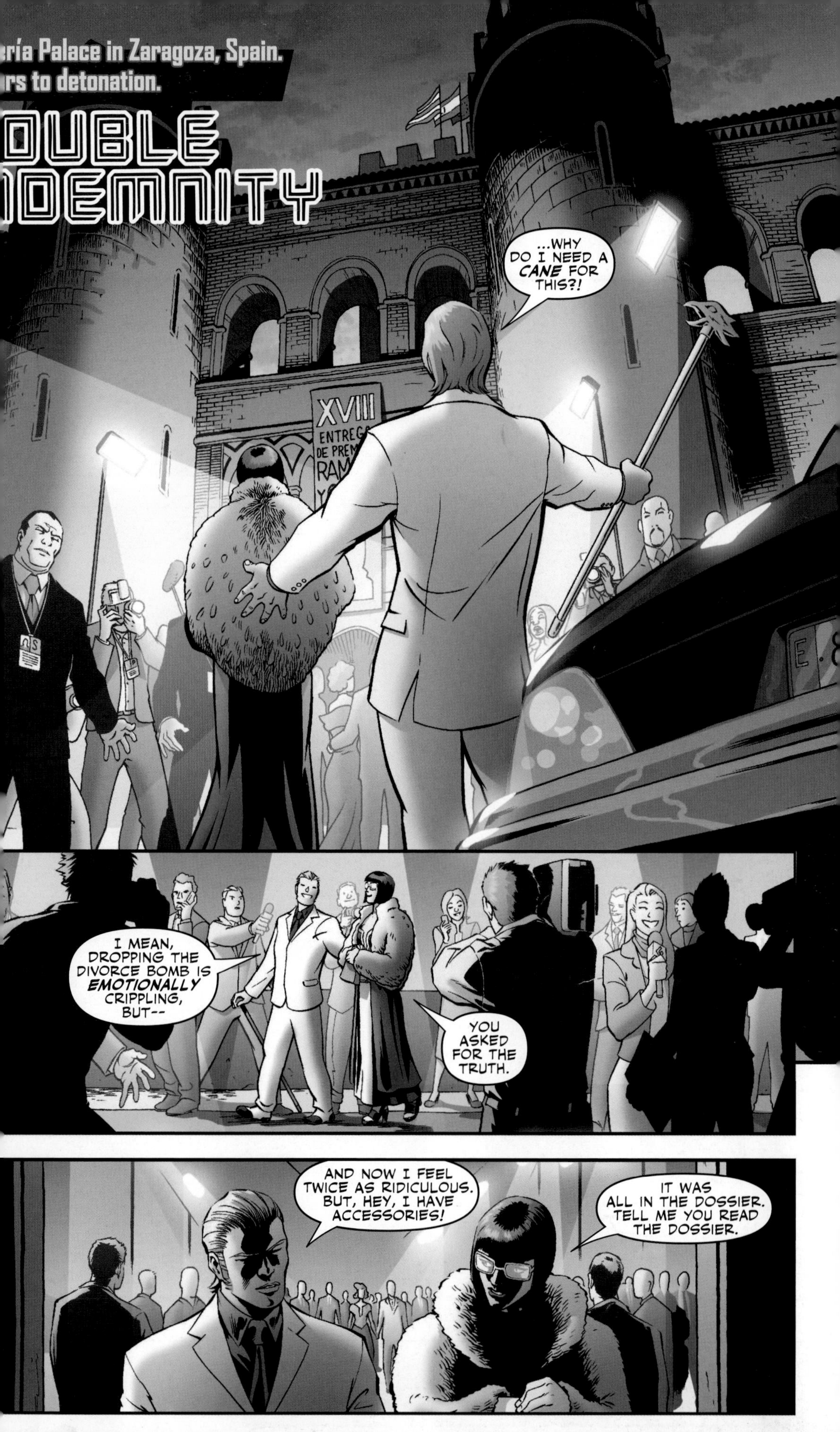
ría Palace in Zaragoza, Spain.
rs to detonation.
OUBLE
DEMNITY
...WHY DO I NEED A *CANE* FOR THIS?!
XVIII
I MEAN, DROPPING THE DIVORCE BOMB IS ***EMOTIONALLY*** CRIPPLING, BUT--
YOU ASKED FOR THE TRUTH.
AND NOW I FEEL TWICE AS RIDICULOUS. BUT, HEY, I HAVE ACCESSORIES!
IT WAS ALL IN THE DOSSIER. TELL ME YOU READ THE DOSSIER.

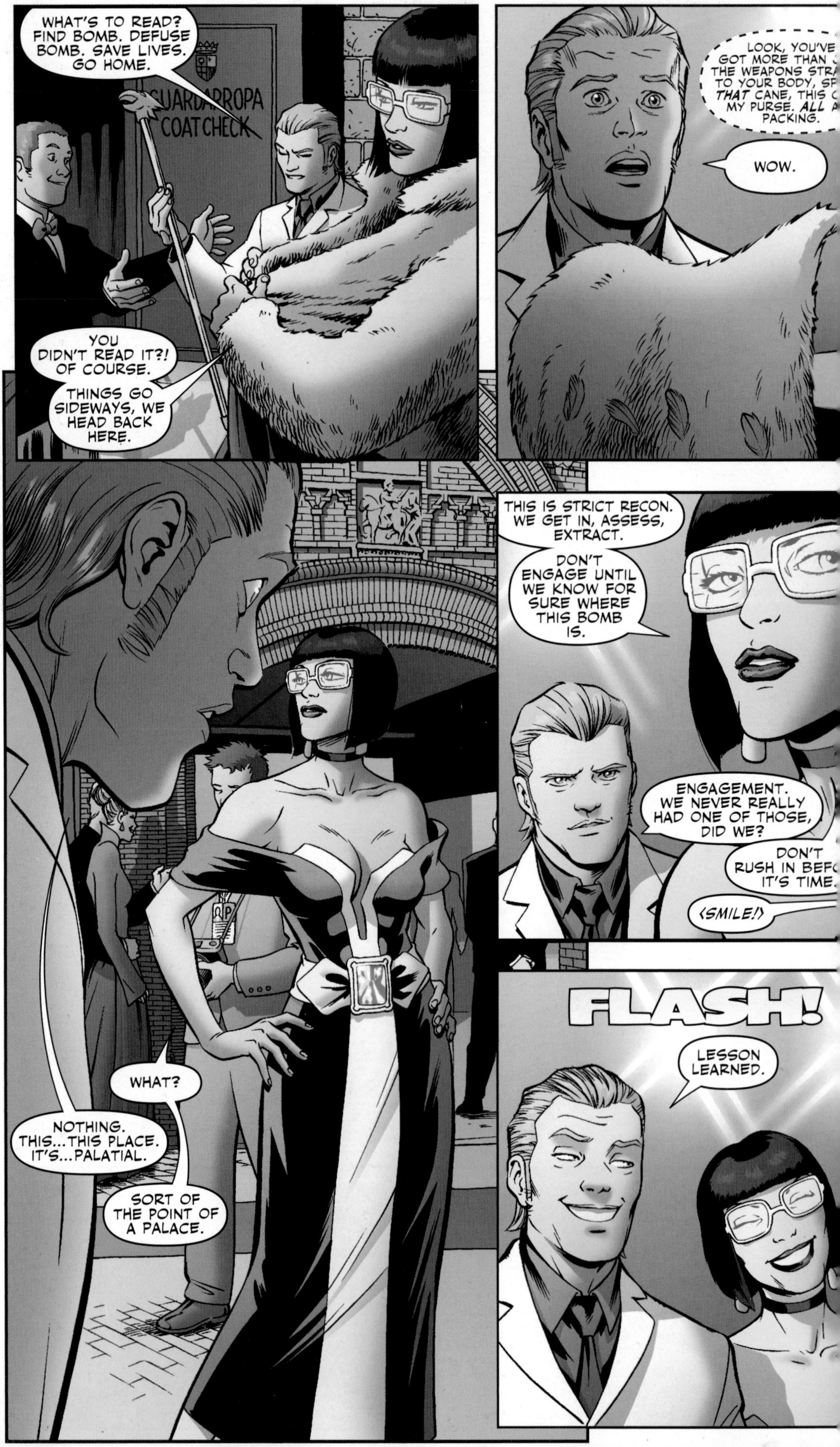
WHAT'S TO READ? FIND BOMB. DEFUSE BOMB. SAVE LIVES. GO HOME.
GUARDARROPA
COAT CHECK
YOU DIDN'T READ IT?! OF COURSE.
THINGS GO SIDEWAYS, WE HEAD BACK HERE.
LOOK, YOU'VE GOT MORE THAN THE WEAPONS STR TO YOUR BODY, SP THAT CANE, THIS MY PURSE. ALL PACKING.
WOW.
WHAT?
NOTHING. THIS...THIS PLACE. IT'S...PALATIAL.
SORT OF THE POINT OF A PALACE.
THIS IS STRICT RECON. WE GET IN, ASSESS, EXTRACT.
DON'T ENGAGE UNTIL WE KNOW FOR SURE WHERE THIS BOMB IS.
ENGAGEMENT. WE NEVER REALLY HAD ONE OF THOSE, DID WE?
DON'T RUSH IN BEF IT'S TIME.
<SMILE!>
FLASH!
LESSON LEARNED.

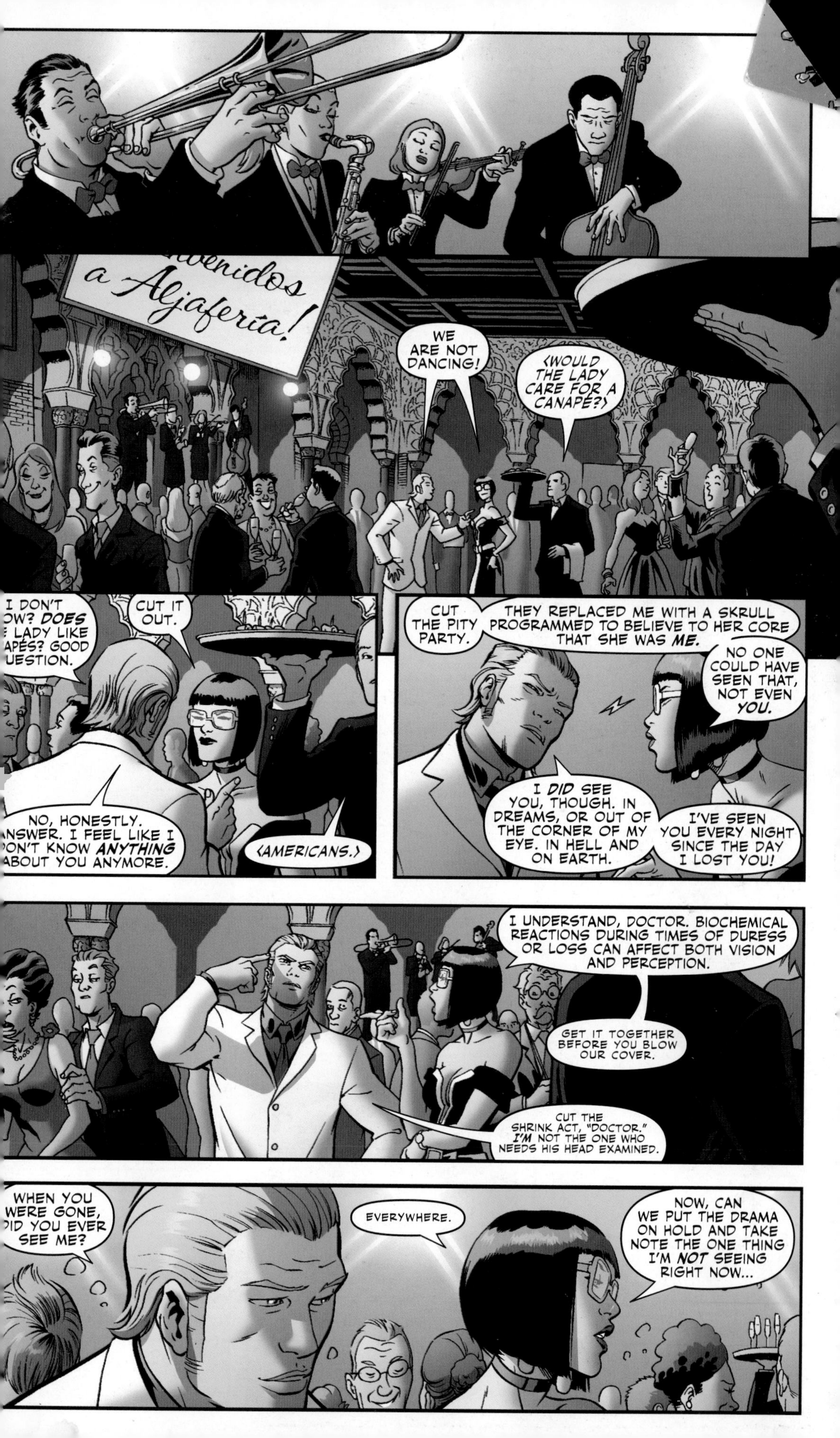
a Aljafería!
WE ARE NOT DANCING!
<WOULD THE LADY CARE FOR A CANAPÉ?>
I DON'T
OW? DOES
LADY LIKE
APÉS? GOOD
UESTION.
CUT IT OUT.
NO, HONESTLY.
NSWER. I FEEL LIKE I
ON'T KNOW ANYTHING
ABOUT YOU ANYMORE.
<AMERICANS.>
CUT THE PITY PARTY.
THEY REPLACED ME WITH A SKRULL PROGRAMMED TO BELIEVE TO HER CORE THAT SHE WAS ME.
NO ONE COULD HAVE SEEN THAT, NOT EVEN YOU.
I DID SEE YOU, THOUGH. IN DREAMS, OR OUT OF THE CORNER OF MY EYE. IN HELL AND ON EARTH.
I'VE SEEN YOU EVERY NIGHT SINCE THE DAY I LOST YOU!
I UNDERSTAND, DOCTOR. BIOCHEMICAL REACTIONS DURING TIMES OF DURESS OR LOSS CAN AFFECT BOTH VISION AND PERCEPTION.
GET IT TOGETHER BEFORE YOU BLOW OUR COVER.
CUT THE SHRINK ACT, "DOCTOR." I'M NOT THE ONE WHO NEEDS HIS HEAD EXAMINED.
WHEN YOU WERE GONE, DID YOU EVER SEE ME?
EVERYWHERE.
NOW, CAN WE PUT THE DRAMA ON HOLD AND TAKE NOTE THE ONE THING I'M NOT SEEING RIGHT NOW...

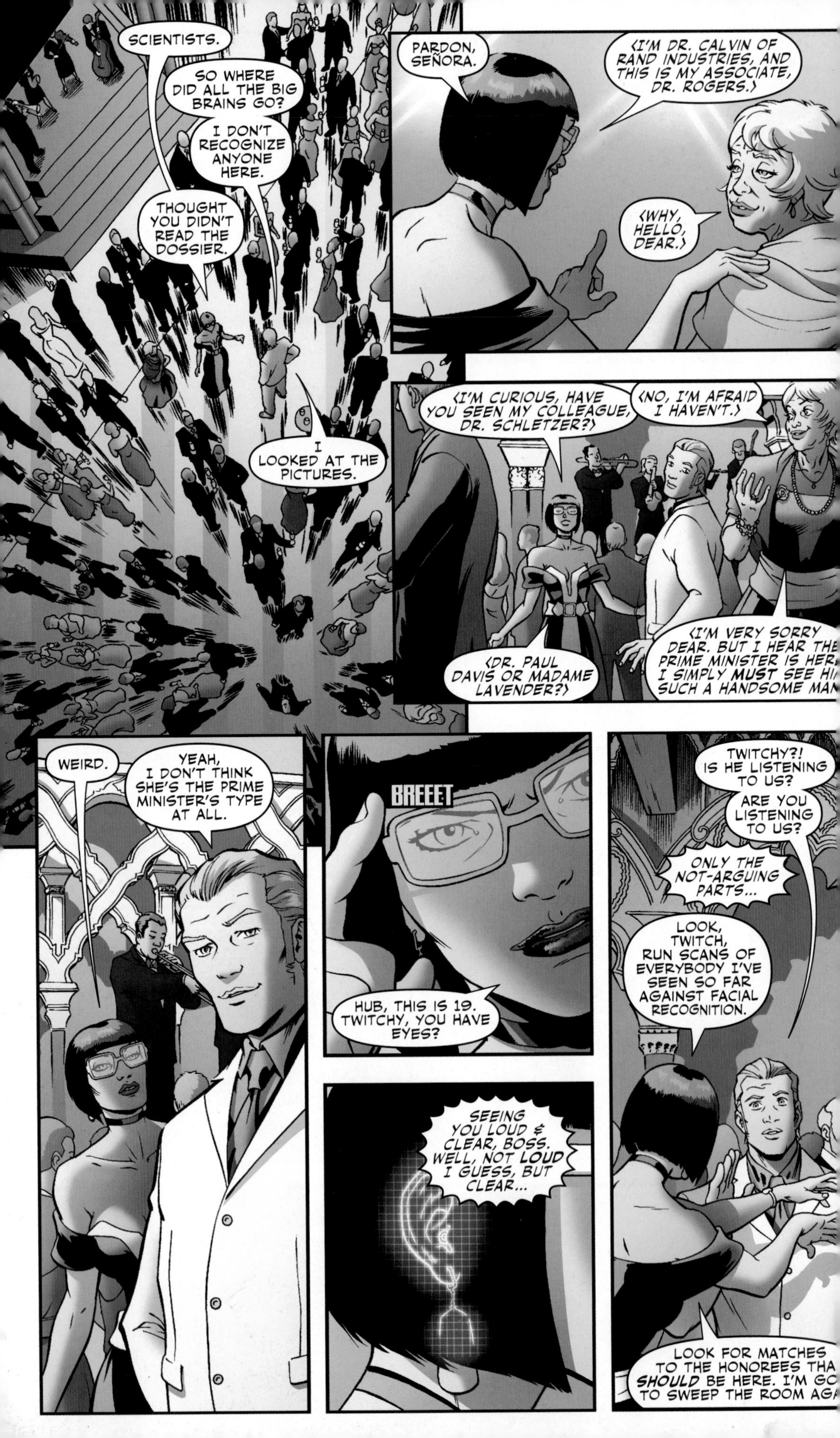
SCIENTISTS.
SO WHERE DID ALL THE BIG BRAINS GO?
I DON'T RECOGNIZE ANYONE HERE.
THOUGHT YOU DIDN'T READ THE DOSSIER.
I LOOKED AT THE PICTURES.
PARDON, SEÑORA.
‹I'M DR. CALVIN OF RAND INDUSTRIES, AND THIS IS MY ASSOCIATE, DR. ROGERS.›
‹WHY, HELLO, DEAR.›
‹I'M CURIOUS, HAVE YOU SEEN MY COLLEAGUE, DR. SCHLETZER?›
‹NO, I'M AFRAID I HAVEN'T.›
‹DR. PAUL DAVIS OR MADAME LAVENDER?›
‹I'M VERY SORRY DEAR. BUT I HEAR THE PRIME MINISTER IS HER I SIMPLY MUST SEE HI SUCH A HANDSOME MAN
WEIRD.
YEAH, I DON'T THINK SHE'S THE PRIME MINISTER'S TYPE AT ALL.
BREEET
HUB, THIS IS 19. TWITCHY, YOU HAVE EYES?
SEEING YOU LOUD & CLEAR, BOSS. WELL, NOT LOUD I GUESS, BUT CLEAR...
TWITCHY?! IS HE LISTENING TO US?
ARE YOU LISTENING TO US?
ONLY THE NOT-ARGUING PARTS...
LOOK, TWITCH, RUN SCANS OF EVERYBODY I'VE SEEN SO FAR AGAINST FACIAL RECOGNITION.
LOOK FOR MATCHES TO THE HONOREES THA SHOULD BE HERE. I'M GO TO SWEEP THE ROOM AG

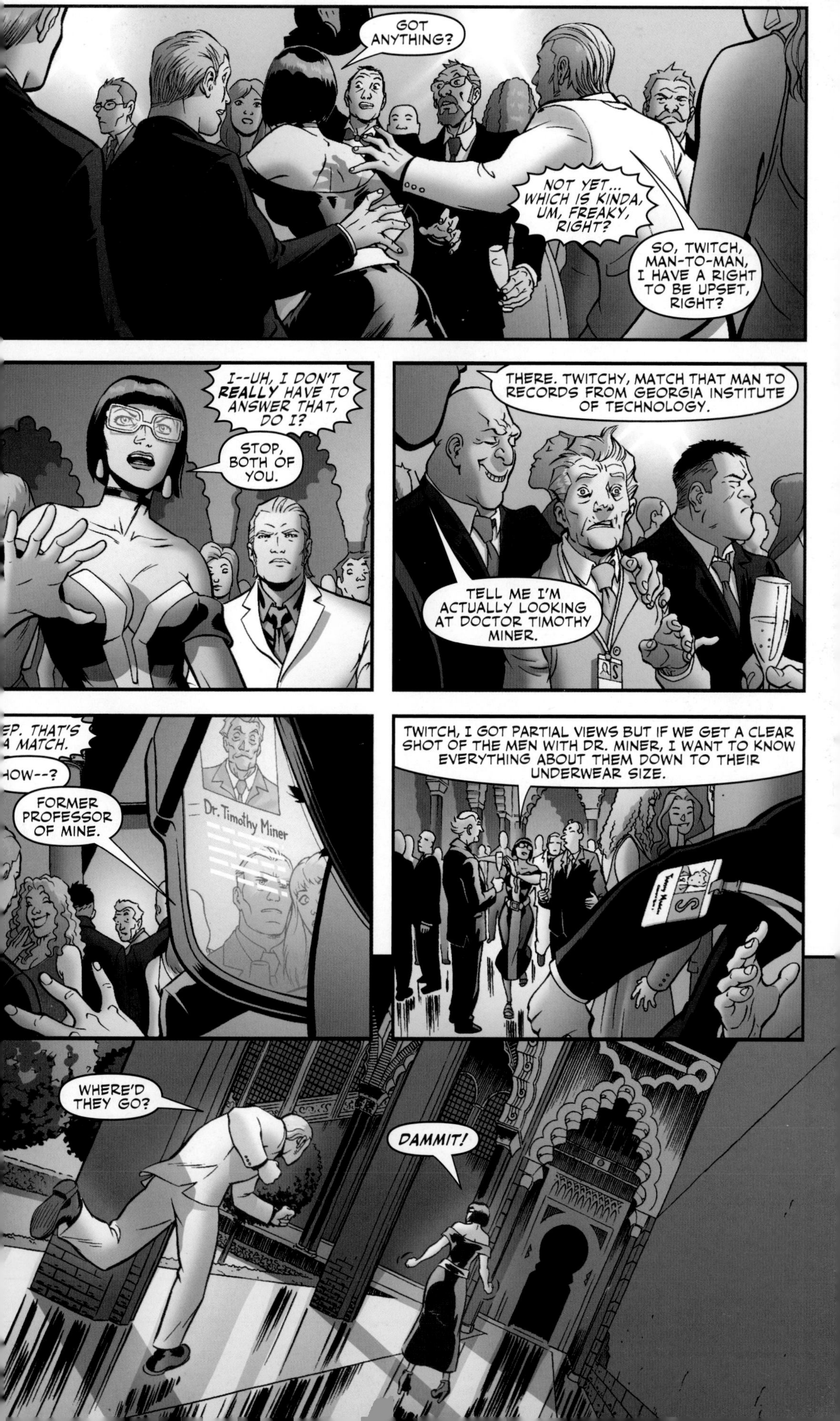
GOT ANYTHING?
NOT YET... WHICH IS KINDA, UM, FREAKY, RIGHT?
SO, TWITCH, MAN-TO-MAN, I HAVE A RIGHT TO BE UPSET, RIGHT?
I--UH, I DON'T REALLY HAVE TO ANSWER THAT, DO I?
STOP, BOTH OF YOU.
THERE. TWITCHY, MATCH THAT MAN TO RECORDS FROM GEORGIA INSTITUTE OF TECHNOLOGY.
TELL ME I'M ACTUALLY LOOKING AT DOCTOR TIMOTHY MINER.
EP. THAT'S A MATCH.
HOW--?
FORMER PROFESSOR OF MINE.
Dr. Timothy Miner
TWITCH, I GOT PARTIAL VIEWS BUT IF WE GET A CLEAR SHOT OF THE MEN WITH DR. MINER, I WANT TO KNOW EVERYTHING ABOUT THEM DOWN TO THEIR UNDERWEAR SIZE.
WHERE'D THEY GO?
DAMMIT!

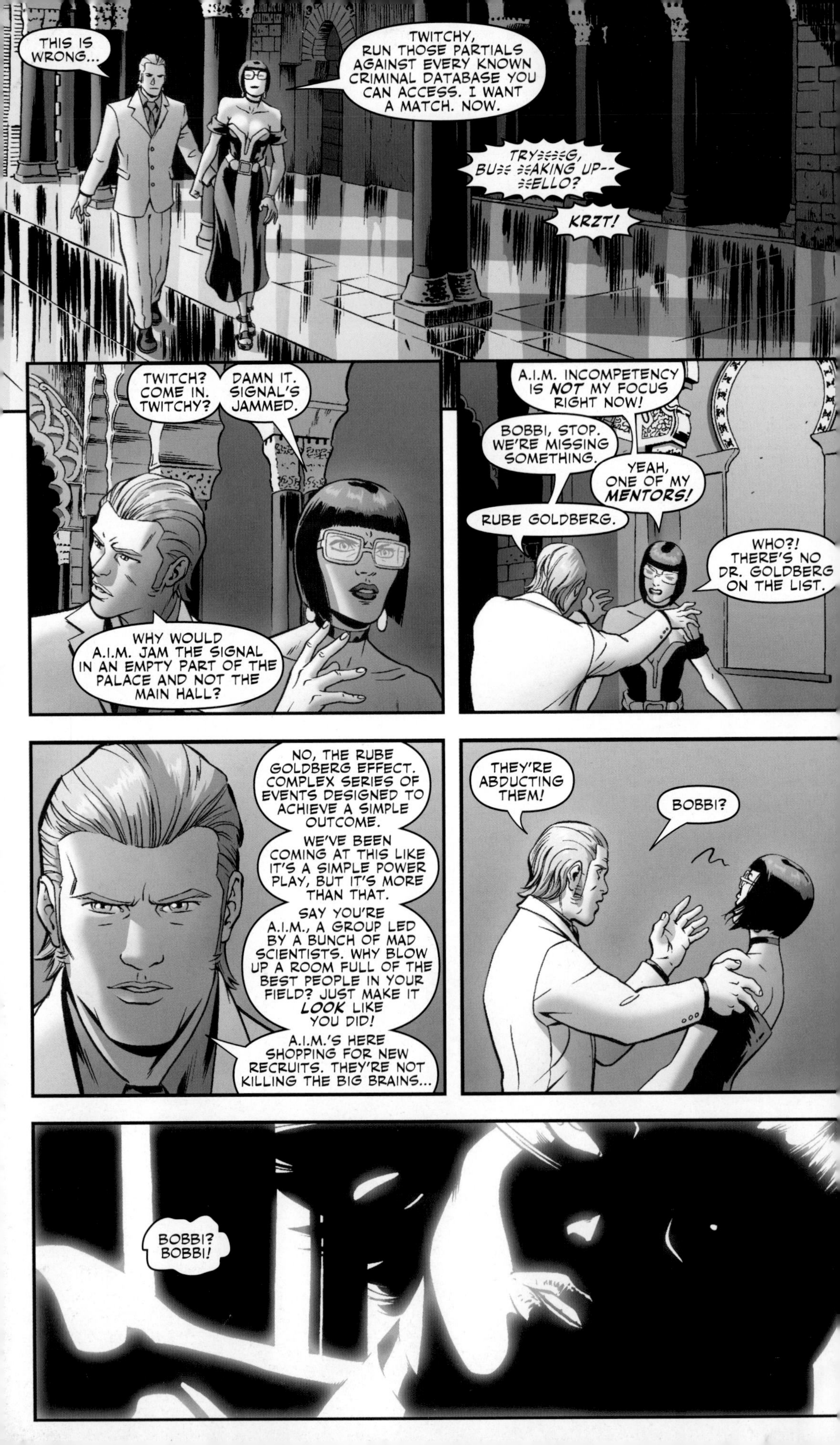
THIS IS WRONG...
TWITCHY, RUN THOSE PARTIALS AGAINST EVERY KNOWN CRIMINAL DATABASE YOU CAN ACCESS. I WANT A MATCH. NOW.
TRY≋≋≋G, BU≋≋ ≋AKING UP-- ≋ELLO?
KRZT!
TWITCH? COME IN. TWITCHY?
DAMN IT. SIGNAL'S JAMMED.
WHY WOULD A.I.M. JAM THE SIGNAL IN AN EMPTY PART OF THE PALACE AND NOT THE MAIN HALL?
A.I.M. INCOMPETENCY IS NOT MY FOCUS RIGHT NOW!
BOBBI, STOP. WE'RE MISSING SOMETHING.
YEAH, ONE OF MY MENTORS!
RUBE GOLDBERG.
WHO?! THERE'S NO DR. GOLDBERG ON THE LIST.
NO, THE RUBE GOLDBERG EFFECT. COMPLEX SERIES OF EVENTS DESIGNED TO ACHIEVE A SIMPLE OUTCOME.
WE'VE BEEN COMING AT THIS LIKE IT'S A SIMPLE POWER PLAY, BUT IT'S MORE THAN THAT.
SAY YOU'RE A.I.M., A GROUP LED BY A BUNCH OF MAD SCIENTISTS. WHY BLOW UP A ROOM FULL OF THE BEST PEOPLE IN YOUR FIELD? JUST MAKE IT LOOK LIKE YOU DID!
A.I.M.'S HERE SHOPPING FOR NEW RECRUITS. THEY'RE NOT KILLING THE BIG BRAINS...
THEY'RE ABDUCTING THEM!
BOBBI?
BOBBI? BOBBI!

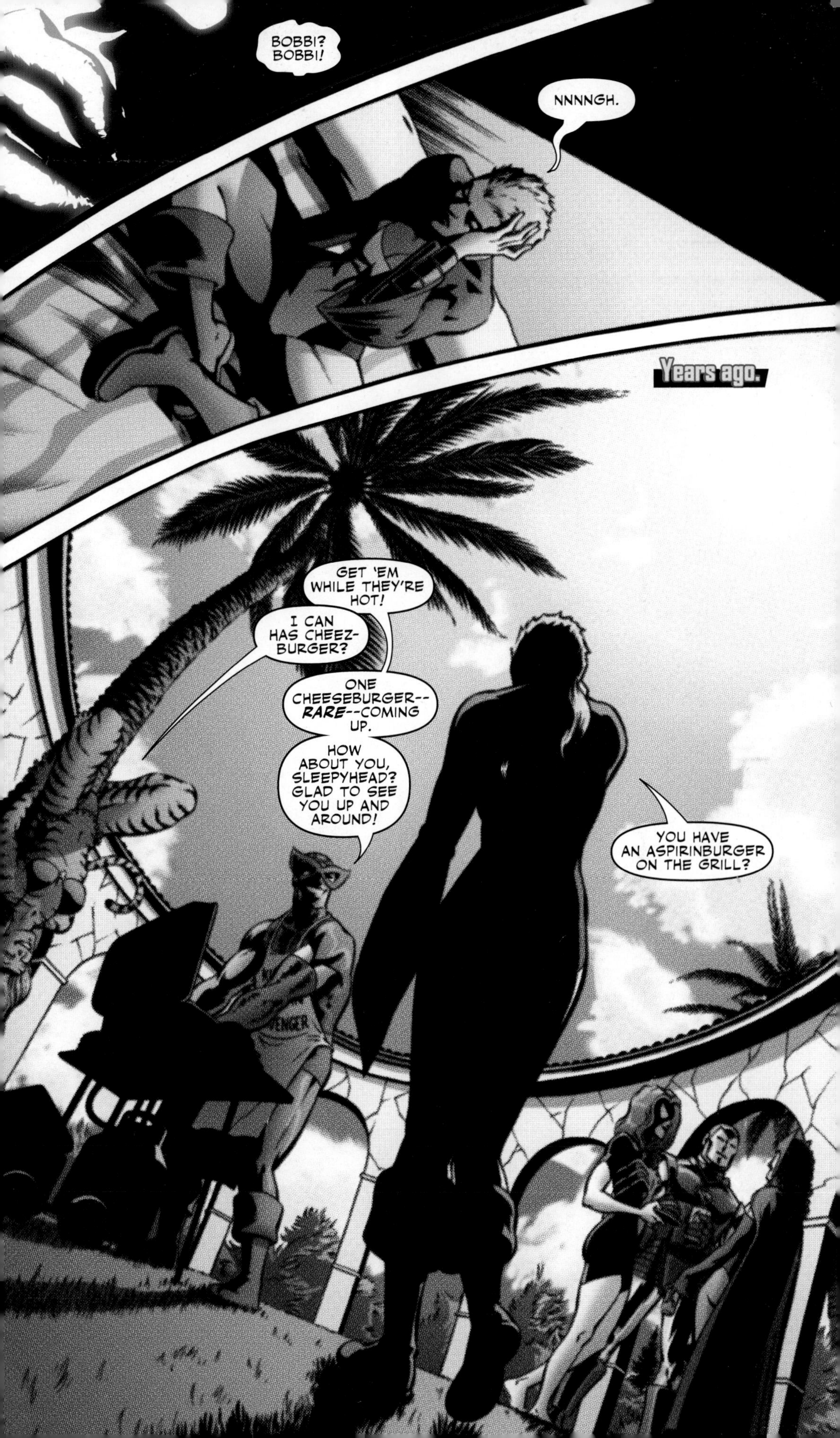
BOBBI? BOBBI!
NNNNGH.
Years ago.
GET 'EM WHILE THEY'RE HOT!
I CAN HAS CHEEZ-BURGER?
ONE CHEESEBURGER-- *RARE*--COMING UP.
HOW ABOUT YOU, SLEEPYHEAD? GLAD TO SEE YOU UP AND AROUND!
YOU HAVE AN ASPIRINBURGER ON THE GRILL?

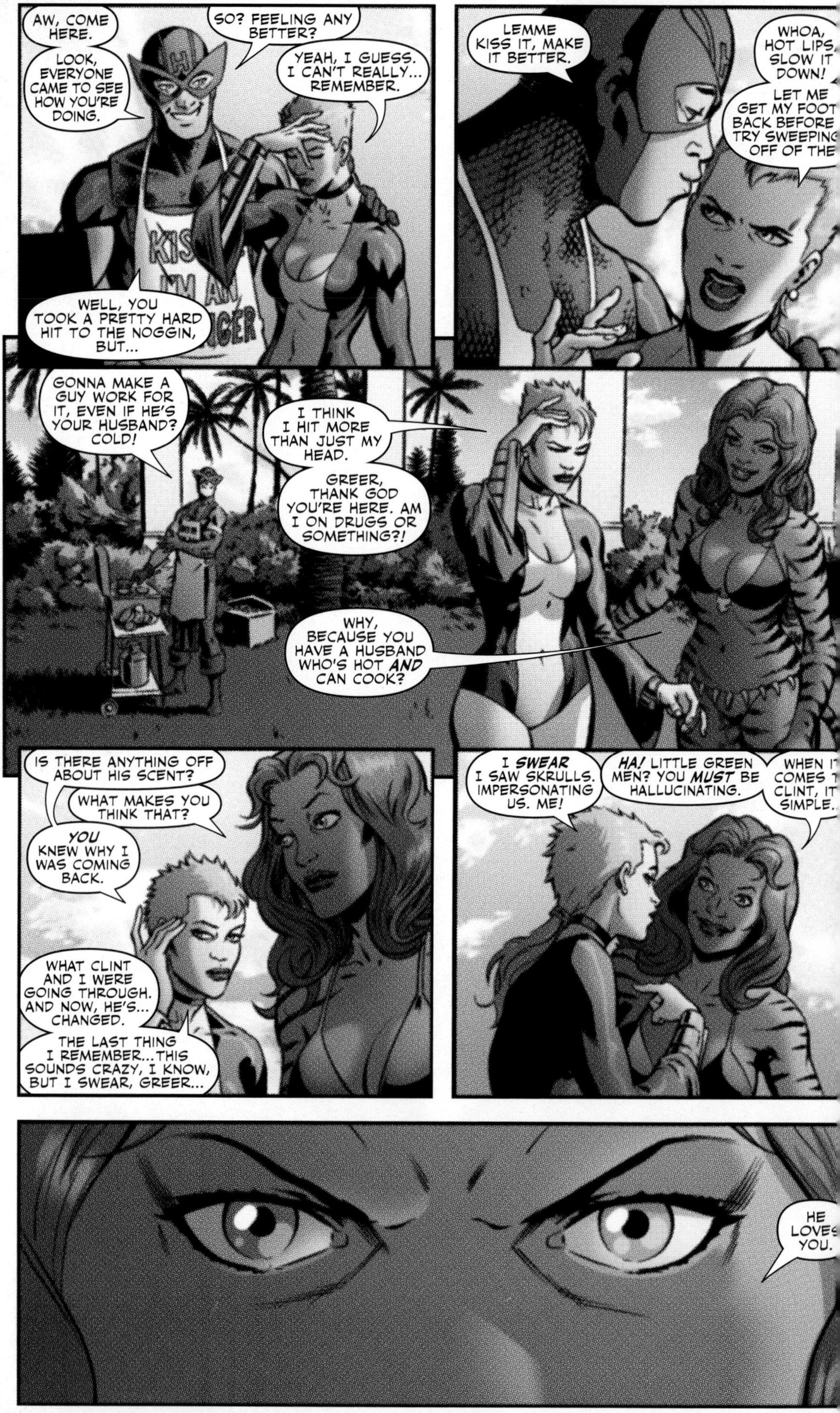
AW, COME HERE.
LOOK, EVERYONE CAME TO SEE HOW YOU'RE DOING.
SO? FEELING ANY BETTER?
YEAH, I GUESS. I CAN'T REALLY... REMEMBER.
WELL, YOU TOOK A PRETTY HARD HIT TO THE NOGGIN, BUT...
LEMME KISS IT, MAKE IT BETTER.
WHOA, HOT LIPS, SLOW IT DOWN!
LET ME GET MY FOOT BACK BEFORE TRY SWEEPING OFF OF THE
GONNA MAKE A GUY WORK FOR IT, EVEN IF HE'S YOUR HUSBAND? COLD!
I THINK I HIT MORE THAN JUST MY HEAD.
GREER, THANK GOD YOU'RE HERE. AM I ON DRUGS OR SOMETHING?!
WHY, BECAUSE YOU HAVE A HUSBAND WHO'S HOT AND CAN COOK?
IS THERE ANYTHING OFF ABOUT HIS SCENT?
WHAT MAKES YOU THINK THAT?
YOU KNEW WHY I WAS COMING BACK.
WHAT CLINT AND I WERE GOING THROUGH. AND NOW, HE'S... CHANGED.
THE LAST THING I REMEMBER...THIS SOUNDS CRAZY, I KNOW, BUT I SWEAR, GREER...
I SWEAR I SAW SKRULLS. IMPERSONATING US. ME!
HA! LITTLE GREEN MEN? YOU MUST BE HALLUCINATING.
WHEN IT COMES T CLINT, IT SIMPLE.
HE LOVES YOU.

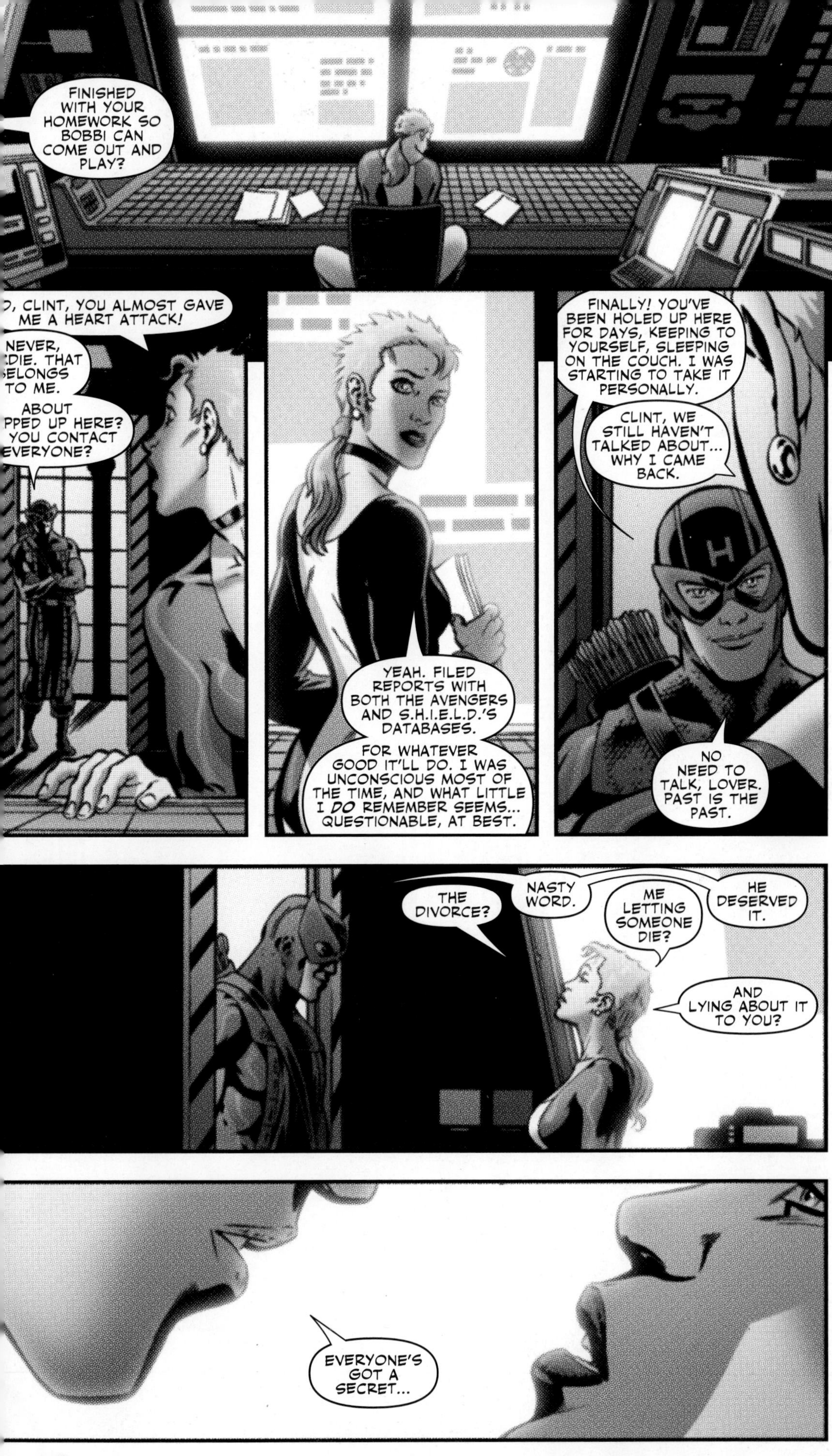

FINISHED WITH YOUR HOMEWORK SO BOBBI CAN COME OUT AND PLAY?
O, CLINT, YOU ALMOST GAVE ME A HEART ATTACK!
NEVER, DIE. THAT ELONGS TO ME.
ABOUT PPED UP HERE? YOU CONTACT EVERYONE?
YEAH. FILED REPORTS WITH BOTH THE AVENGERS AND S.H.I.E.L.D.'S DATABASES.
FOR WHATEVER GOOD IT'LL DO. I WAS UNCONSCIOUS MOST OF THE TIME, AND WHAT LITTLE I *DO* REMEMBER SEEMS... QUESTIONABLE, AT BEST.
FINALLY! YOU'VE BEEN HOLED UP HERE FOR DAYS, KEEPING TO YOURSELF, SLEEPING ON THE COUCH. I WAS STARTING TO TAKE IT PERSONALLY.
CLINT, WE STILL HAVEN'T TALKED ABOUT... WHY I CAME BACK.
NO NEED TO TALK, LOVER. PAST IS THE PAST.
THE DIVORCE?
NASTY WORD.
ME LETTING SOMEONE DIE?
HE DESERVED IT.
AND LYING ABOUT IT TO YOU?
EVERYONE'S GOT A SECRET...

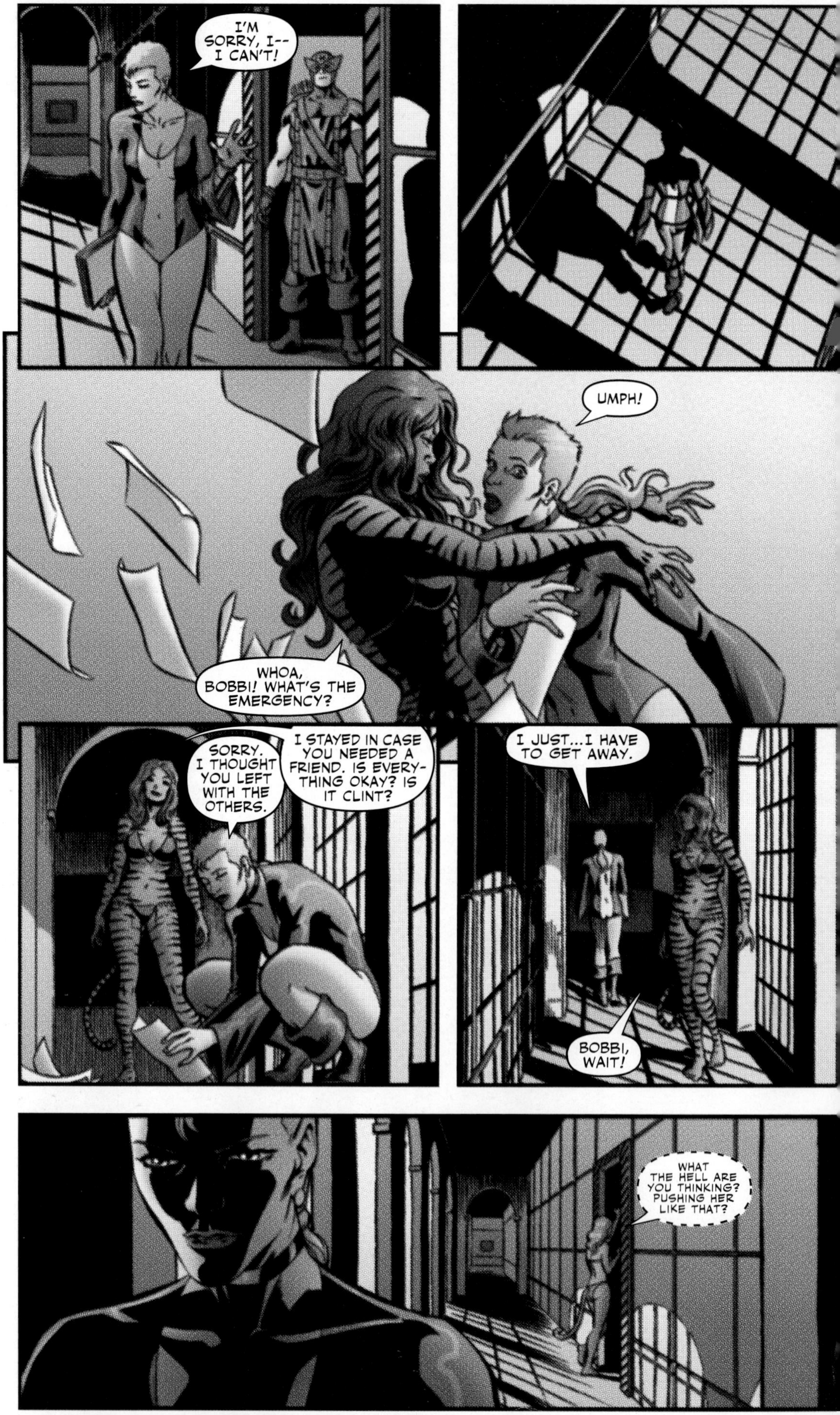
I'M SORRY, I-- I CAN'T!
UMPH!
WHOA, BOBBI! WHAT'S THE EMERGENCY?
SORRY. I THOUGHT YOU LEFT WITH THE OTHERS.
I STAYED IN CASE YOU NEEDED A FRIEND. IS EVERY-THING OKAY? IS IT CLINT?
I JUST...I HAVE TO GET AWAY.
BOBBI, WAIT!
WHAT THE HELL ARE YOU THINKING? PUSHING HER LIKE THAT?

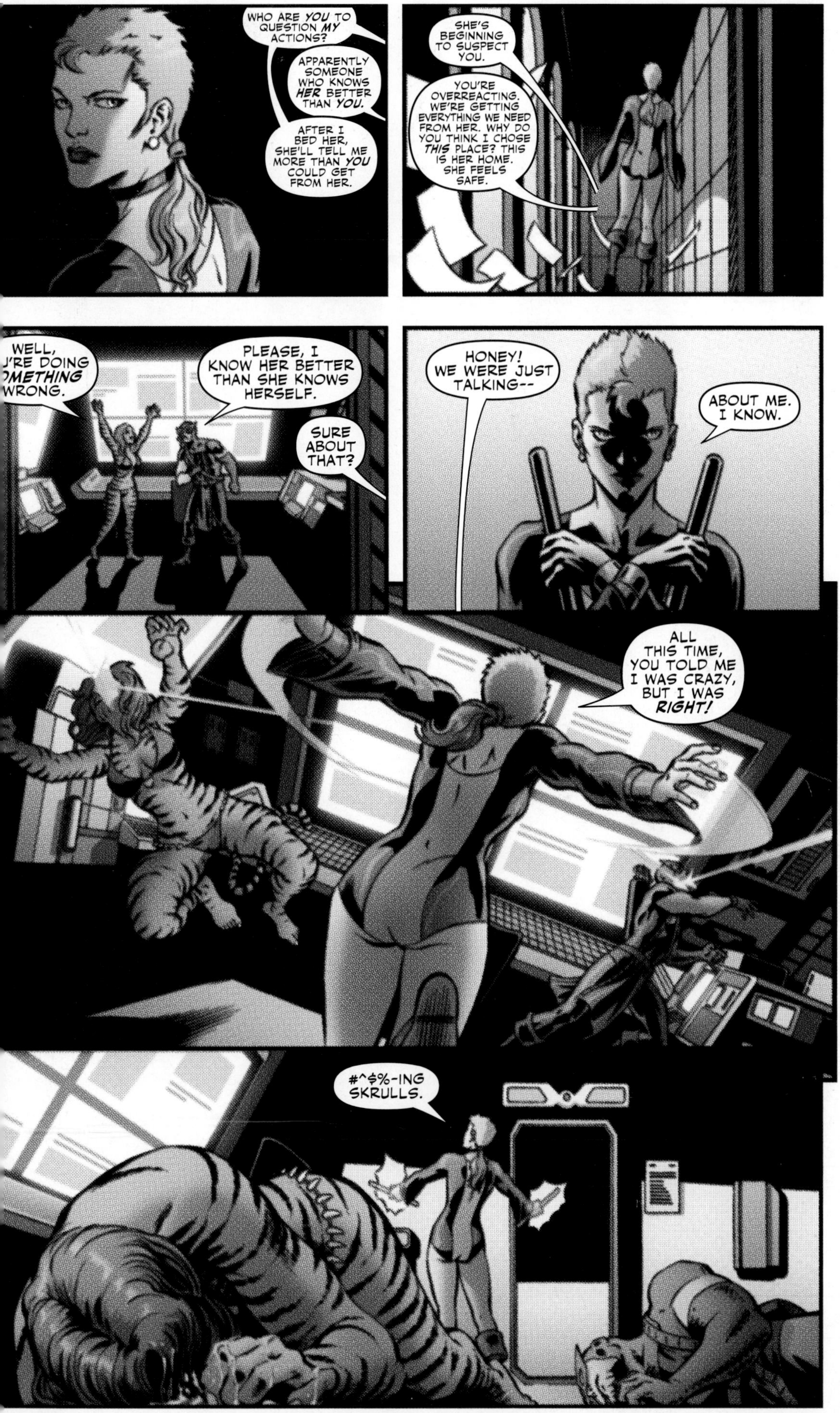
WHO ARE YOU TO QUESTION MY ACTIONS?
APPARENTLY SOMEONE WHO KNOWS HER BETTER THAN YOU.
AFTER I BED HER, SHE'LL TELL ME MORE THAN YOU COULD GET FROM HER.
SHE'S BEGINNING TO SUSPECT YOU.
YOU'RE OVERREACTING. WE'RE GETTING EVERYTHING WE NEED FROM HER. WHY DO YOU THINK I CHOSE THIS PLACE? THIS IS HER HOME. SHE FEELS SAFE.
WELL, 'RE DOING OMETHING WRONG.
PLEASE, I KNOW HER BETTER THAN SHE KNOWS HERSELF.
SURE ABOUT THAT?
HONEY! WE WERE JUST TALKING--
ABOUT ME. I KNOW.
ALL THIS TIME, YOU TOLD ME I WAS CRAZY, BUT I WAS RIGHT!
#^$%-ING SKRULLS.

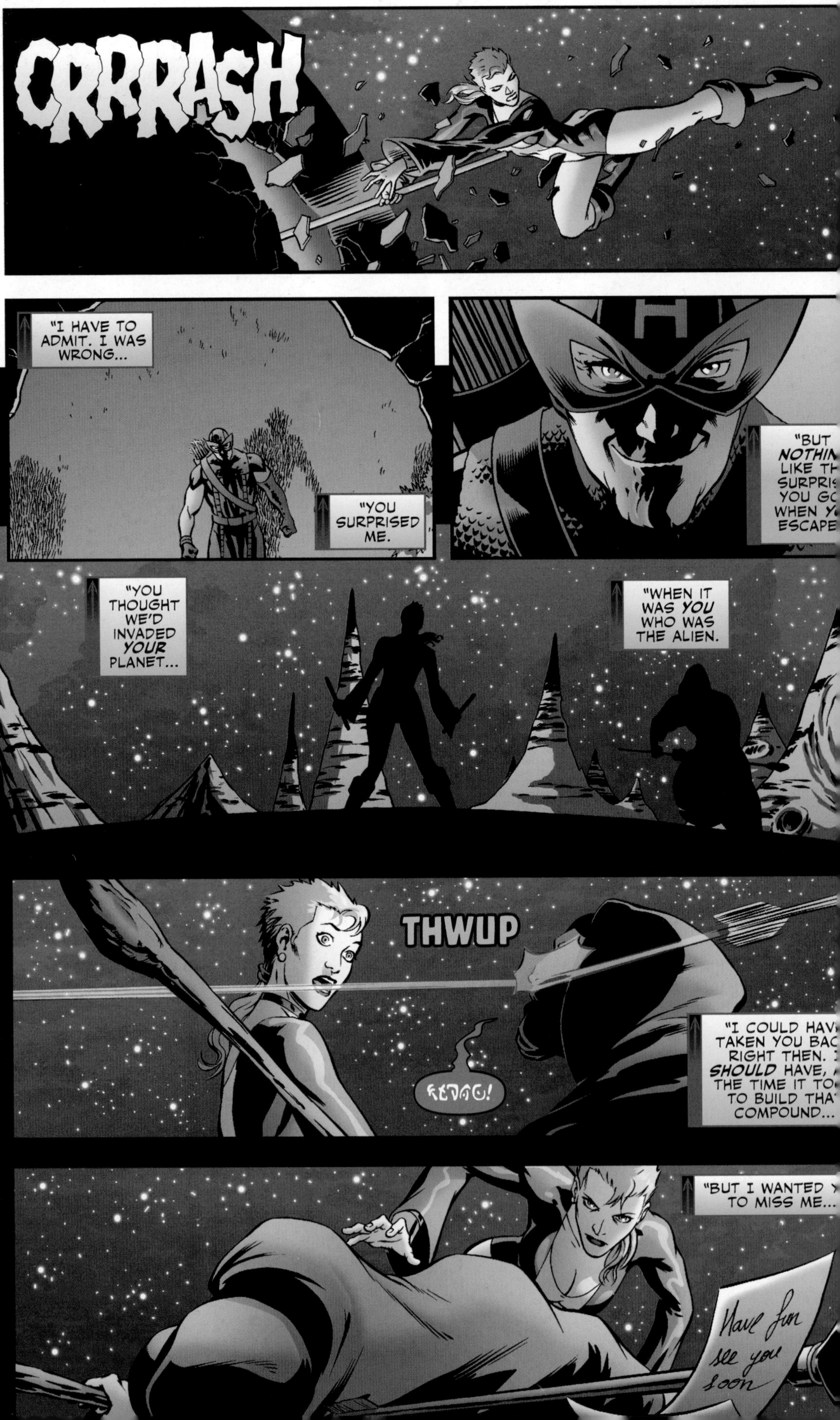
CRRRASH
"I HAVE TO ADMIT. I WAS WRONG...
"YOU SURPRISED ME.
"BUT NOTHIN LIKE TH SURPRIS YOU GO WHEN Y ESCAPE
"YOU THOUGHT WE'D INVADED YOUR PLANET...
"WHEN IT WAS YOU WHO WAS THE ALIEN.
THWUP
"I COULD HAV TAKEN YOU BAC RIGHT THEN. I SHOULD HAVE, THE TIME IT TO TO BUILD THA COMPOUND...
"BUT I WANTED TO MISS ME...
Have fun see you soon

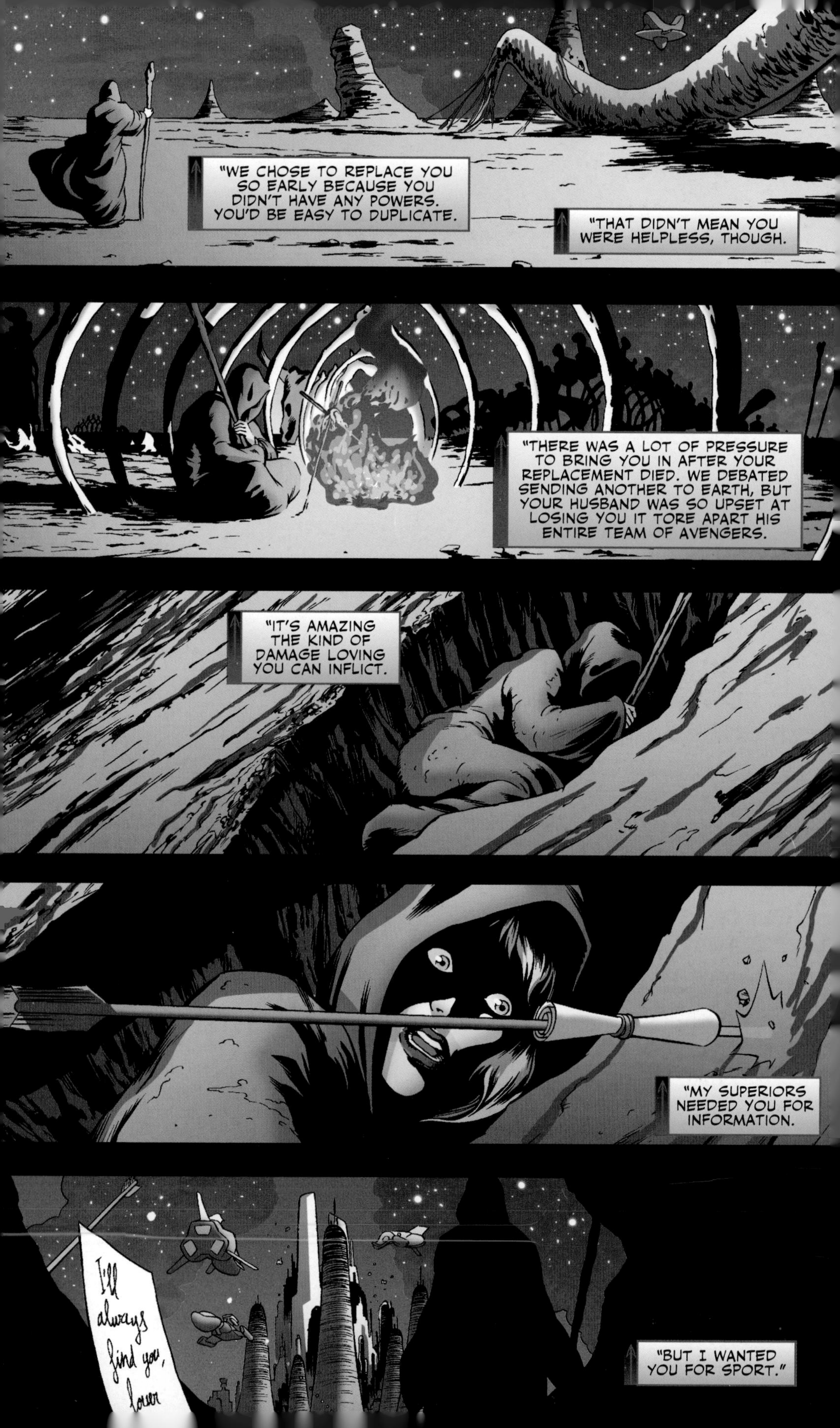
"WE CHOSE TO REPLACE YOU SO EARLY BECAUSE YOU DIDN'T HAVE ANY POWERS. YOU'D BE EASY TO DUPLICATE.
"THAT DIDN'T MEAN YOU WERE HELPLESS, THOUGH.
"THERE WAS A LOT OF PRESSURE TO BRING YOU IN AFTER YOUR REPLACEMENT DIED. WE DEBATED SENDING ANOTHER TO EARTH, BUT YOUR HUSBAND WAS SO UPSET AT LOSING YOU IT TORE APART HIS ENTIRE TEAM OF AVENGERS.
"IT'S AMAZING THE KIND OF DAMAGE LOVING YOU CAN INFLICT.
"MY SUPERIORS NEEDED YOU FOR INFORMATION.
I'll always find you, lover
"BUT I WANTED YOU FOR SPORT."

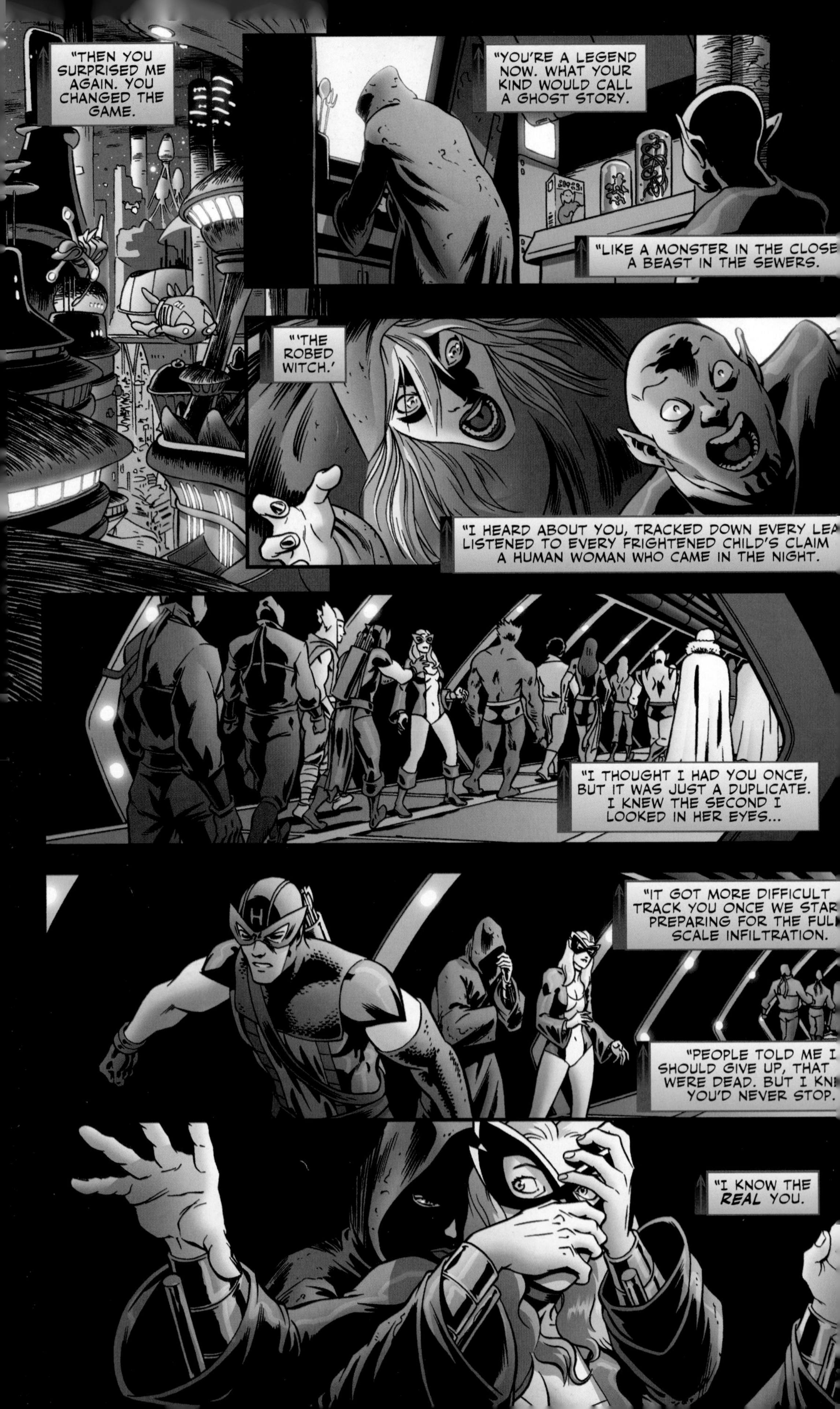
"THEN YOU SURPRISED ME AGAIN. YOU CHANGED THE GAME.
"YOU'RE A LEGEND NOW. WHAT YOUR KIND WOULD CALL A GHOST STORY.
"LIKE A MONSTER IN THE CLOSE A BEAST IN THE SEWERS.
"'THE ROBED WITCH.'
"I HEARD ABOUT YOU, TRACKED DOWN EVERY LEA LISTENED TO EVERY FRIGHTENED CHILD'S CLAIM A HUMAN WOMAN WHO CAME IN THE NIGHT.
"I THOUGHT I HAD YOU ONCE, BUT IT WAS JUST A DUPLICATE. I KNEW THE SECOND I LOOKED IN HER EYES...
"IT GOT MORE DIFFICULT TRACK YOU ONCE WE STAR PREPARING FOR THE FUL SCALE INFILTRATION.
"PEOPLE TOLD ME I SHOULD GIVE UP, THAT WERE DEAD. BUT I KN YOU'D NEVER STOP.
"I KNOW THE *REAL* YOU.

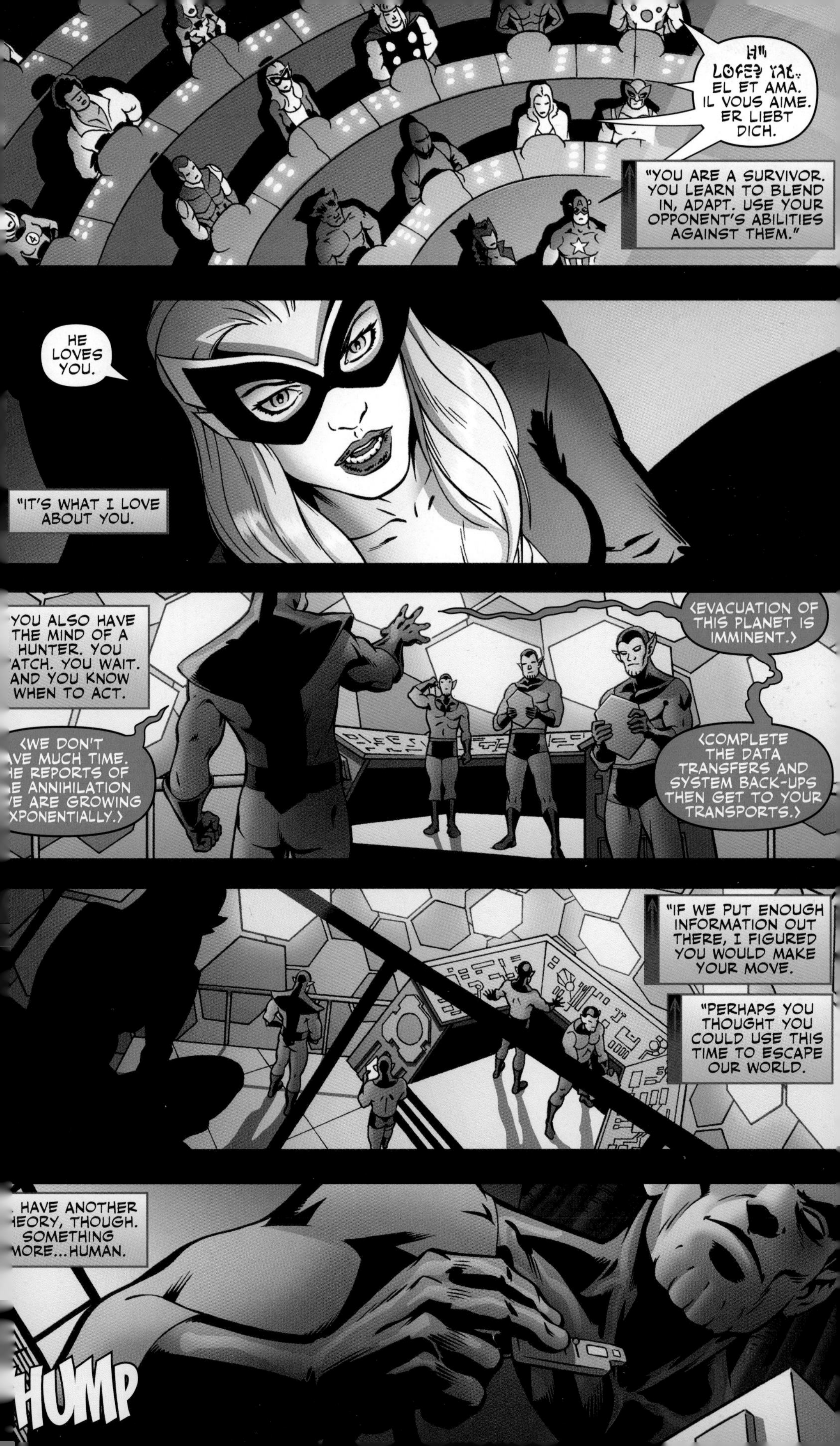
EL ET AMA. IL VOUS AIME. ER LIEBT DICH.
"YOU ARE A SURVIVOR. YOU LEARN TO BLEND IN, ADAPT. USE YOUR OPPONENT'S ABILITIES AGAINST THEM."
HE LOVES YOU.
"IT'S WHAT I LOVE ABOUT YOU.
YOU ALSO HAVE THE MIND OF A HUNTER. YOU ATCH. YOU WAIT. AND YOU KNOW WHEN TO ACT.
<EVACUATION OF THIS PLANET IS IMMINENT.>
<WE DON'T AVE MUCH TIME. HE REPORTS OF E ANNIHILATION VE ARE GROWING XPONENTIALLY.>
<COMPLETE THE DATA TRANSFERS AND SYSTEM BACK-UPS THEN GET TO YOUR TRANSPORTS.>
"IF WE PUT ENOUGH INFORMATION OUT THERE, I FIGURED YOU WOULD MAKE YOUR MOVE.
"PERHAPS YOU THOUGHT YOU COULD USE THIS TIME TO ESCAPE OUR WORLD.
HAVE ANOTHER HEORY, THOUGH. SOMETHING MORE...HUMAN.
HUMP

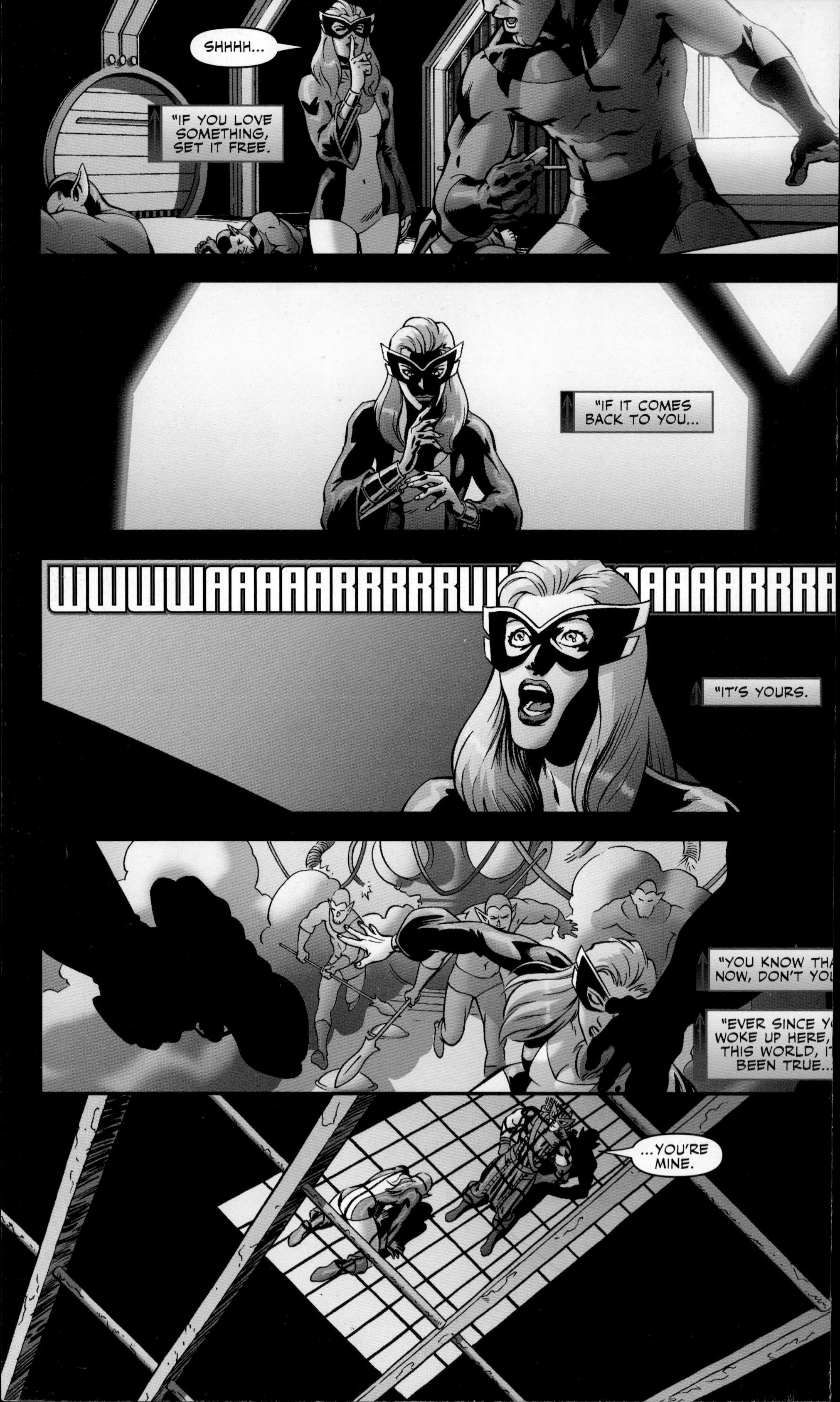
SHHHH...
"IF YOU LOVE SOMETHING, SET IT FREE.
"IF IT COMES BACK TO YOU...
WWWWAAAAARRRRRU
AAAAARRRR
"IT'S YOURS.
"YOU KNOW THA
NOW, DON'T YO
"EVER SINCE Y
WOKE UP HERE,
THIS WORLD, I
BEEN TRUE...
...YOU'RE MINE.

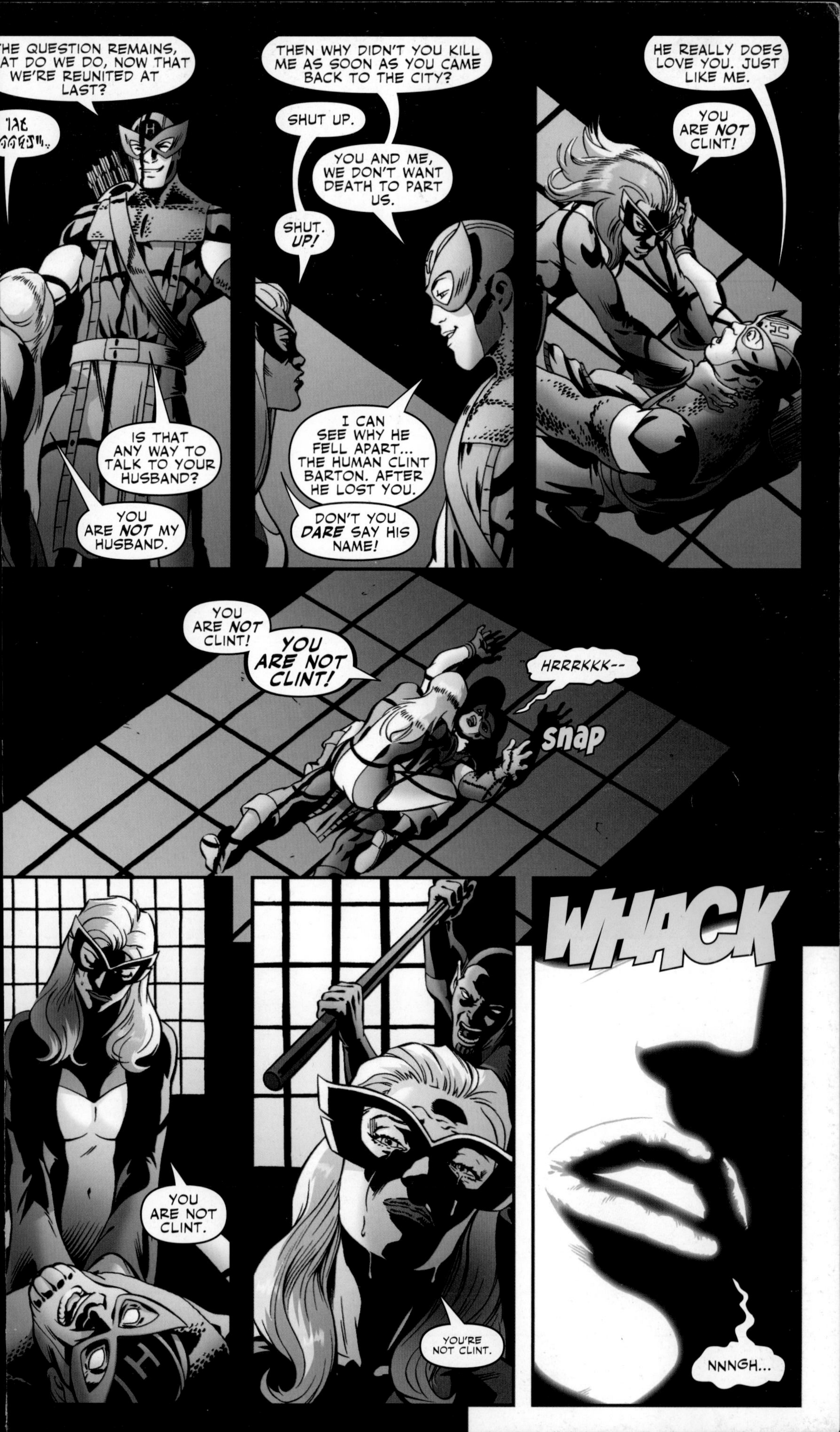

THE QUESTION REMAINS, AT DO WE DO, NOW THAT WE'RE REUNITED AT LAST?
IS THAT ANY WAY TO TALK TO YOUR HUSBAND?
YOU ARE NOT MY HUSBAND.
THEN WHY DIDN'T YOU KILL ME AS SOON AS YOU CAME BACK TO THE CITY?
SHUT UP.
YOU AND ME, WE DON'T WANT DEATH TO PART US.
SHUT. UP!
I CAN SEE WHY HE FELL APART... THE HUMAN CLINT BARTON. AFTER HE LOST YOU.
DON'T YOU DARE SAY HIS NAME!
HE REALLY DOES LOVE YOU. JUST LIKE ME.
YOU ARE NOT CLINT!
YOU ARE NOT CLINT!
YOU ARE NOT CLINT!
HRRRKKK--
snap
YOU ARE NOT CLINT.
YOU'RE NOT CLINT.
WHACK
NNNGH...

HRRRNNN...

WELCOME BACK.

Today. 90 minutes to detonation.

WHAT...WHAT HAPPENED?

I'M THINKING "BIOCHEMICAL REACTION." YOU FAINTED.

WHAT'S THE MATTER? LOOK LIKE YOU'VE SEEN A GHOST.

Y--YEAH.

LISTEN, THIS IS THE WORST TIMING EVER, I KNOW, BUT...

THERE SOMETH I CAN SHAKE

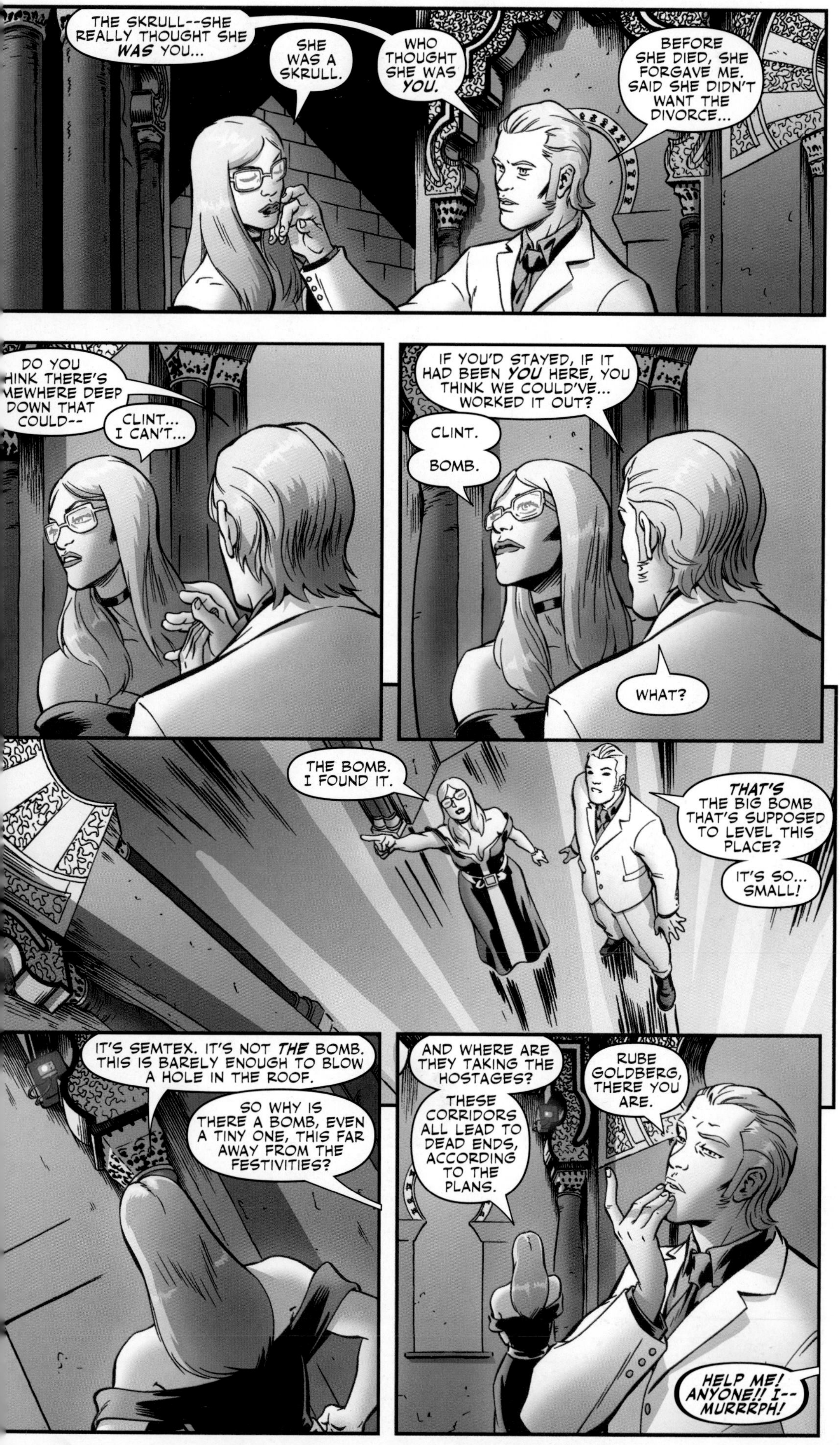
THE SKRULL--SHE REALLY THOUGHT SHE *WAS* YOU...
SHE WAS A SKRULL.
WHO THOUGHT SHE WAS *YOU.*
BEFORE SHE DIED, SHE FORGAVE ME. SAID SHE DIDN'T WANT THE DIVORCE...
DO YOU HINK THERE'S MEWHERE DEEP DOWN THAT COULD--
CLINT... I CAN'T...
IF YOU'D STAYED, IF IT HAD BEEN *YOU* HERE, YOU THINK WE COULD'VE... WORKED IT OUT?
CLINT.
BOMB.
WHAT?
THE BOMB. I FOUND IT.
THAT'S THE BIG BOMB THAT'S SUPPOSED TO LEVEL THIS PLACE?
IT'S SO... SMALL!
IT'S SEMTEX. IT'S NOT *THE* BOMB. THIS IS BARELY ENOUGH TO BLOW A HOLE IN THE ROOF.
SO WHY IS THERE A BOMB, EVEN A TINY ONE, THIS FAR AWAY FROM THE FESTIVITIES?
AND WHERE ARE THEY TAKING THE HOSTAGES?
THESE CORRIDORS ALL LEAD TO DEAD ENDS, ACCORDING TO THE PLANS.
RUBE GOLDBERG, THERE YOU ARE.
HELP ME! ANYONE!! I-- MURRRPH!

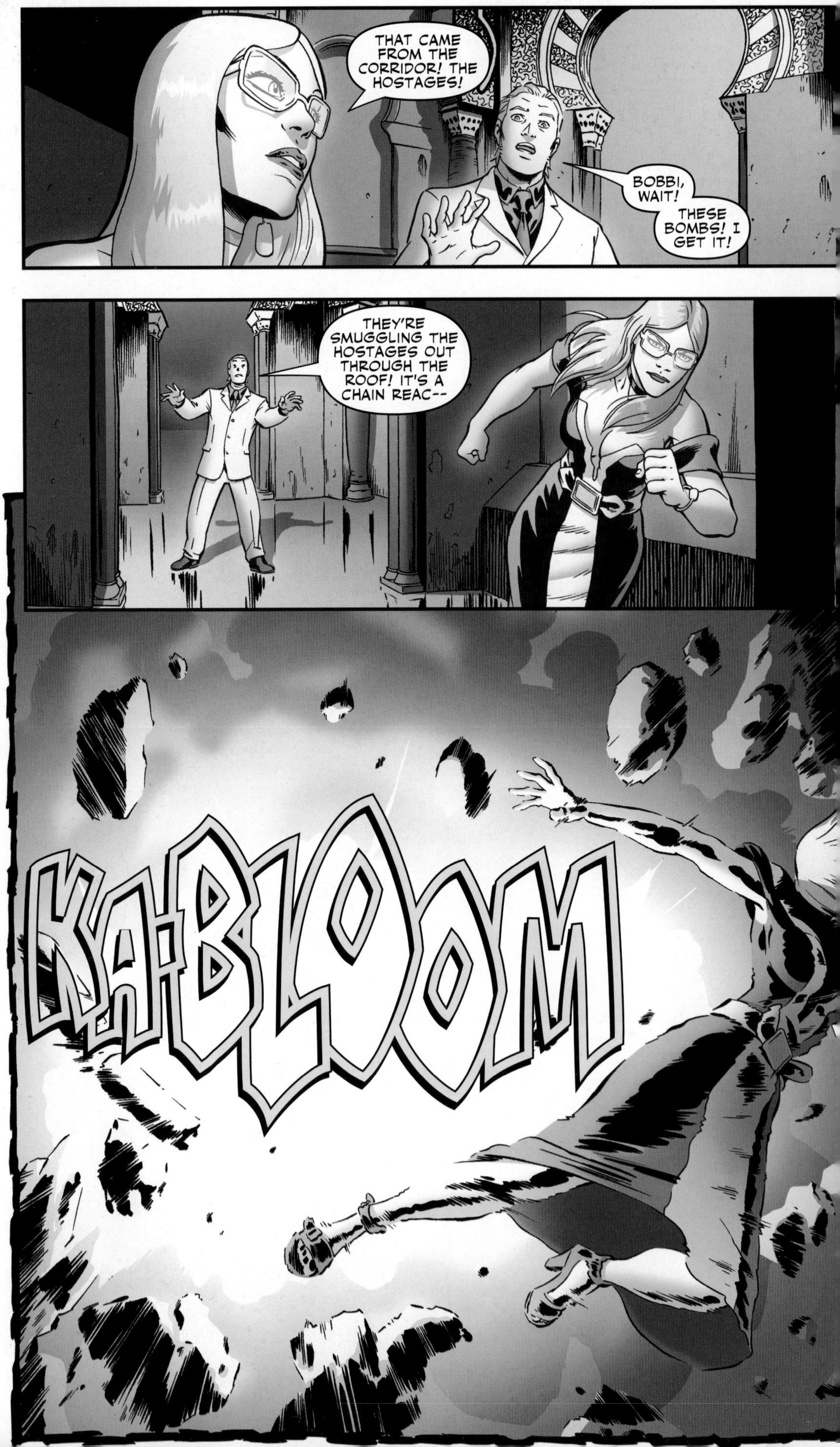
THAT CAME FROM THE CORRIDOR! THE HOSTAGES!
BOBBI, WAIT!
THESE BOMBS! I GET IT!
THEY'RE SMUGGLING THE HOSTAGES OUT THROUGH THE ROOF! IT'S A CHAIN REAC--
KA-BLOOM

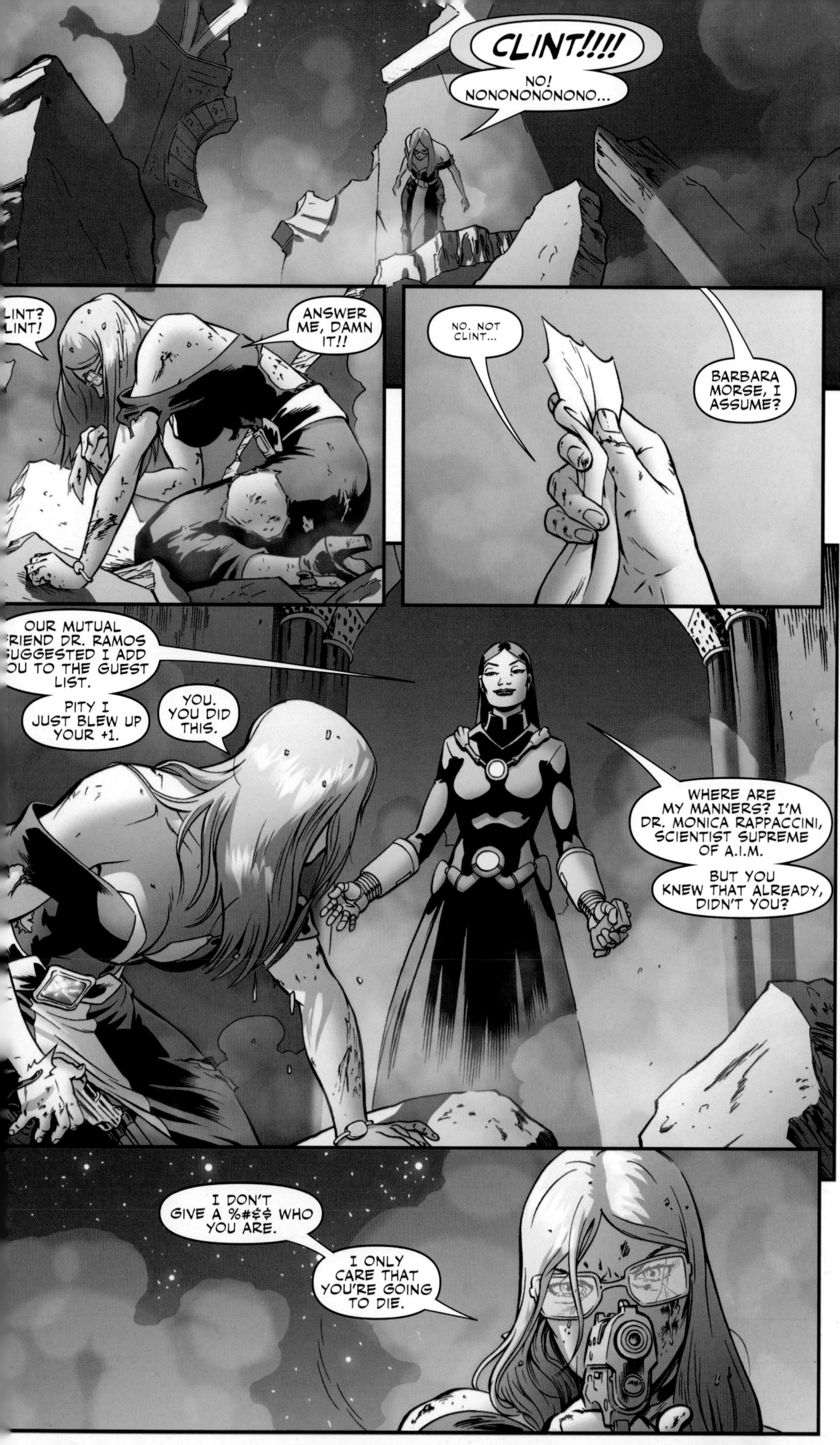

CLINT!!!!
NO! NONONONONONO...
LINT? LINT!
ANSWER ME, DAMN IT!!
NO. NOT CLINT...
BARBARA MORSE, I ASSUME?
OUR MUTUAL FRIEND DR. RAMOS SUGGESTED I ADD OU TO THE GUEST LIST.
PITY I JUST BLEW UP YOUR +1.
YOU. YOU DID THIS.
WHERE ARE MY MANNERS? I'M DR. MONICA RAPPACCINI, SCIENTIST SUPREME OF A.I.M.
BUT YOU KNEW THAT ALREADY, DIDN'T YOU?
I DON'T GIVE A %#&$ WHO YOU ARE.
I ONLY CARE THAT YOU'RE GOING TO DIE.

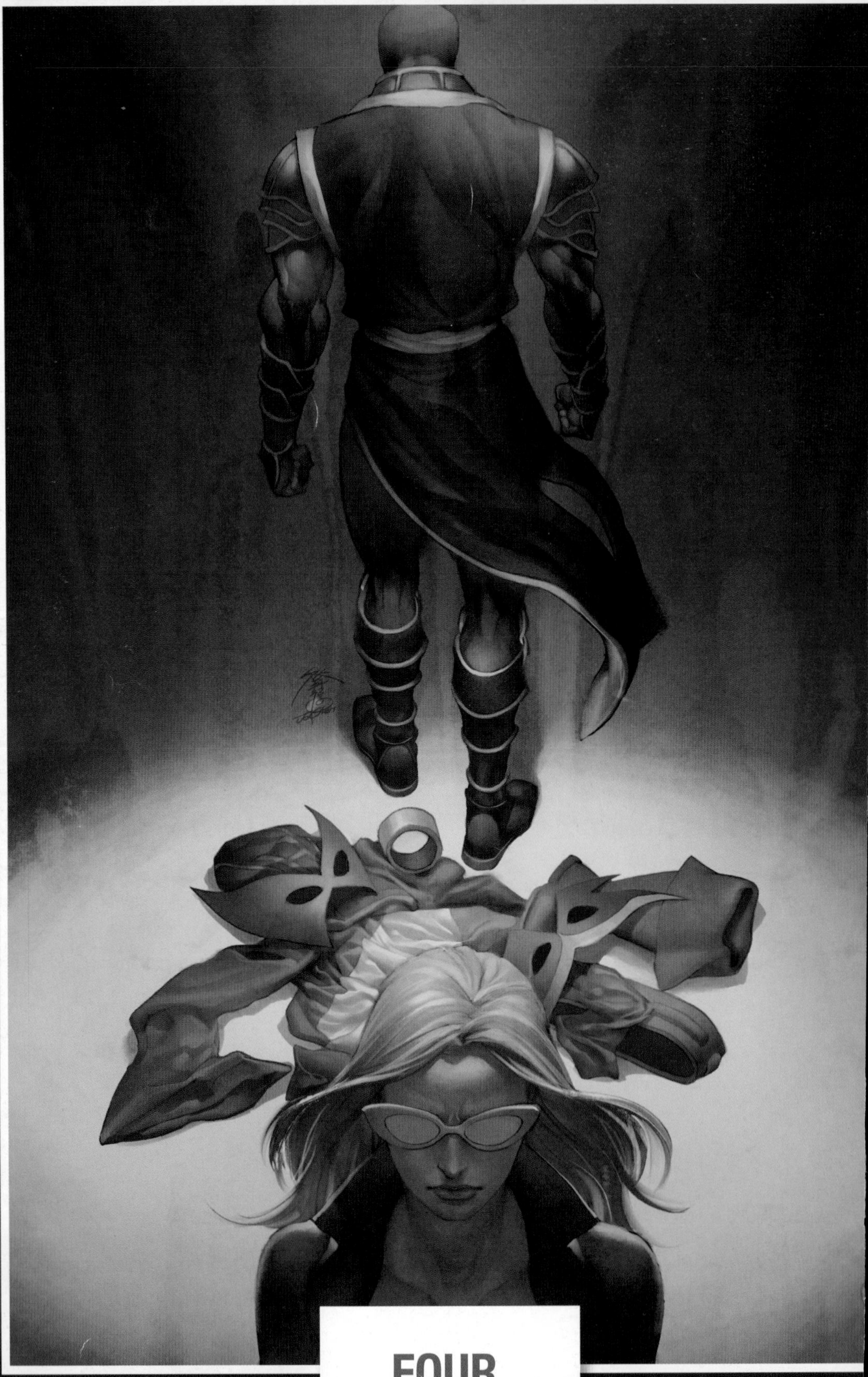

FOUR

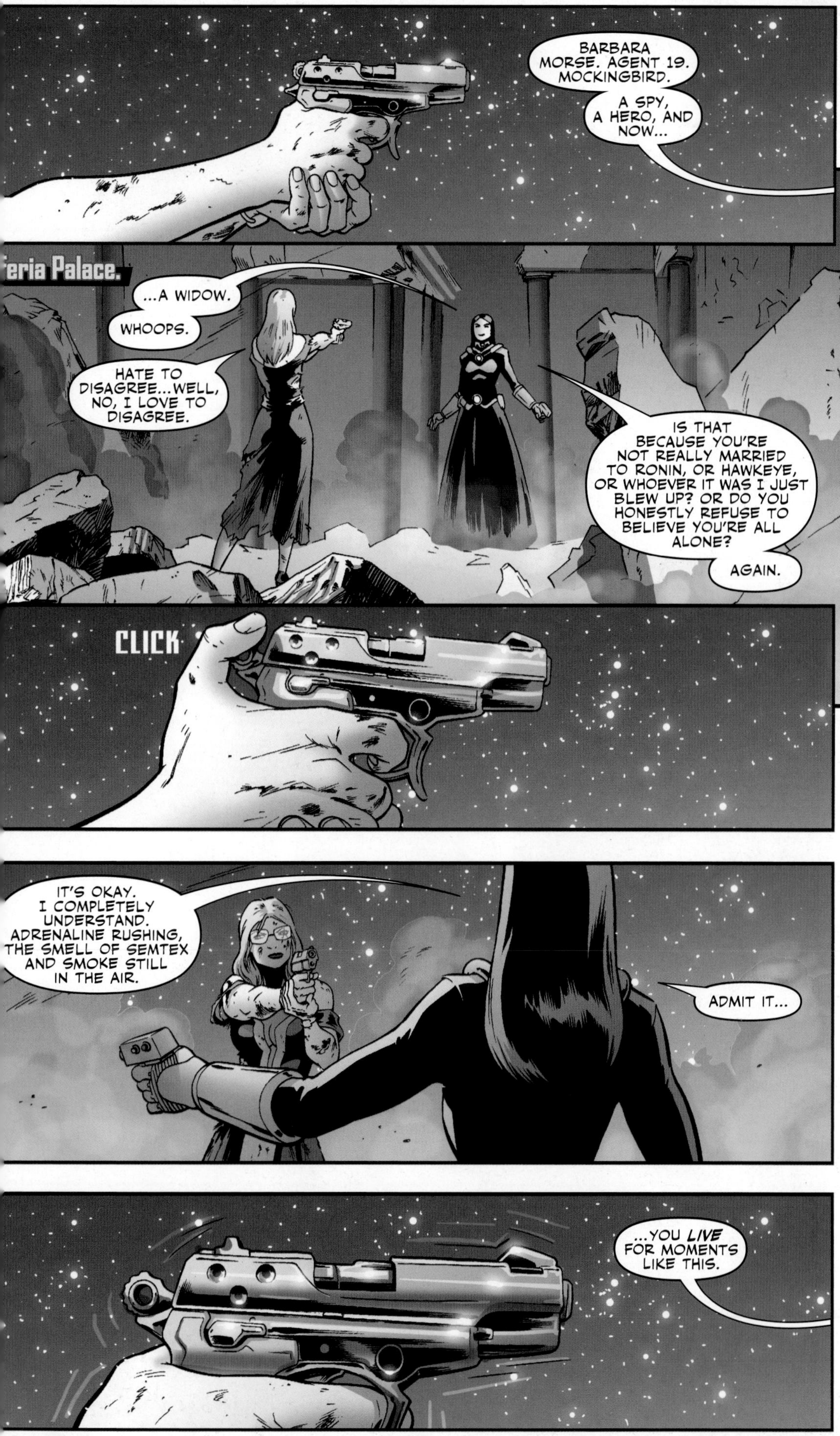
BARBARA MORSE. AGENT 19. MOCKINGBIRD.
A SPY, A HERO, AND NOW...
...A WIDOW.
WHOOPS.
eria Palace.
HATE TO DISAGREE...WELL, NO, I LOVE TO DISAGREE.
IS THAT BECAUSE YOU'RE NOT REALLY MARRIED TO RONIN, OR HAWKEYE, OR WHOEVER IT WAS I JUST BLEW UP? OR DO YOU HONESTLY REFUSE TO BELIEVE YOU'RE ALL ALONE?
AGAIN.
CLICK
IT'S OKAY. I COMPLETELY UNDERSTAND. ADRENALINE RUSHING, THE SMELL OF SEMTEX AND SMOKE STILL IN THE AIR.
ADMIT IT...
...YOU *LIVE* FOR MOMENTS LIKE THIS.

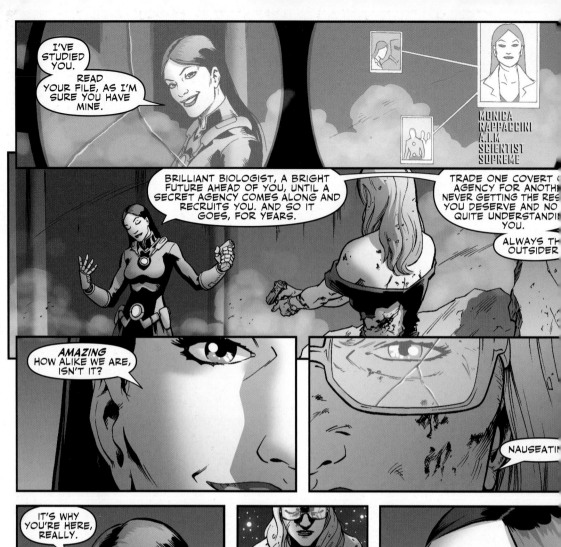

I'VE STUDIED YOU.

READ YOUR FILE, AS I'M SURE YOU HAVE MINE.

MONICA RAPPACCINI
A.I.M
SCIENTIST SUPREME

BRILLIANT BIOLOGIST, A BRIGHT FUTURE AHEAD OF YOU, UNTIL A SECRET AGENCY COMES ALONG AND RECRUITS YOU. AND SO IT GOES, FOR YEARS.

TRADE ONE COVERT AGENCY FOR ANOTHE NEVER GETTING THE RES YOU DESERVE AND NO QUITE UNDERSTANDIN YOU.

ALWAYS TH OUTSIDER

AMAZING HOW ALIKE WE ARE, ISN'T IT?

NAUSEATIN

IT'S WHY YOU'RE HERE, REALLY.

WHY DO YOU THINK THAT OLD HACK DR. MINER WAS ON THE GUEST LIST?

IT'S NOT LIKE YOU HAVE A MAILING ADDRESS. I HAD TO MAKE SURE YOU WOULD COME.

HERE I THOUGHT YOUR CALLING CARD WAS THAT DIRTY BOMB.

NO, MY DEAR, THAT'S JUS THE PROVERB ICING ON T CAKE.

I RARELY ENTER THE FIELD MYSELF, BUT I WANTED TO *PERSONALLY* OFFER YOU THE CHOICE YOU NEVER HAD: COME WITH ME.

BE THE SCIENTIST YOU WERE *MEANT* TO BE. THE PERSON YOU'VE ALWAYS *WANTED* TO BE.

YOU MUST NOT HAVE STUDIE ME VERY WELL, MONICA...

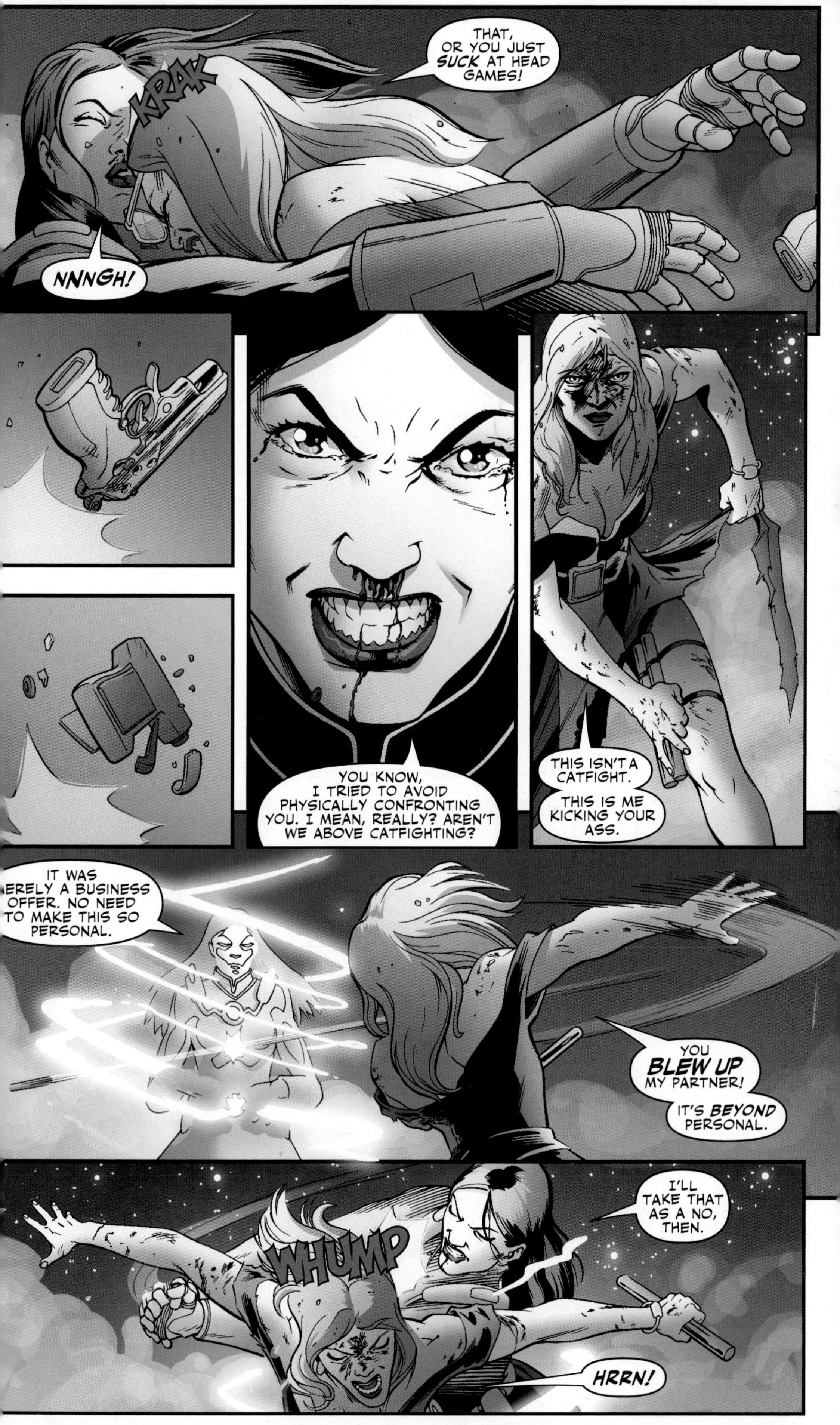
THAT, OR YOU JUST SUCK AT HEAD GAMES!
KRAK
NNNGH!
YOU KNOW, I TRIED TO AVOID PHYSICALLY CONFRONTING YOU. I MEAN, REALLY? AREN'T WE ABOVE CATFIGHTING?
THIS ISN'T A CATFIGHT.
THIS IS ME KICKING YOUR ASS.
IT WAS ERELY A BUSINESS OFFER. NO NEED TO MAKE THIS SO PERSONAL.
YOU BLEW UP MY PARTNER!
IT'S BEYOND PERSONAL.
I'LL TAKE THAT AS A NO, THEN.
WHUMP
HRRN!

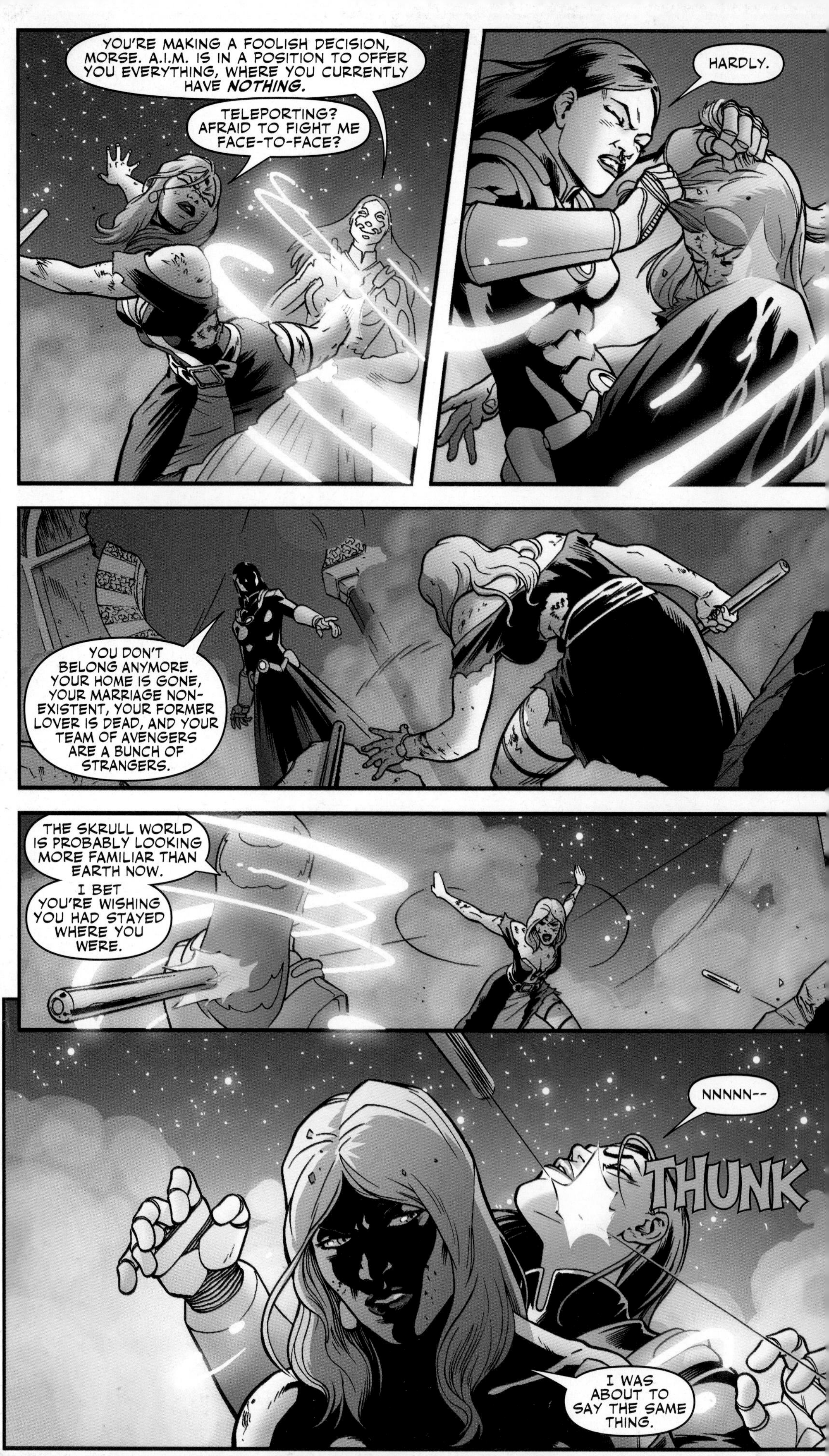
YOU'RE MAKING A FOOLISH DECISION, MORSE. A.I.M. IS IN A POSITION TO OFFER YOU EVERYTHING, WHERE YOU CURRENTLY HAVE *NOTHING.*
TELEPORTING? AFRAID TO FIGHT ME FACE-TO-FACE?
HARDLY.
YOU DON'T BELONG ANYMORE. YOUR HOME IS GONE, YOUR MARRIAGE NON-EXISTENT, YOUR FORMER LOVER IS DEAD, AND YOUR TEAM OF AVENGERS ARE A BUNCH OF STRANGERS.
THE SKRULL WORLD IS PROBABLY LOOKING MORE FAMILIAR THAN EARTH NOW.
I BET YOU'RE WISHING YOU HAD STAYED WHERE YOU WERE.
NNNNN--
THUNK
I WAS ABOUT TO SAY THE SAME THING.

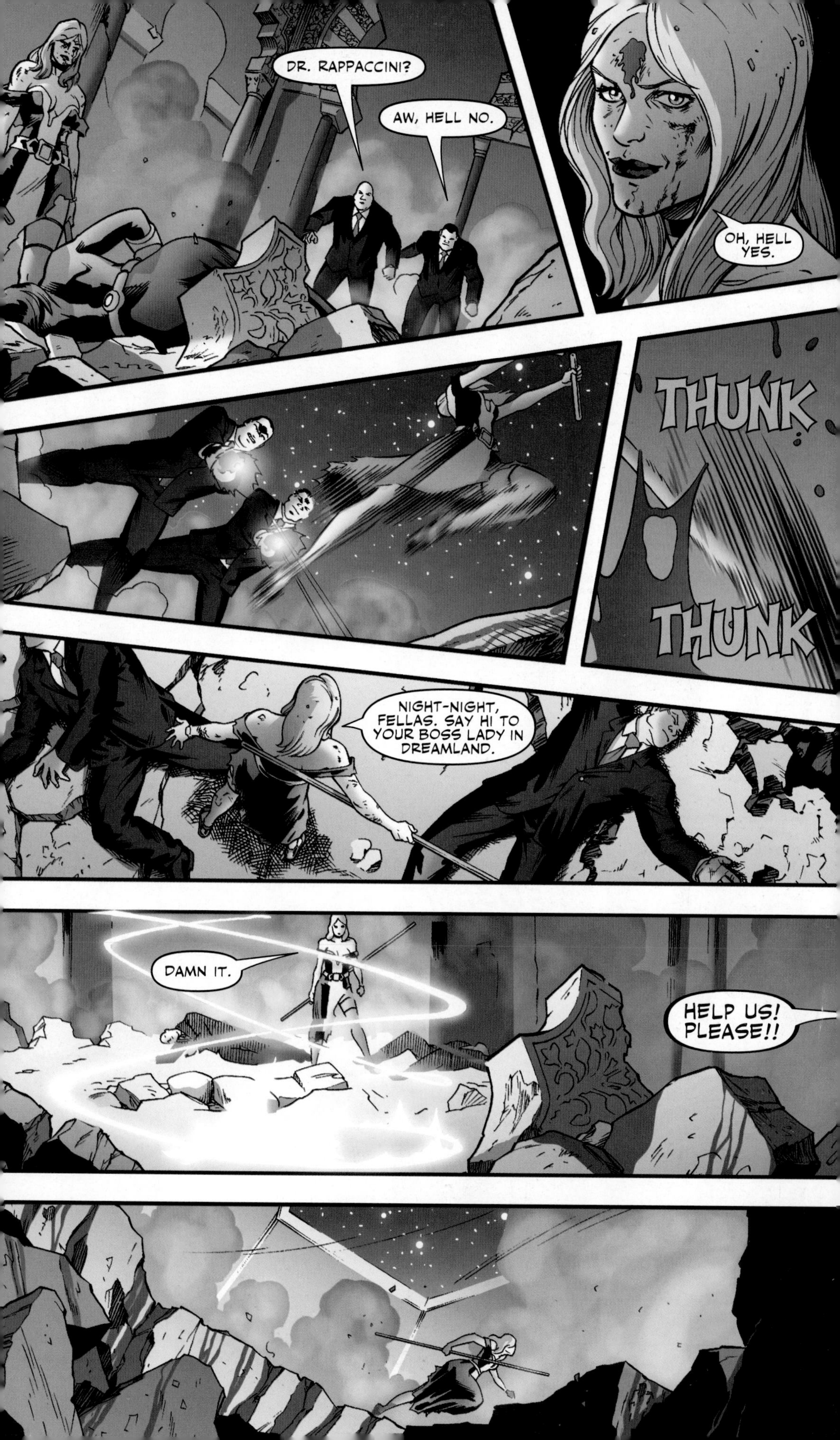
DR. RAPPACCINI?
AW, HELL NO.
OH, HELL YES.
THUNK
THUNK
NIGHT-NIGHT, FELLAS. SAY HI TO YOUR BOSS LADY IN DREAMLAND.
DAMN IT.
HELP US! PLEASE!!

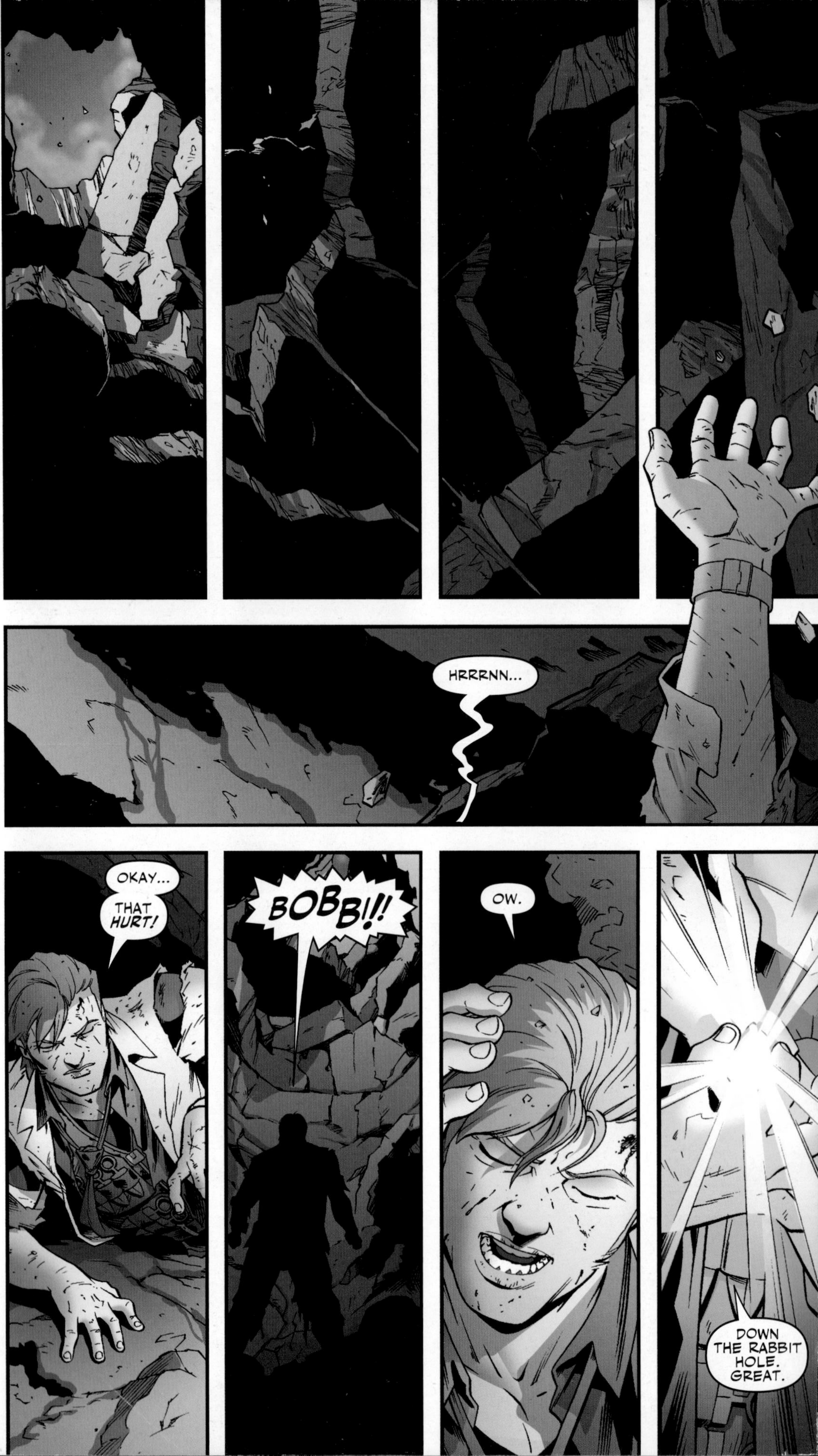
HRRRNN...
OKAY... THAT HURT!
BOBBI!!
OW.
DOWN THE RABBIT HOLE. GREAT.

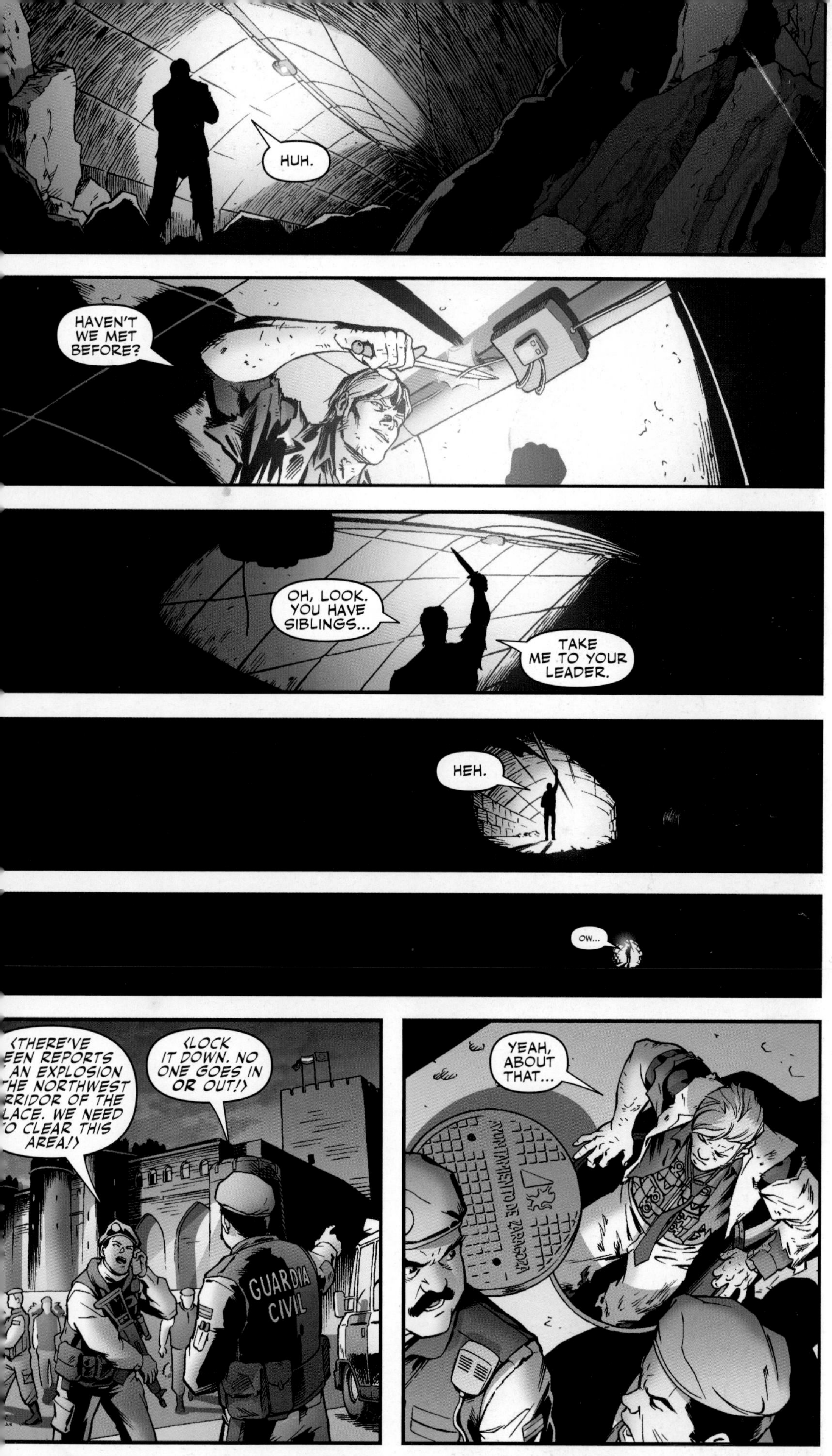
HUH.
HAVEN'T WE MET BEFORE?
OH, LOOK. YOU HAVE SIBLINGS...
TAKE ME TO YOUR LEADER.
HEH.
OW...
‹THERE'VE EEN REPORTS AN EXPLOSION THE NORTHWEST RRIDOR OF THE LACE. WE NEED TO CLEAR THIS AREA!›
‹LOCK IT DOWN. NO ONE GOES IN OR OUT!›
GUARDIA CIVIL
YEAH, ABOUT THAT...
AYUNTAMIENTO DE ZARAGOZA

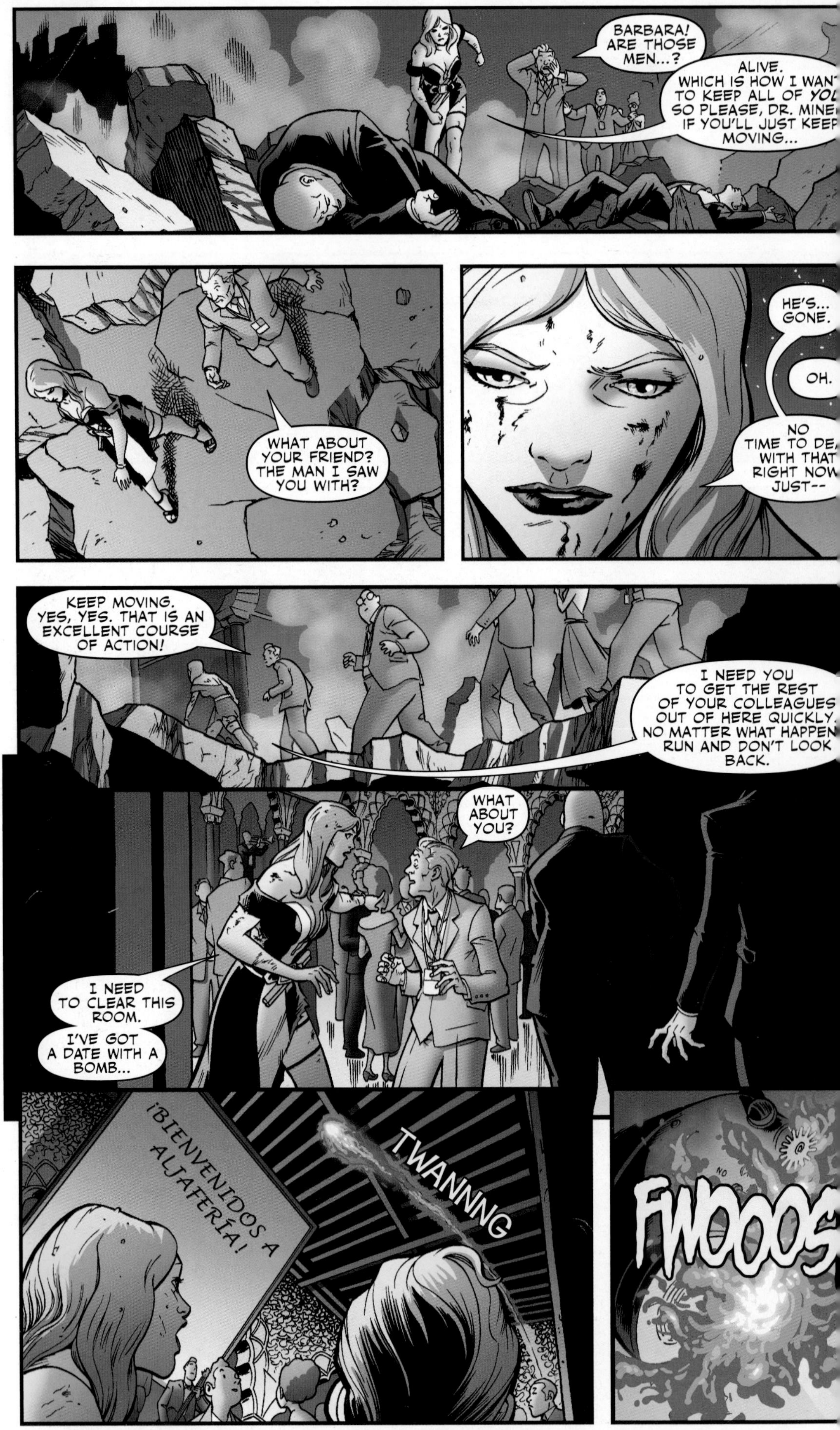
BARBARA! ARE THOSE MEN...?
ALIVE. WHICH IS HOW I WANT TO KEEP ALL OF YOU. SO PLEASE, DR. MINE, IF YOU'LL JUST KEEP MOVING...
WHAT ABOUT YOUR FRIEND? THE MAN I SAW YOU WITH?
HE'S... GONE.
OH.
NO TIME TO DEAL WITH THAT RIGHT NOW. JUST--
KEEP MOVING. YES, YES. THAT IS AN EXCELLENT COURSE OF ACTION!
I NEED YOU TO GET THE REST OF YOUR COLLEAGUES OUT OF HERE QUICKLY. NO MATTER WHAT HAPPENS, RUN AND DON'T LOOK BACK.
WHAT ABOUT YOU?
I NEED TO CLEAR THIS ROOM.
I'VE GOT A DATE WITH A BOMB...
¡BIENVENIDOS A ALJAFERÍA!
TWANNNG
FWOOOS

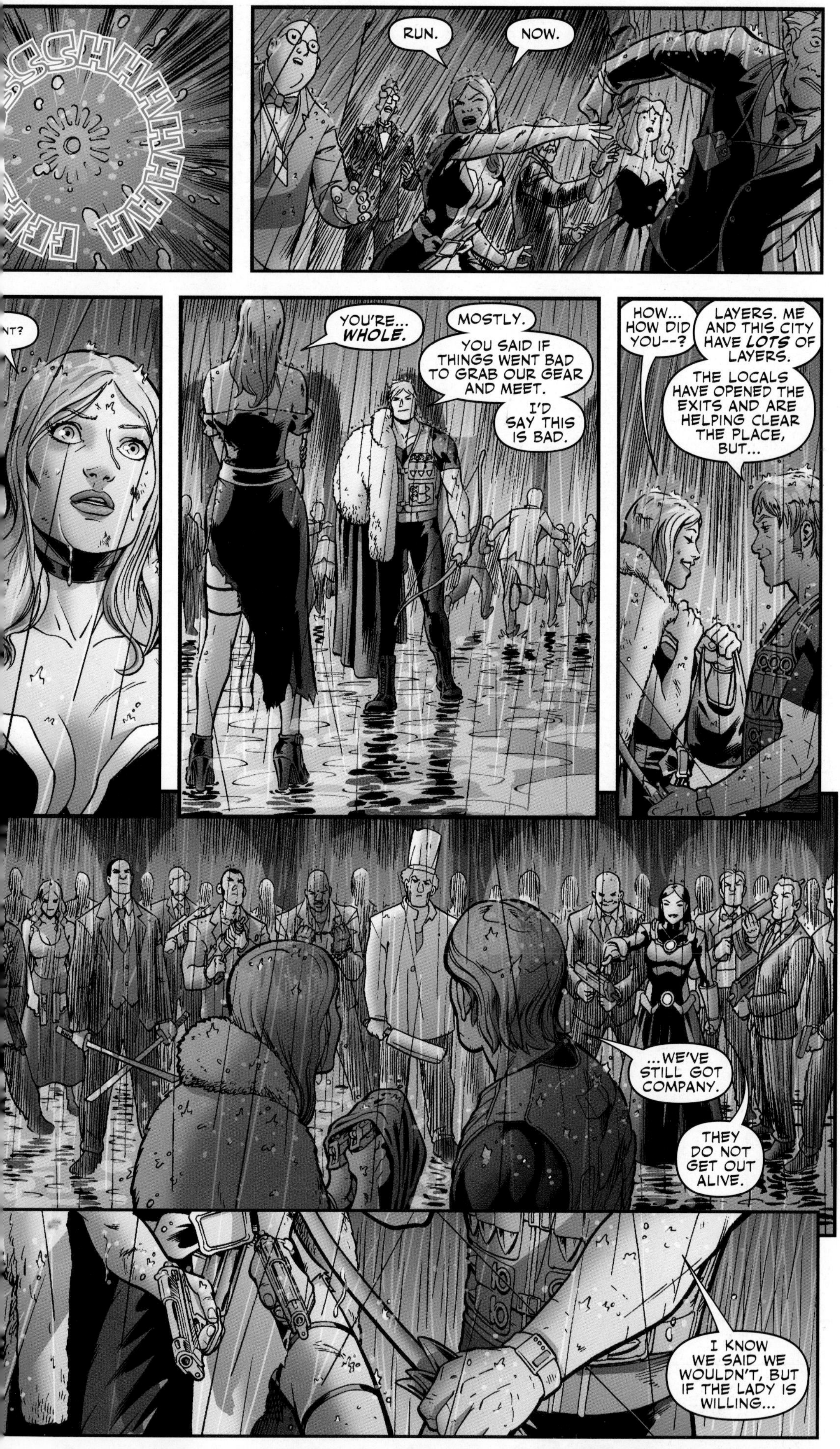
RUN.
NOW.
YOU'RE... *WHOLE.*
MOSTLY.
YOU SAID IF THINGS WENT BAD TO GRAB OUR GEAR AND MEET.
I'D SAY THIS IS BAD.
HOW... HOW DID YOU--?
LAYERS. ME AND THIS CITY HAVE *LOTS* OF LAYERS.
THE LOCALS HAVE OPENED THE EXITS AND ARE HELPING CLEAR THE PLACE, BUT...
...WE'VE STILL GOT COMPANY.
THEY DO NOT GET OUT ALIVE.
I KNOW WE SAID WE WOULDN'T, BUT IF THE LADY IS WILLING...

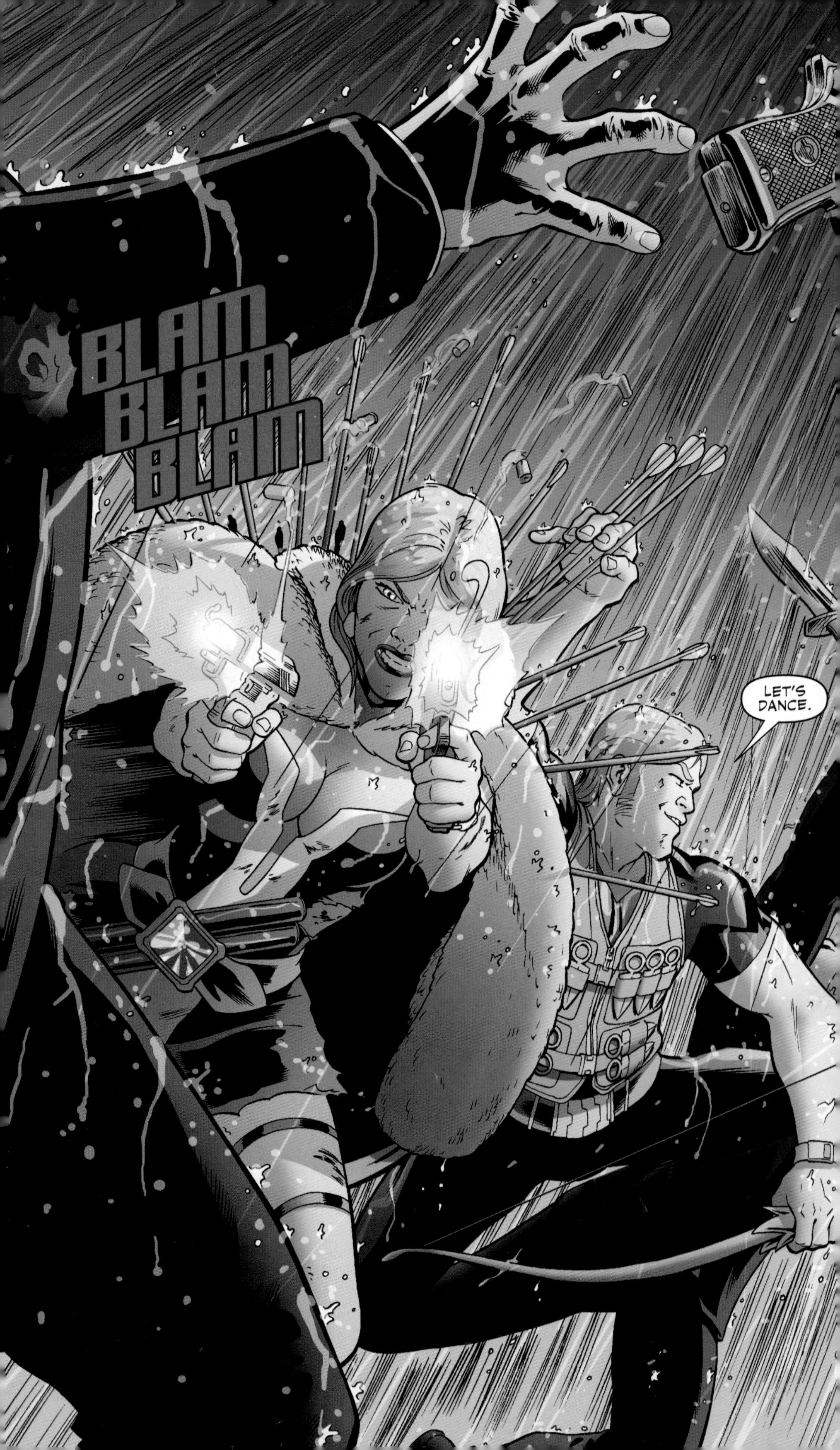
BLAM
BLAM
BLAM
LET'S DANCE.

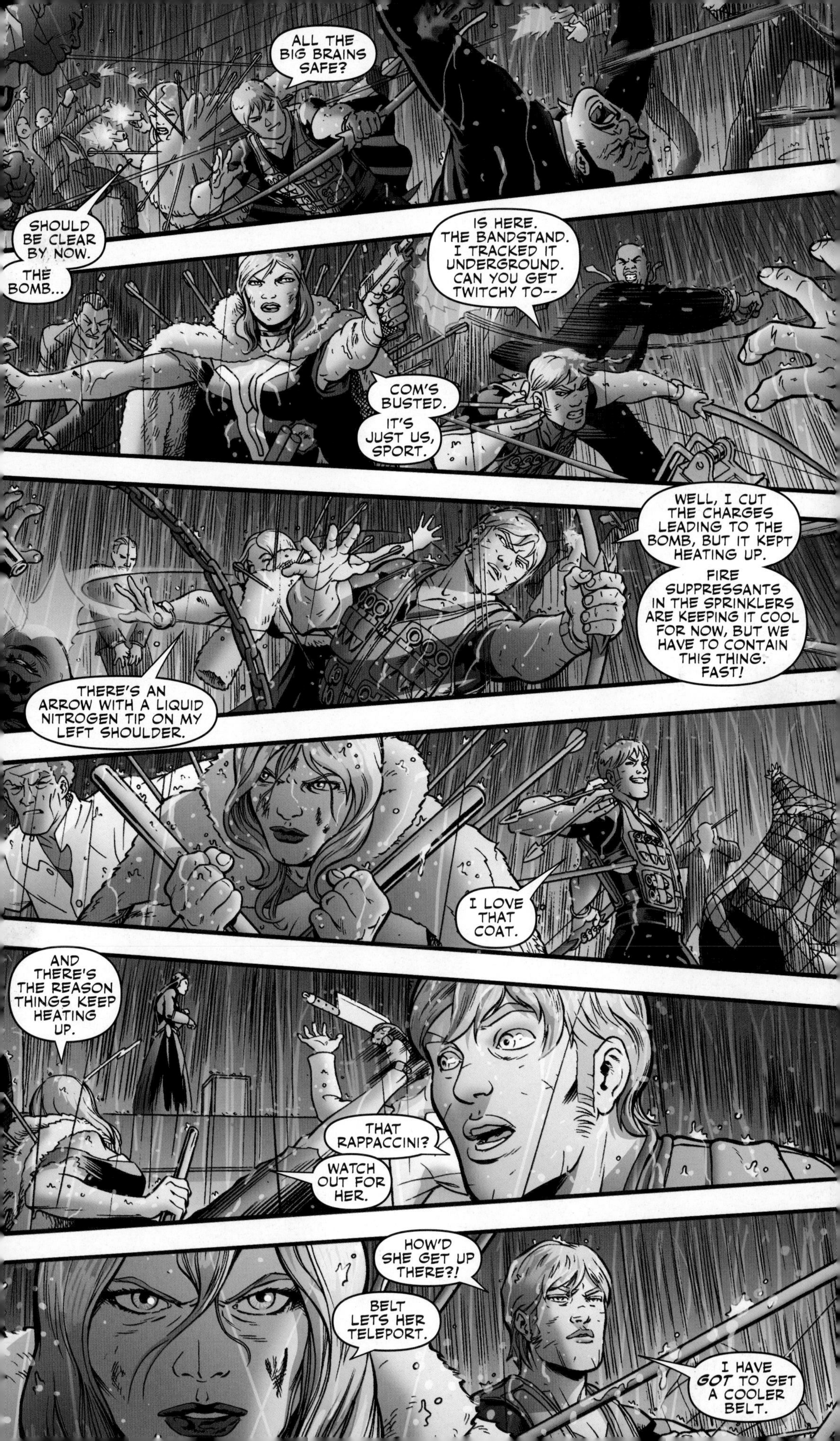
ALL THE BIG BRAINS SAFE?
SHOULD BE CLEAR BY NOW.
THE BOMB...
IS HERE. THE BANDSTAND. I TRACKED IT UNDERGROUND. CAN YOU GET TWITCHY TO--
COM'S BUSTED.
IT'S JUST US, SPORT.
WELL, I CUT THE CHARGES LEADING TO THE BOMB, BUT IT KEPT HEATING UP.
FIRE SUPPRESSANTS IN THE SPRINKLERS ARE KEEPING IT COOL FOR NOW, BUT WE HAVE TO CONTAIN THIS THING. FAST!
THERE'S AN ARROW WITH A LIQUID NITROGEN TIP ON MY LEFT SHOULDER.
I LOVE THAT COAT.
AND THERE'S THE REASON THINGS KEEP HEATING UP.
THAT RAPPACCINI?
WATCH OUT FOR HER.
HOW'D SHE GET UP THERE?!
BELT LETS HER TELEPORT.
I HAVE GOT TO GET A COOLER BELT.

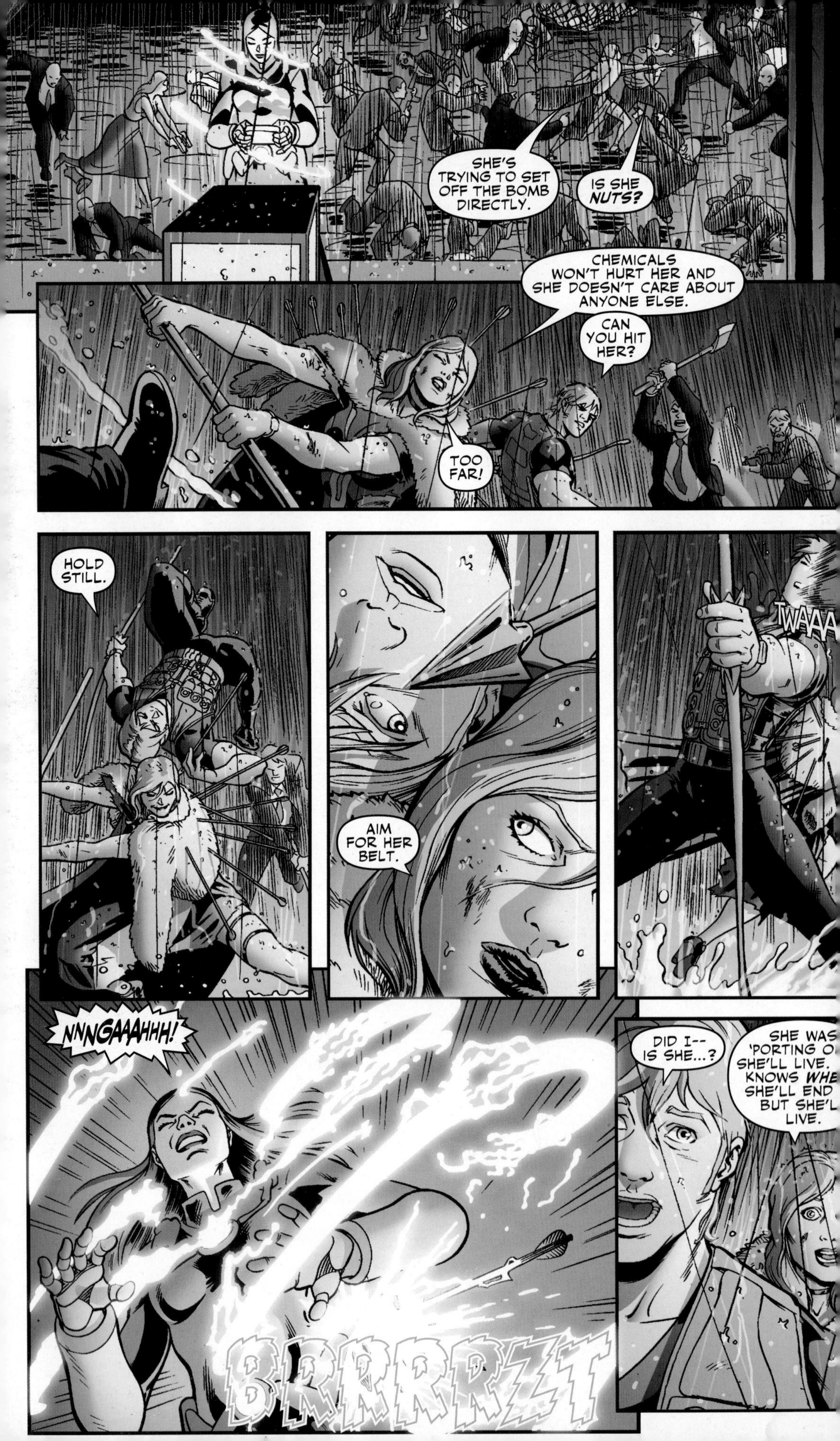
SHE'S TRYING TO SET OFF THE BOMB DIRECTLY.
IS SHE NUTS?
CHEMICALS WON'T HURT HER AND SHE DOESN'T CARE ABOUT ANYONE ELSE.
CAN YOU HIT HER?
TOO FAR!
HOLD STILL.
AIM FOR HER BELT.
NNNGAAAHHH!
BRRRRZZT
DID I-- IS SHE...?
SHE WAS 'PORTING O SHE'LL LIVE. KNOWS WHE SHE'LL END BUT SHE'L LIVE.

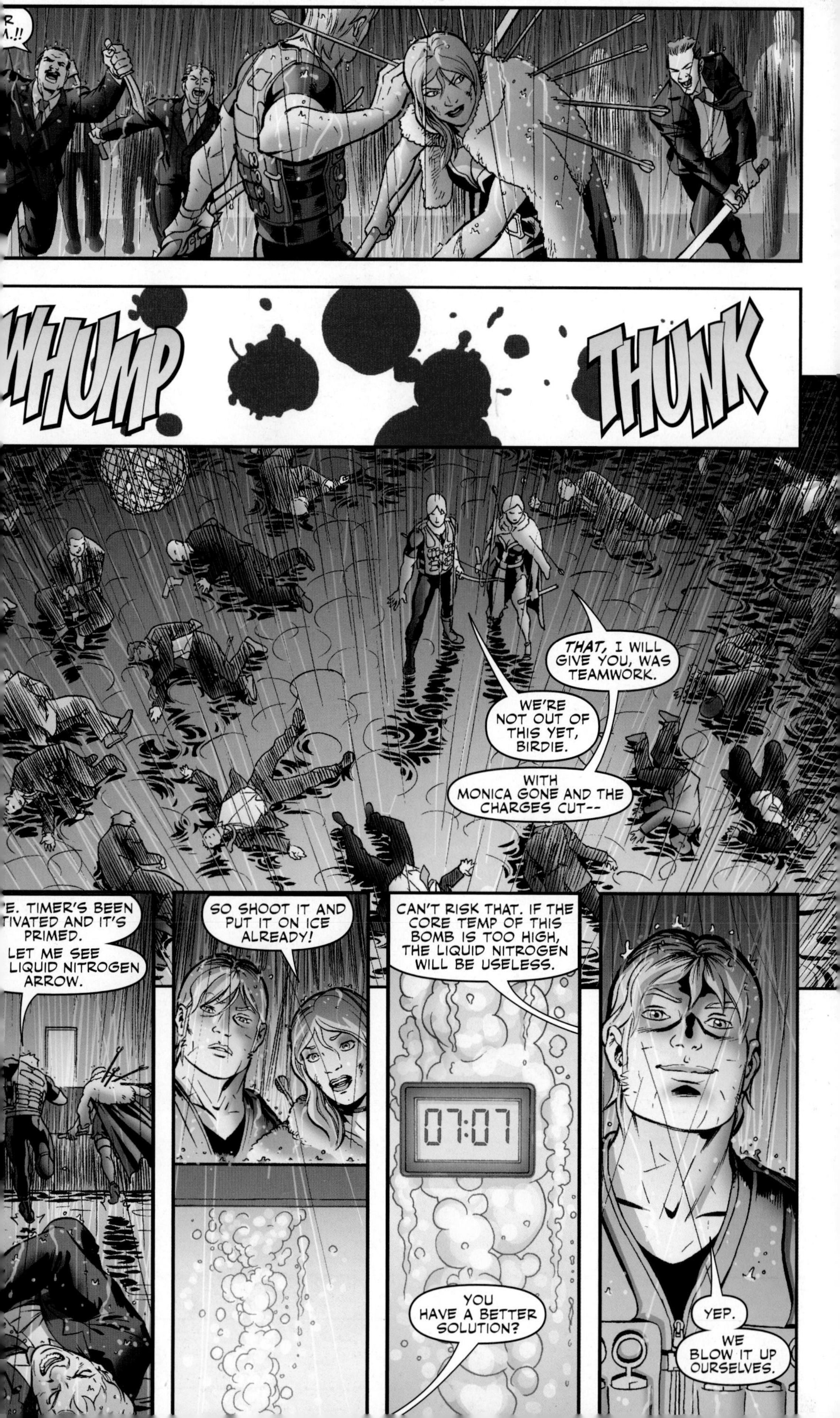
WHUMP
THUNK
THAT, I WILL GIVE YOU, WAS TEAMWORK.
WE'RE NOT OUT OF THIS YET, BIRDIE.
WITH MONICA GONE AND THE CHARGES CUT--
E. TIMER'S BEEN TIVATED AND IT'S PRIMED.
LET ME SEE LIQUID NITROGEN ARROW.
SO SHOOT IT AND PUT IT ON ICE ALREADY!
CAN'T RISK THAT. IF THE CORE TEMP OF THIS BOMB IS TOO HIGH, THE LIQUID NITROGEN WILL BE USELESS.
07:07
YOU HAVE A BETTER SOLUTION?
YEP.
WE BLOW IT UP OURSELVES.

OKAY, YOU'RE NOT AS WHOLE AS I THOUGHT BECAUSE YOU MUST HAVE LEFT YOUR *BRAIN* UNDERGROUND!

WHAT DOES THE W.C.A. DO, BOBBI? YOU SAID IT YOURSELF.

WE CAST A WIDER NET.

TO CONTAIN THE EXPLOSION?! THERE'S ONLY A HANDFUL OF WAYS TO CONTAIN THE AMOUNT OF RADIOLOGICAL TOXINS A BLAST LIKE THIS WILL RELEASE.

YOU NEE—

RUBE GOLDBERG.

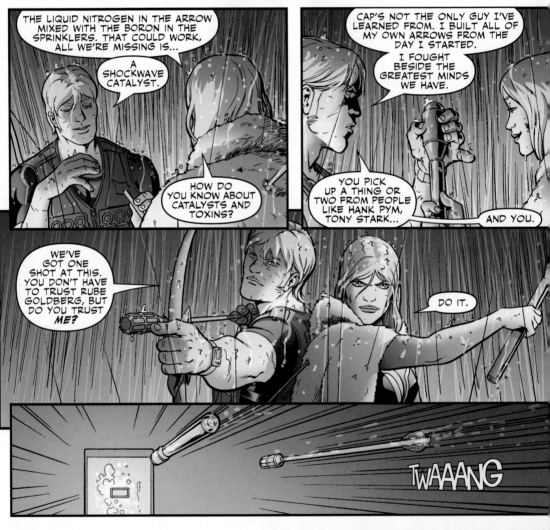

THE LIQUID NITROGEN IN THE ARROW MIXED WITH THE BORON IN THE SPRINKLERS. THAT COULD WORK, ALL WE'RE MISSING IS...

A SHOCKWAVE CATALYST.

HOW DO YOU KNOW ABOUT CATALYSTS AND TOXINS?

CAP'S NOT THE ONLY GUY I'VE LEARNED FROM. I BUILT ALL OF MY OWN ARROWS FROM THE DAY I STARTED.

I FOUGHT BESIDE THE GREATEST MINDS WE HAVE.

YOU PICK UP A THING OR TWO FROM PEOPLE LIKE HANK PYM, TONY STARK...

AND YOU.

WE'VE GOT ONE SHOT AT THIS. YOU DON'T HAVE TO TRUST RUBE GOLDBERG, BUT DO YOU TRUST *ME?*

DO IT.

TWAAANG

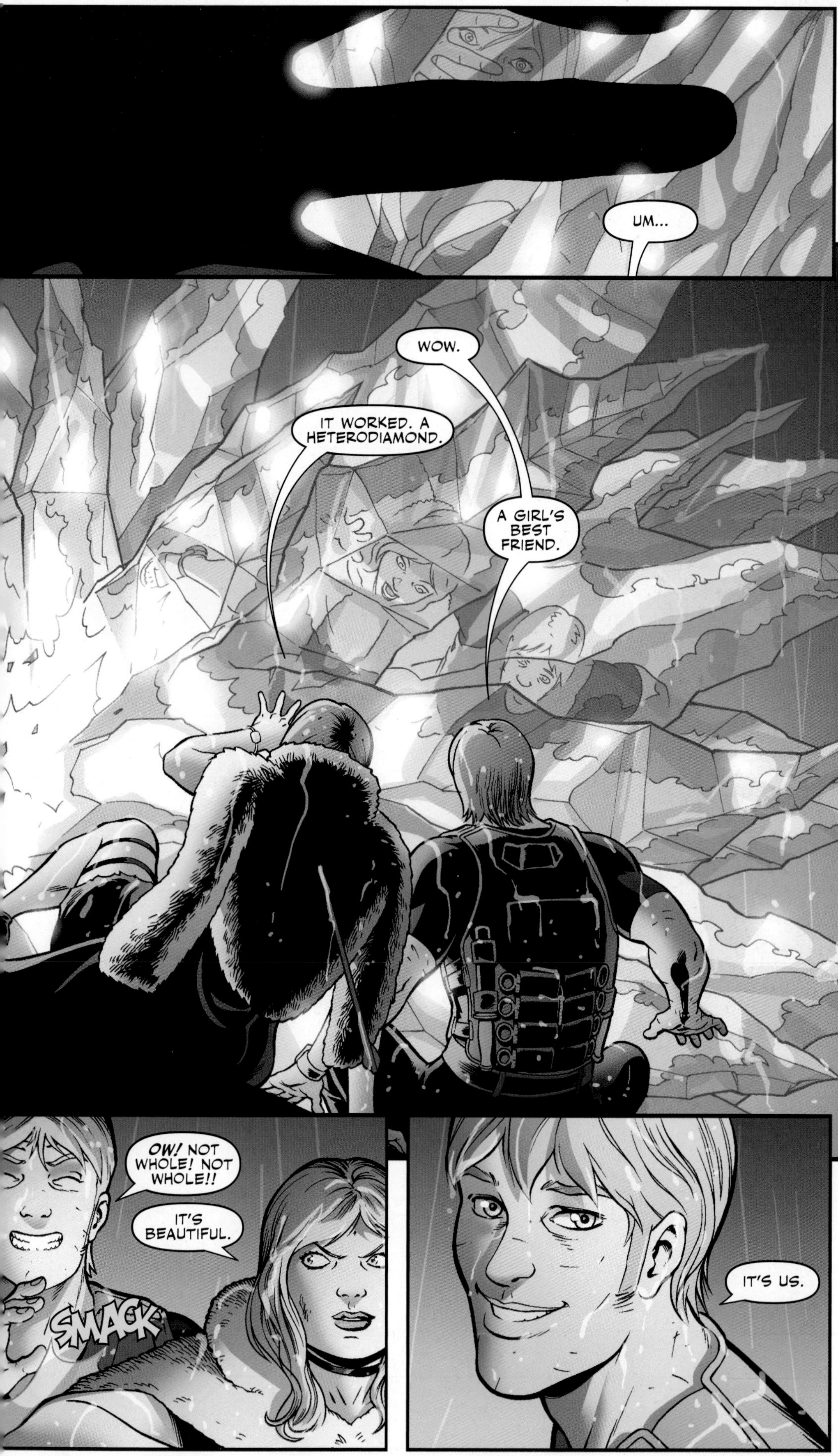
UM...
WOW.
IT WORKED. A HETERODIAMOND.
A GIRL'S BEST FRIEND.
OW! NOT WHOLE! NOT WHOLE!!
SMACK
IT'S BEAUTIFUL.
IT'S US.

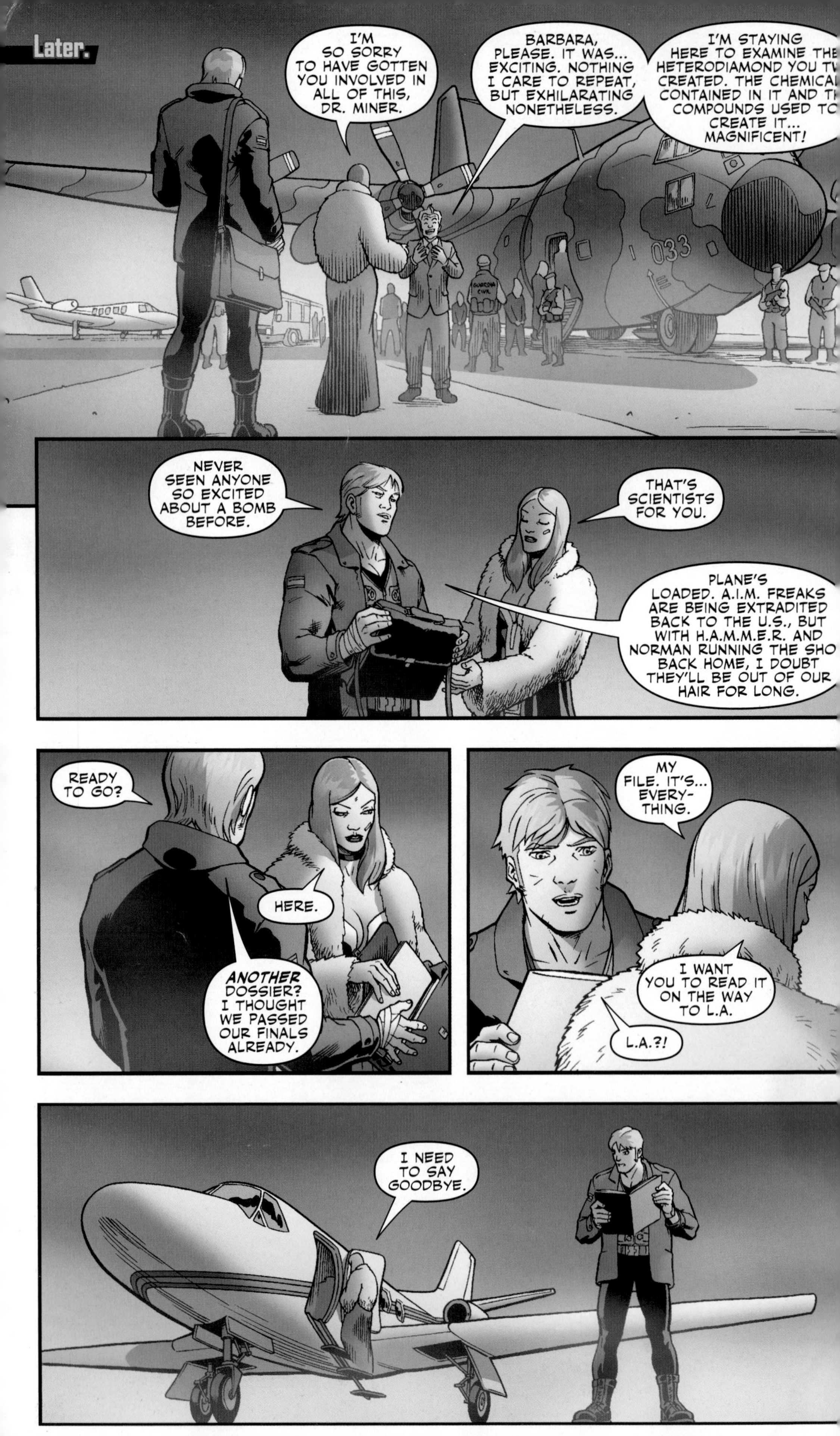

Later.
I'M SO SORRY TO HAVE GOTTEN YOU INVOLVED IN ALL OF THIS, DR. MINER.
BARBARA, PLEASE. IT WAS... EXCITING. NOTHING I CARE TO REPEAT, BUT EXHILARATING NONETHELESS.
I'M STAYING HERE TO EXAMINE THE HETERODIAMOND YOU TW CREATED. THE CHEMICAL CONTAINED IN IT AND TH COMPOUNDS USED TO CREATE IT... MAGNIFICENT!
033
NEVER SEEN ANYONE SO EXCITED ABOUT A BOMB BEFORE.
THAT'S SCIENTISTS FOR YOU.
PLANE'S LOADED. A.I.M. FREAKS ARE BEING EXTRADITED BACK TO THE U.S., BUT WITH H.A.M.M.E.R. AND NORMAN RUNNING THE SHO BACK HOME, I DOUBT THEY'LL BE OUT OF OUR HAIR FOR LONG.
READY TO GO?
HERE.
ANOTHER DOSSIER? I THOUGHT WE PASSED OUR FINALS ALREADY.
MY FILE. IT'S... EVERYTHING.
I WANT YOU TO READ IT ON THE WAY TO L.A.
L.A.?!
I NEED TO SAY GOODBYE.

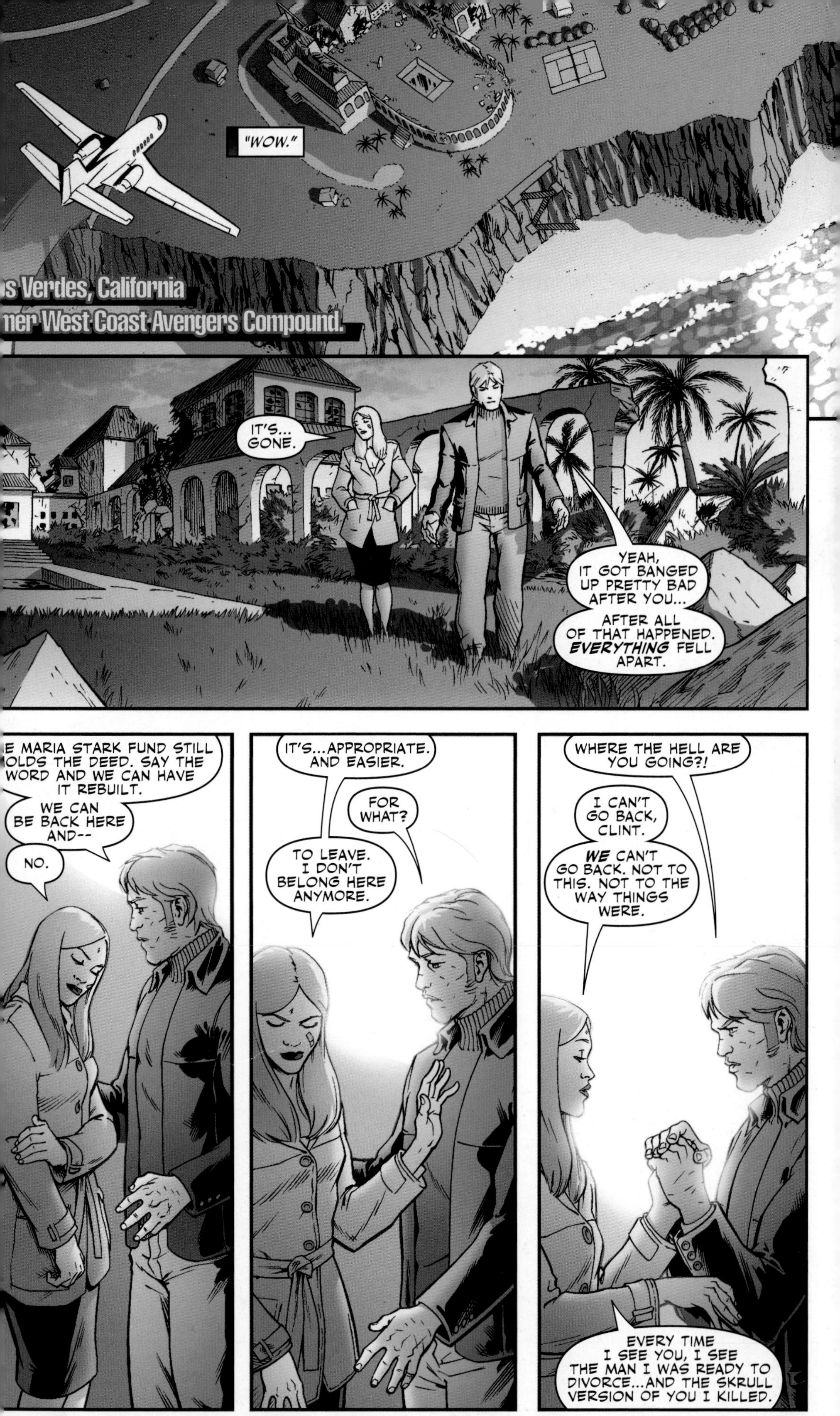
"WOW."
s Verdes, California
ner West Coast Avengers Compound.
IT'S... GONE.
YEAH, IT GOT BANGED UP PRETTY BAD AFTER YOU...
AFTER ALL OF THAT HAPPENED. EVERYTHING FELL APART.
E MARIA STARK FUND STILL OLDS THE DEED. SAY THE WORD AND WE CAN HAVE IT REBUILT.
WE CAN BE BACK HERE AND--
NO.
IT'S...APPROPRIATE. AND EASIER.
FOR WHAT?
TO LEAVE. I DON'T BELONG HERE ANYMORE.
WHERE THE HELL ARE YOU GOING?!
I CAN'T GO BACK, CLINT.
WE CAN'T GO BACK. NOT TO THIS. NOT TO THE WAY THINGS WERE.
EVERY TIME I SEE YOU, I SEE THE MAN I WAS READY TO DIVORCE...AND THE SKRULL VERSION OF YOU I KILLED.

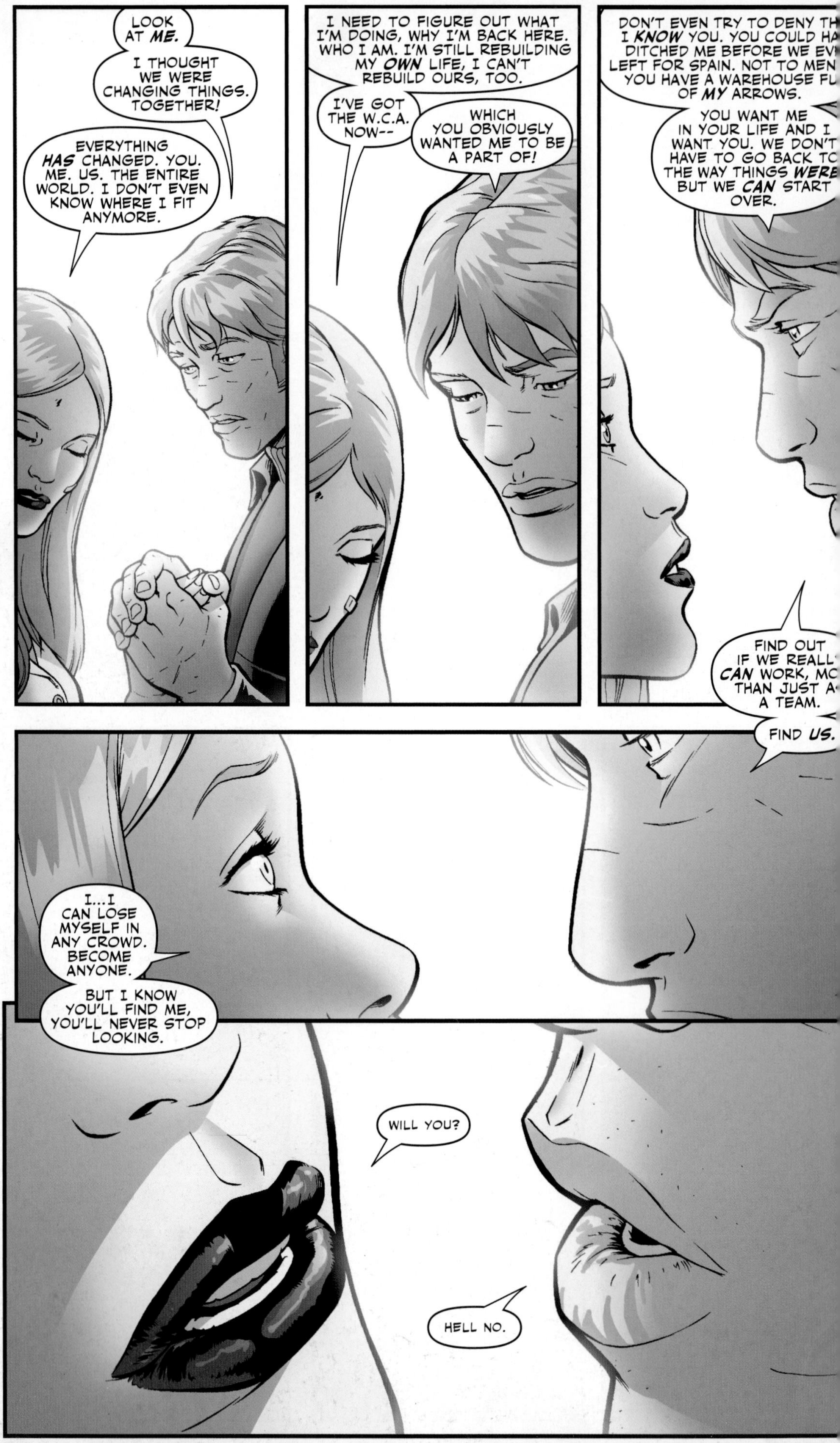

LOOK AT *ME.*
I THOUGHT WE WERE CHANGING THINGS. TOGETHER!
EVERYTHING *HAS* CHANGED. YOU. ME. US. THE ENTIRE WORLD. I DON'T EVEN KNOW WHERE I FIT ANYMORE.
I NEED TO FIGURE OUT WHAT I'M DOING, WHY I'M BACK HERE. WHO I AM. I'M STILL REBUILDING MY *OWN* LIFE, I CAN'T REBUILD OURS, TOO.
I'VE GOT THE W.C.A. NOW--
WHICH YOU OBVIOUSLY WANTED ME TO BE A PART OF!
DON'T EVEN TRY TO DENY TH I *KNOW* YOU. YOU COULD HA DITCHED ME BEFORE WE EV LEFT FOR SPAIN. NOT TO MEN YOU HAVE A WAREHOUSE FU OF *MY* ARROWS.
YOU WANT ME IN YOUR LIFE AND I WANT YOU. WE DON'T HAVE TO GO BACK TO THE WAY THINGS *WERE* BUT WE *CAN* START OVER.
FIND OUT IF WE REALL *CAN* WORK, MO THAN JUST A A TEAM.
FIND *US.*
I...I CAN LOSE MYSELF IN ANY CROWD. BECOME ANYONE.
BUT I KNOW YOU'LL FIND ME, YOU'LL NEVER STOP LOOKING.
WILL YOU?
HELL NO.

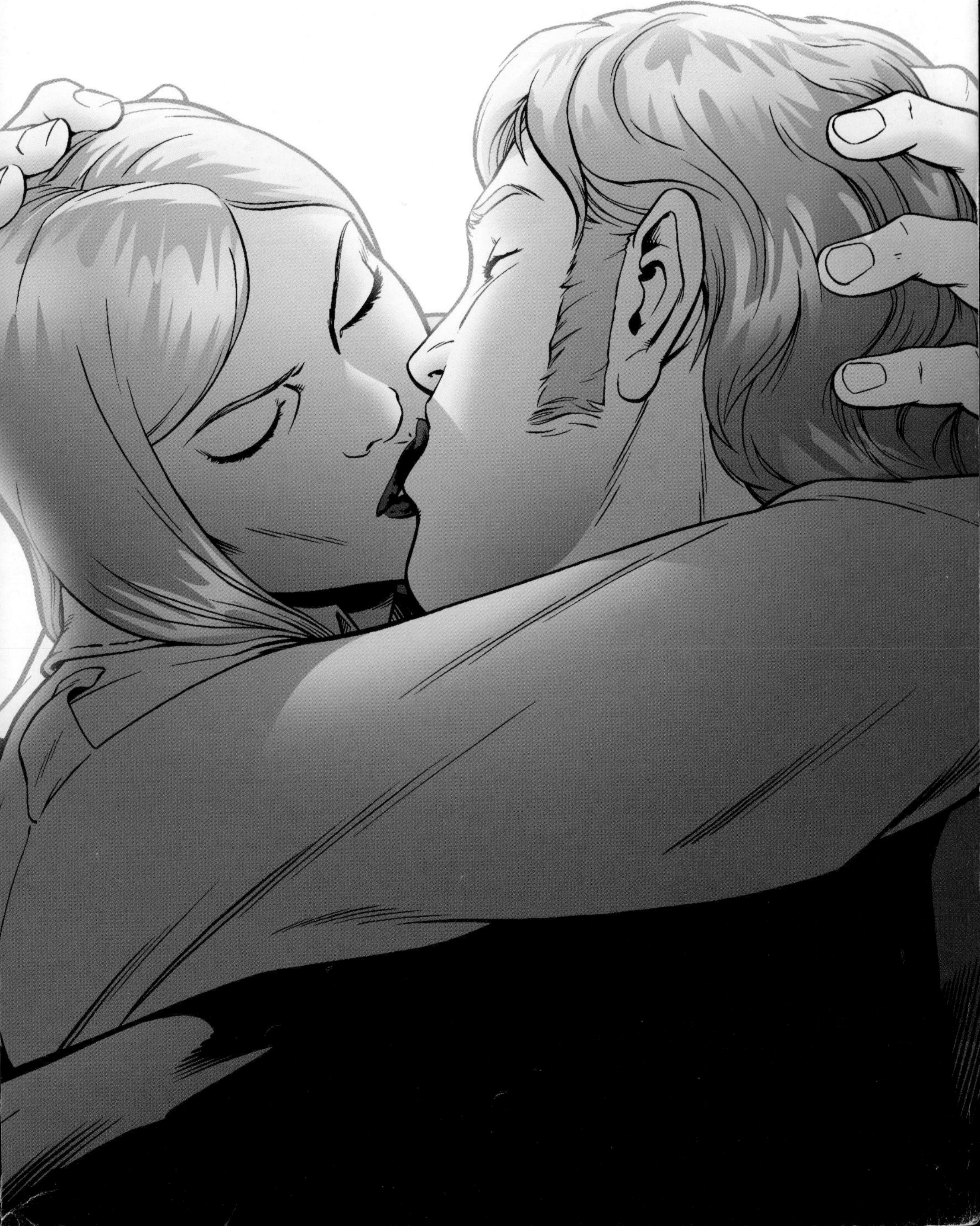

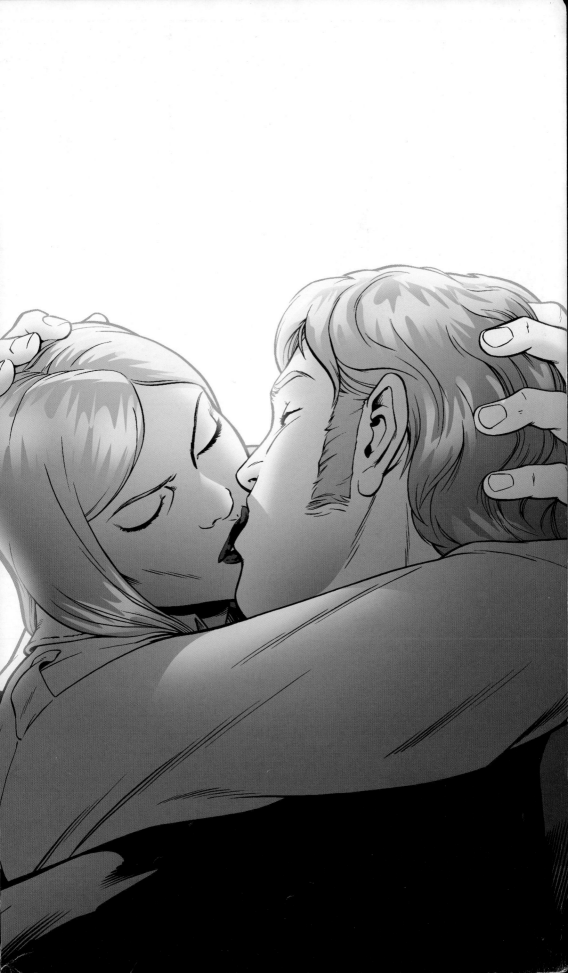

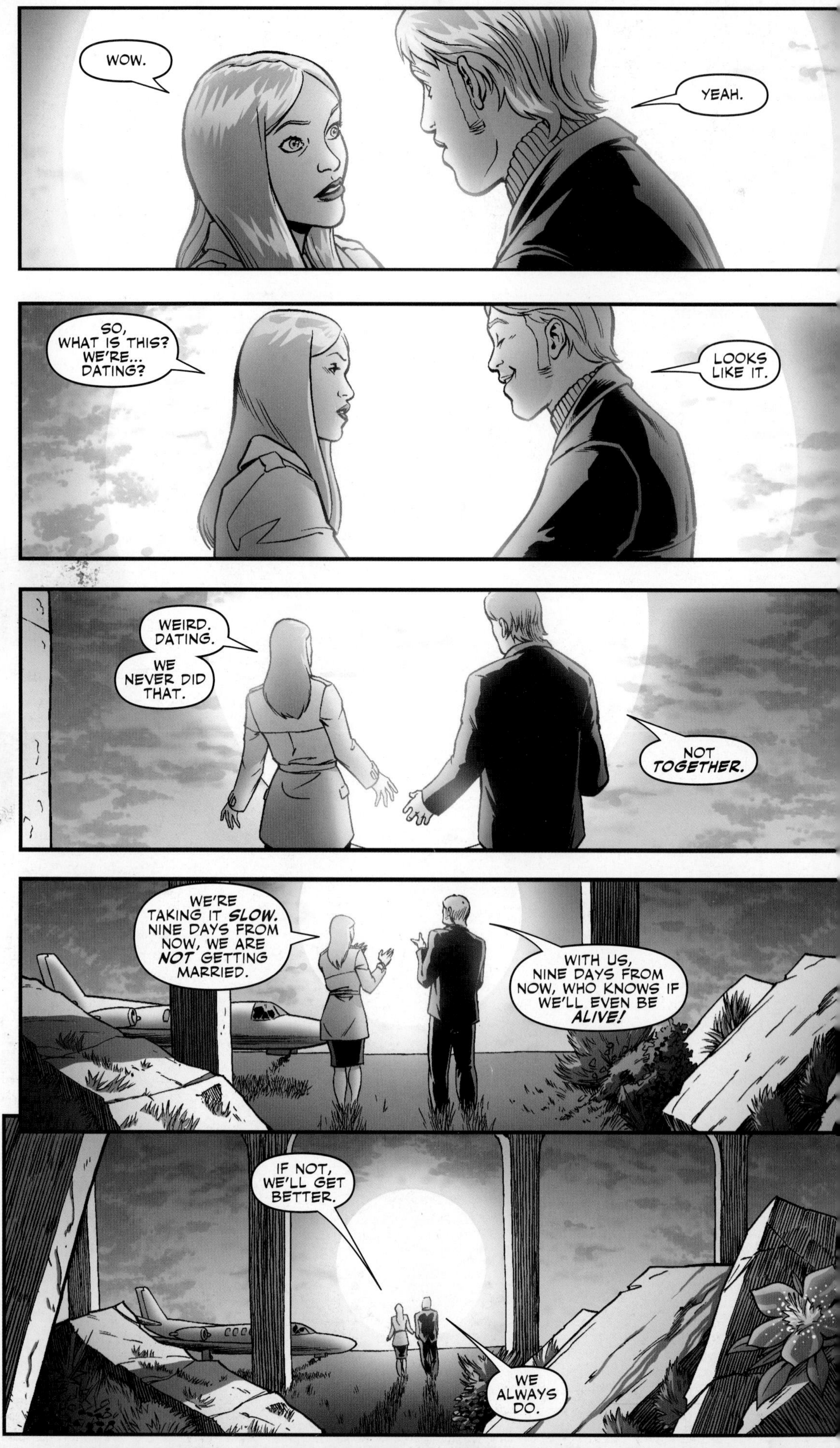
WOW.
YEAH.
SO, WHAT IS THIS? WE'RE... DATING?
LOOKS LIKE IT.
WEIRD. DATING.
WE NEVER DID THAT.
NOT *TOGETHER.*
WE'RE TAKING IT *SLOW.* NINE DAYS FROM NOW, WE ARE *NOT* GETTING MARRIED.
WITH US, NINE DAYS FROM NOW, WHO KNOWS IF WE'LL EVEN BE *ALIVE!*
IF NOT, WE'LL GET BETTER.
WE ALWAYS DO.

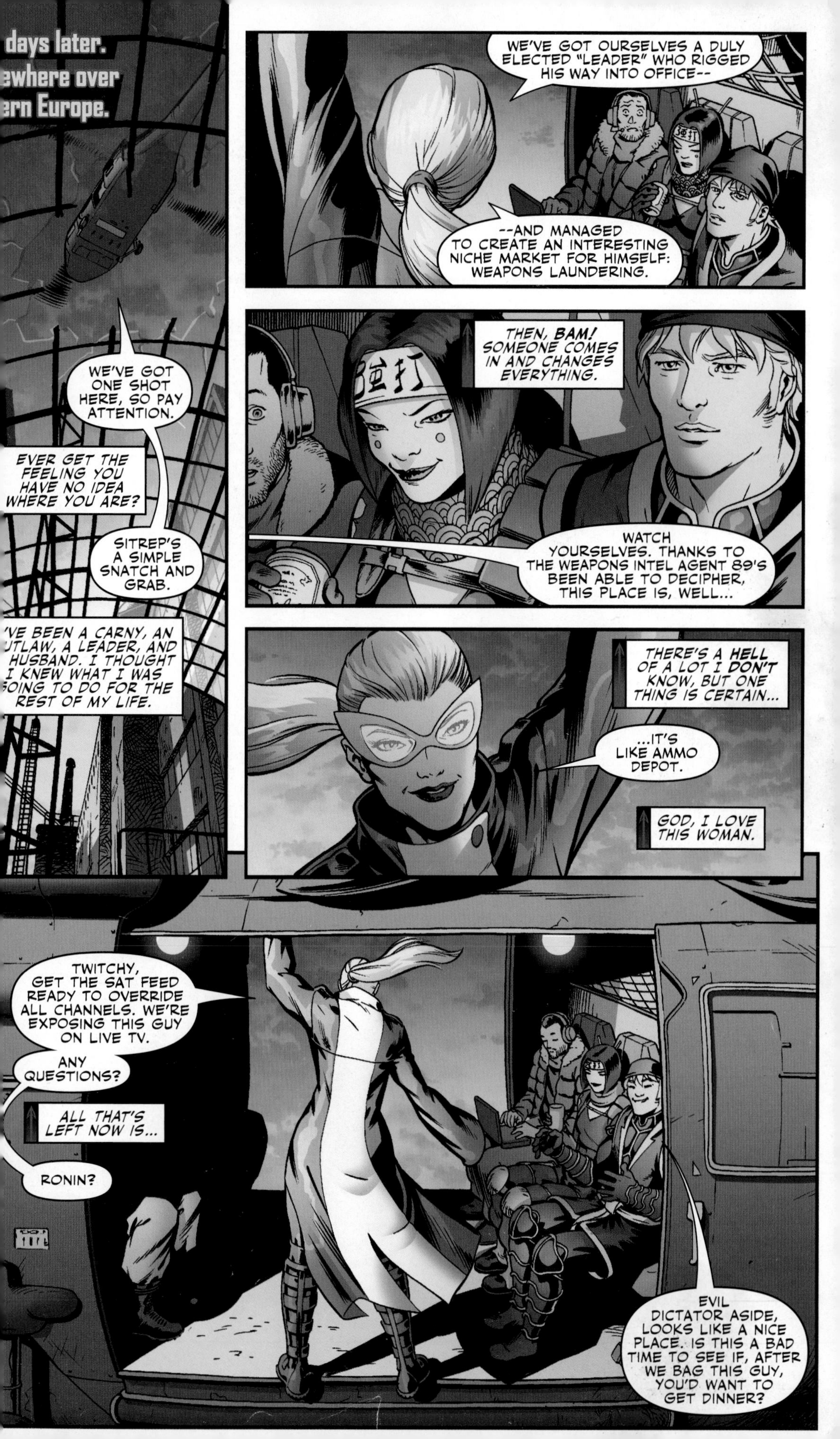
days later.
ewhere over
ern Europe.
WE'VE GOT OURSELVES A DULY ELECTED "LEADER" WHO RIGGED HIS WAY INTO OFFICE--
--AND MANAGED TO CREATE AN INTERESTING NICHE MARKET FOR HIMSELF: WEAPONS LAUNDERING.
WE'VE GOT ONE SHOT HERE, SO PAY ATTENTION.
EVER GET THE FEELING YOU HAVE NO IDEA WHERE YOU ARE?
SITREP'S A SIMPLE SNATCH AND GRAB.
'VE BEEN A CARNY, AN UTLAW, A LEADER, AND HUSBAND. I THOUGHT I KNEW WHAT I WAS GOING TO DO FOR THE REST OF MY LIFE.
THEN, BAM! SOMEONE COMES IN AND CHANGES EVERYTHING.
WATCH YOURSELVES. THANKS TO THE WEAPONS INTEL AGENT 89'S BEEN ABLE TO DECIPHER, THIS PLACE IS, WELL...
THERE'S A HELL OF A LOT I DON'T KNOW, BUT ONE THING IS CERTAIN...
...IT'S LIKE AMMO DEPOT.
GOD, I LOVE THIS WOMAN.
TWITCHY, GET THE SAT FEED READY TO OVERRIDE ALL CHANNELS. WE'RE EXPOSING THIS GUY ON LIVE TV.
ANY QUESTIONS?
ALL THAT'S LEFT NOW IS...
RONIN?
EVIL DICTATOR ASIDE, LOOKS LIKE A NICE PLACE. IS THIS A BAD TIME TO SEE IF, AFTER WE BAG THIS GUY, YOU'D WANT TO GET DINNER?

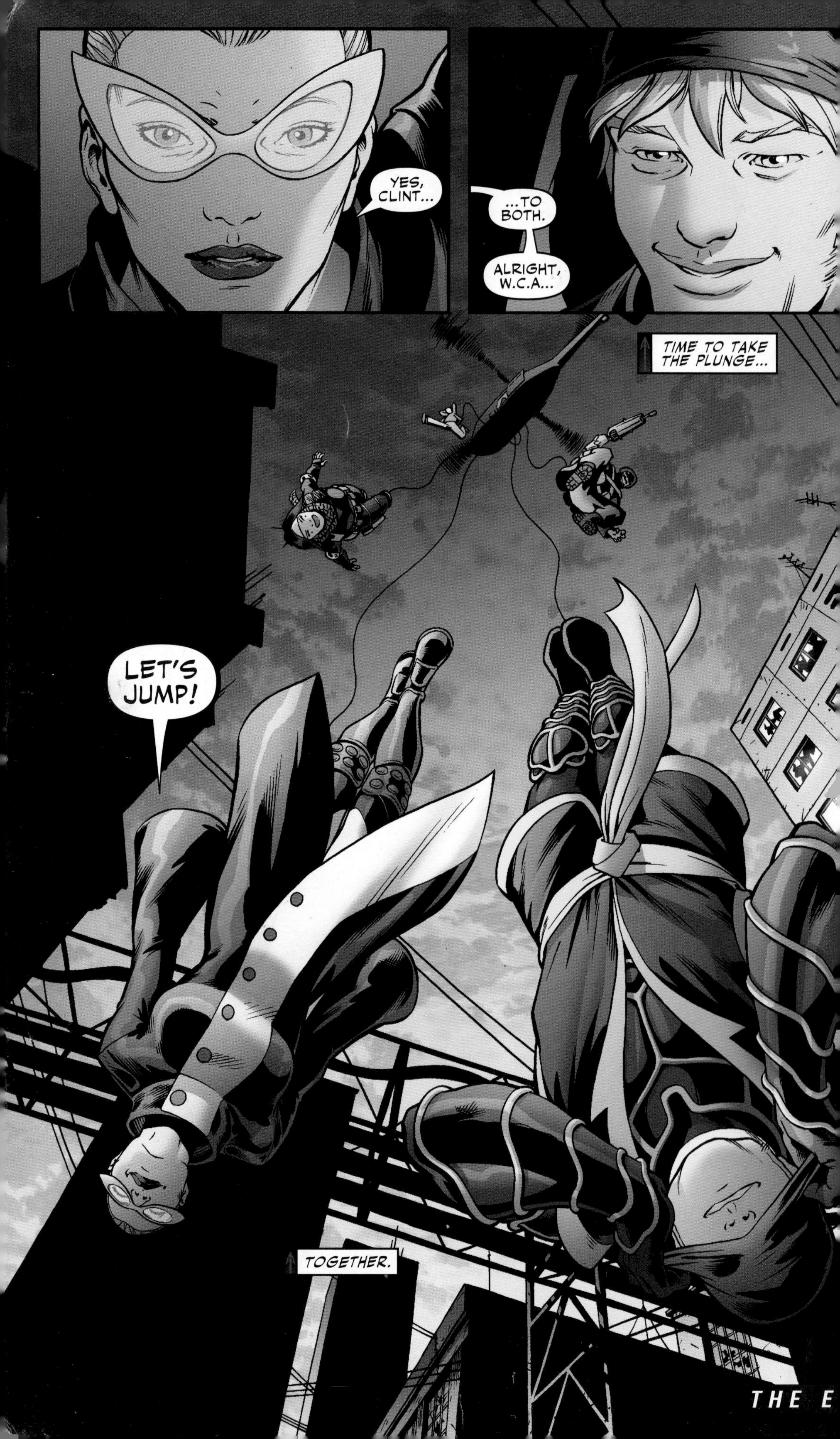
YES, CLINT...
...TO BOTH.
ALRIGHT, W.C.A...
TIME TO TAKE THE PLUNGE...
LET'S JUMP!
TOGETHER.
THE E

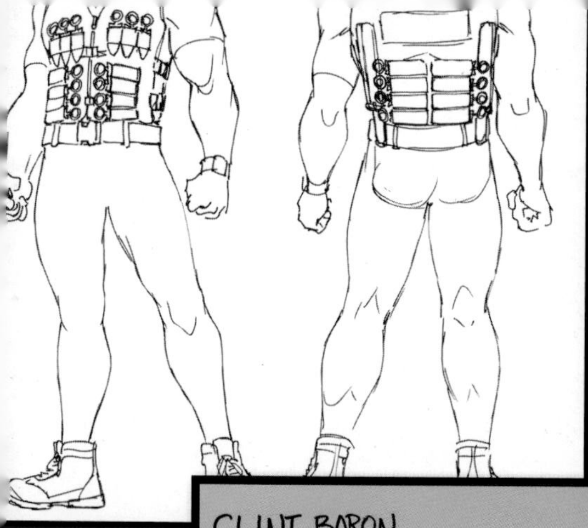

CHARACTER DESIGNS BY DAVID LOPEZ

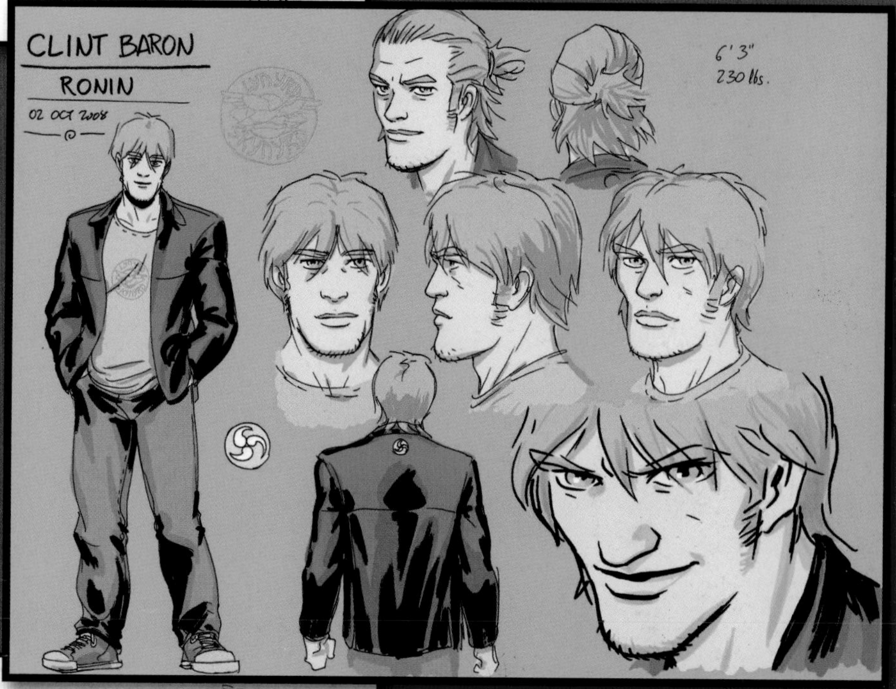
CLINT BARON
RONIN
02 OCT 2008
6' 3"
230 lbs.

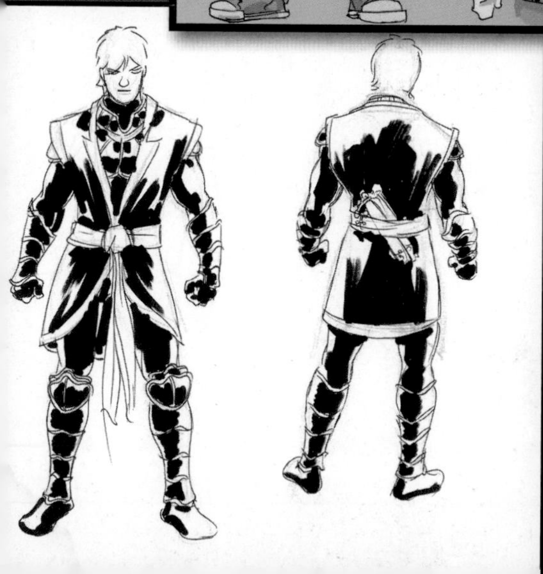

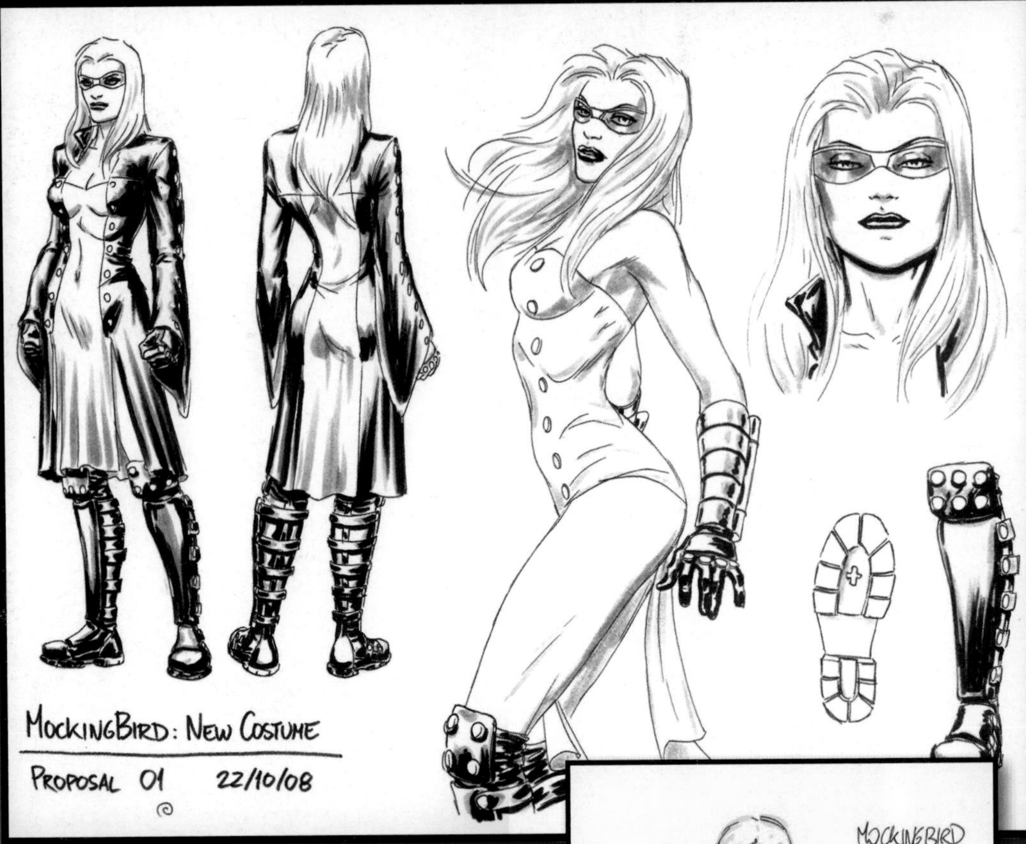
MockingBird: New Costume
Proposal 01 22/10/08

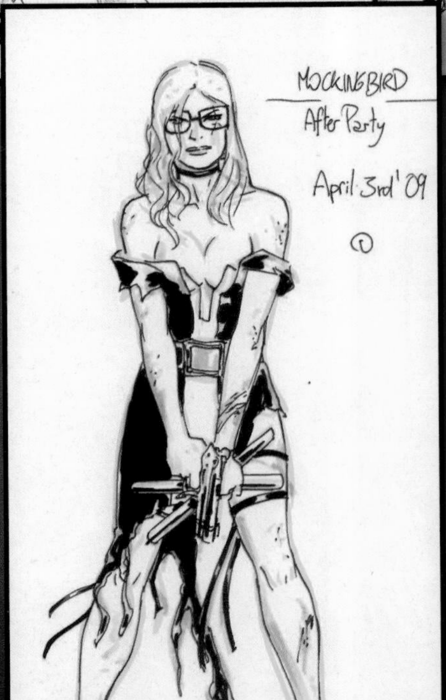
MockingBird
After Party
April 3rd '09

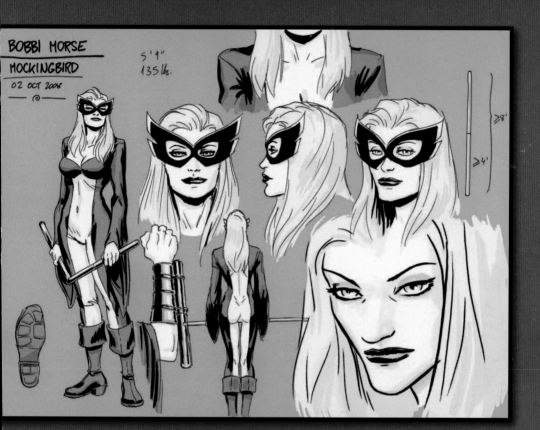

BOBBI MORSE
MOCKINGBIRD
02 OCT 2008

5'9"
135 lbs.

≥8'

≥4'

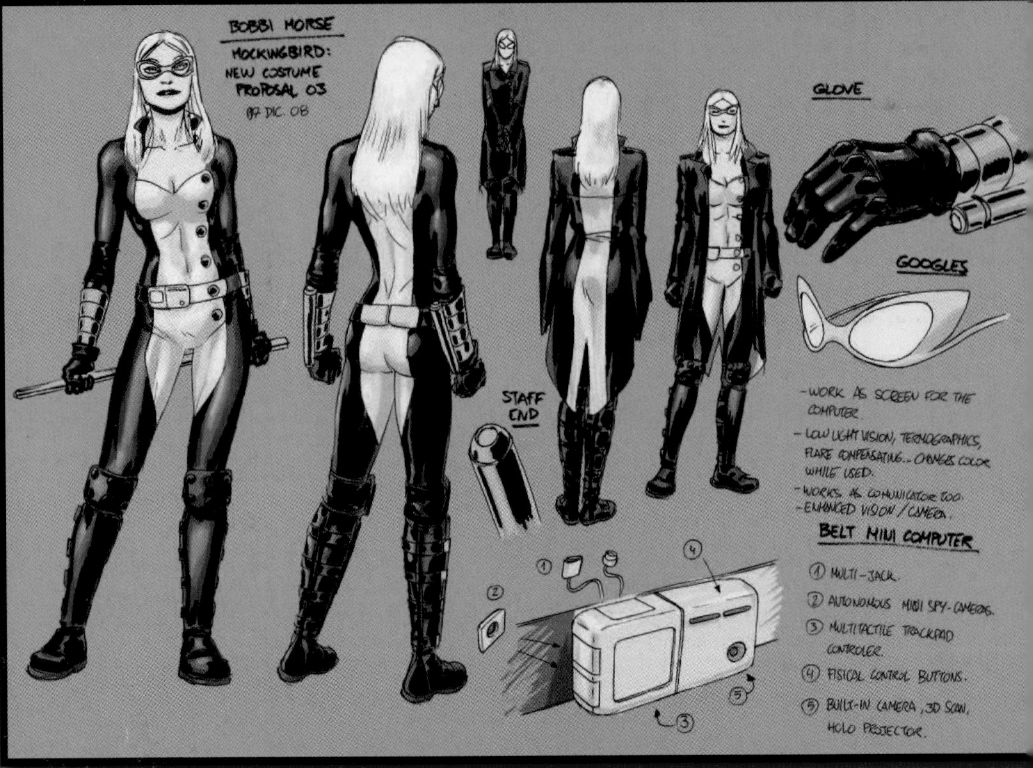
BOBBI MORSE
MOCKINGBIRD:
NEW COSTUME
PROPOSAL 03
07 DIC. 08
GLOVE
GOOGLES
STAFF END
- WORK AS SCREEN FOR THE COMPUTER.
- LOW LIGHT VISION, TERMOGRAPHICS, FLARE COMPENSATING... CHANGES COLOR WHILE USED.
- WORKS AS COMUNICATOR TOO.
- ENHANCED VISION / CAMERA.
BELT MINI COMPUTER
① MULTI-JACK.
② AUTONOMOUS MINI SPY-CAMERAS.
③ MULTITACTILE TRACKPAD CONTROLER.
④ FISICAL CONTROL BUTTONS.
⑤ BUILT-IN CAMERA, 3D SCAN, HOLO PROJECTOR.

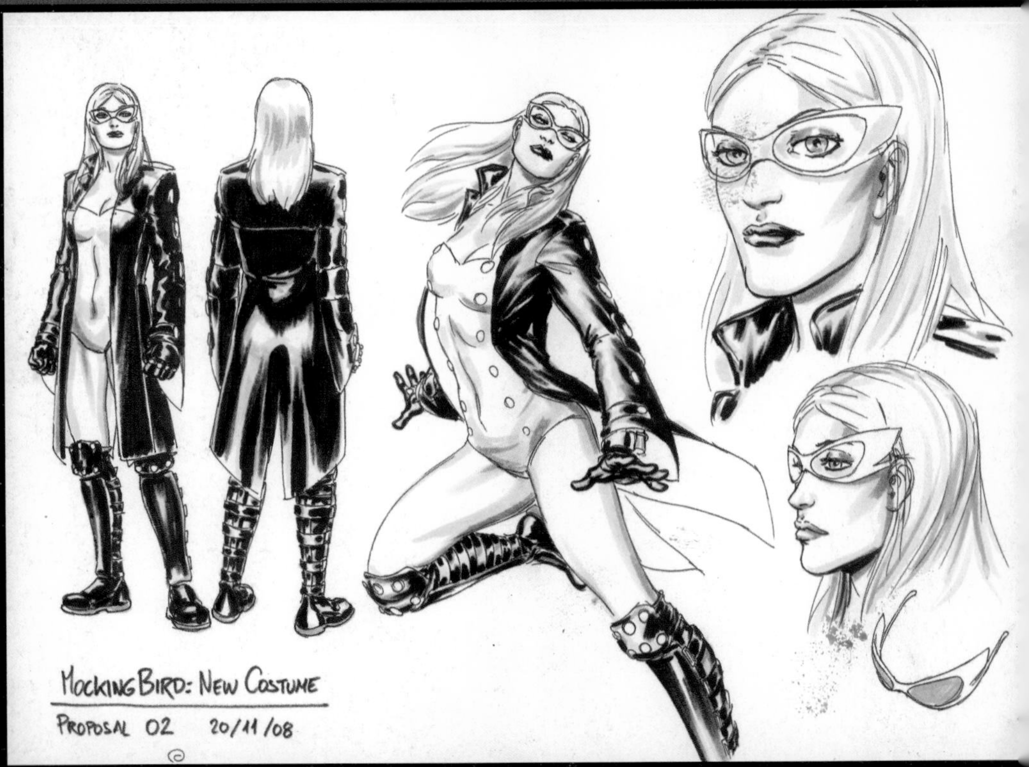
MOCKINGBIRD: NEW COSTUME
PROPOSAL 02 20/11/08

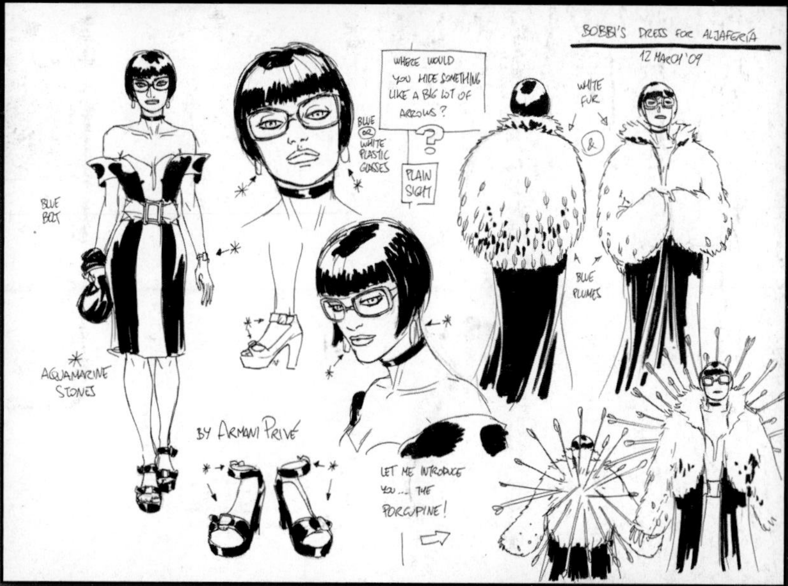
BOBBI'S DRESS FOR ALJAFERÍA
12 MARCH '09
WHERE WOULD YOU HIDE SOMETHING LIKE A BIG LOT OF ARROWS?
?
PLAIN SIGHT!
BLUE OR WHITE PLASTIC GLASSES
WHITE FUR
&
BLUE BELT
BLUE PLUMES
AQUAMARINE STONES
BY ARMANI PRIVÉ
LET ME INTRODUCE YOU... THE PORCUPINE!

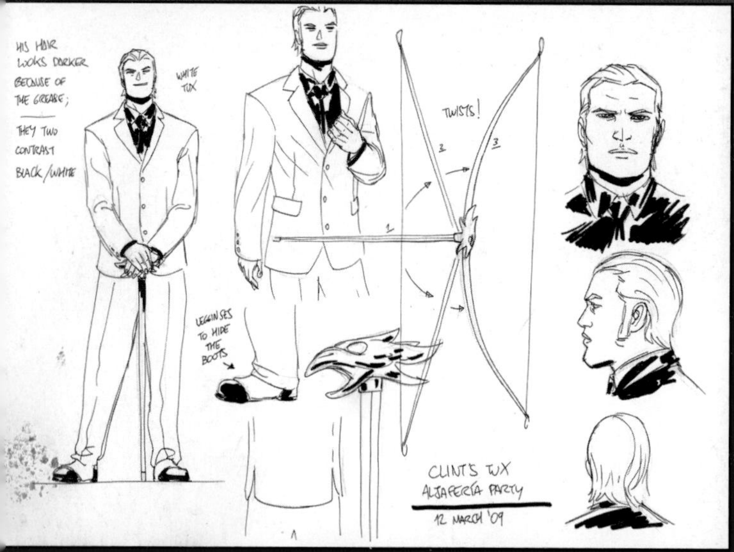
HIS HAIR LOOKS DARKER BECAUSE OF THE GREASE;
THEY TWO CONTRAST BLACK/WHITE
WHITE TUX
TWISTS!
LEGGINSES TO HIDE THE BOOTS
CLINT'S TUX
ALJAFERÍA PARTY
12 MARCH '09

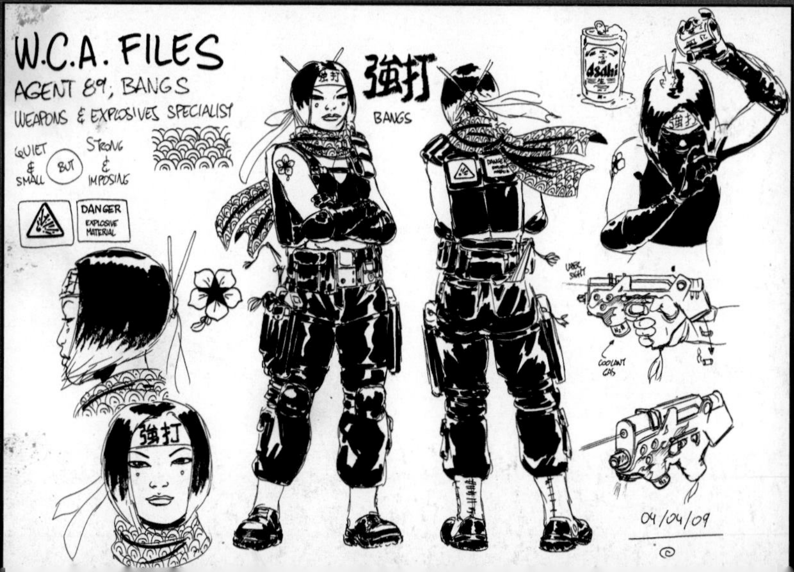
W.C.A. FILES
AGENT 89; BANGS
WEAPONS & EXPLOSIVES SPECIALIST
QUIET & SMALL
BUT
STRONG & IMPOSING
DANGER
EXPLOSIVE MATERIAL
強打
BANGS
Asahi
LASER SIGHT
COOLANT GAS
04/04/09

NEW AVENGERS